Rules, Patterns and Words
Grammar and Lexis in English Language Teaching

CAMBRIDGE LANGUAGE TEACHING LIBRARY

A series covering central issues in language teaching and learning, by authors who have expert knowledge in their field.

In this series:

Rules, Patterns and Words

Grammar and Lexis in English Language Teaching

Dave Willis

CAMBRIDGE
UNIVERSITY PRESS

CAMBRIDGE UNIVERSITY PRESS
Cambridge, New York, Melbourne, Madrid, Cape Town,
Singapore, São Paulo, Delhi, Tokyo, Mexico City

Cambridge University Press
The Edinburgh Building, Cambridge CB2 8RU, UK

Published in the United States of America by Cambridge University Press, New York

www.cambridge.org
Information on this title: www.cambridge.org/9780521536196

First published 2003
4th printing 2009

A catalogue record for this publication is available from the British Library

ISBN 978-0-521-82924-3 Hardback
ISBN 978-0-521-53619-6 Paperback

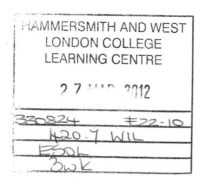

CONTENTS

Contents

Acknowledgements

There are two major influences behind this book. The first is the work of John Sinclair and his COBUILD research team over the last twenty-five years. This research is changing the way language is viewed, in particular the relationship between lexis and grammar. One outcome of the COBUILD research is the work on pattern grammar by Gill Francis, Susan Hunston and Elizabeth Manning which features heavily in Chapter 7.

The second major influence is the work of Michael Halliday. The whole view of language as a meaning system, which informs this book, comes from Halliday. I have attempted to describe language as a functional system, and this again derives from Halliday. In addition to this general influence the detail of very much of the description offered here is based closely on Halliday's work. Michael generously offered to read and comment on a near final version of the book. Most of his comments have been incorporated, although we still differ on the general approach in Chapter 5.

I owe a great debt to colleagues with whom I worked for ten very happy years at the Centre for English Language Studies at Birmingham University: Chris Kennedy, Susan Hunston, Terry Shortall, Murray Knowles, Corony Edwards, Bob Holland, and Carmen Caldas-Coulthard. Talks with these colleagues over the years have helped me in all kinds of ways. I am also grateful for help and insights over the years from two highly valued colleagues, and friends for many years, Malcolm Coulthard and the late David Brazil.

I would like to thank Jane Willis for reading and commenting on developing versions of the book. I have benefited from long discussions which have helped me to clarify and develop my thinking, and without Jane's help the book would certainly have been much less reader friendly than it is. Indeed, without her the book might not have been written at all.

1 What is taught may not be what is learnt: Some preliminary questions

Whenever we do anything in the classroom we are acting on our beliefs about language and language learning. If we ask learners to listen and repeat a particular sentence, we are acting on the belief that such repetition is useful enough to justify the valuable classroom time it takes up, perhaps the belief that it helps rote learning which in turn promotes general language learning. If we give learners grammatical rules or encourage them to discover rules for themselves, we are acting on the belief that rules make a valuable contribution to language description and that this kind of understanding helps promote learning.

Our beliefs about language learning and teaching are shaped by our training, but also by our classroom experience. Unfortunately, learning from experience is not always easy. Teaching is such an absorbing business that it is difficult to stand back and ask appropriate questions about what is happening in the classroom.

My own experience as a language teacher – and also as a learner – suggests to me that learning a language is a much more complex and difficult process than we would like to think. We need to look very carefully at some of the assumptions we make about language learning and about language itself. A first step is to look at what happens in classrooms, and to identify some of the questions that need to be asked.

In the classroom teachers often act on the assumption that language learning is a matter of learning a series of patterns or structures. Learners gradually add to their stock of structures until they have a usable model of the language. They often start with the present tense of *be*, and soon they are exposed to the definite and indefinite articles. At a later stage we add the passive voice and reported speech, and continue until we reach the dizzy heights of the third conditional. The syllabus is presented to learners in a 'logical' order and the language is built up piece by piece until learners have achieved a usable competence, a form of the language which meets their needs.

As teachers, however, we observe that learning proceeds in a much less predictable manner. What is 'taught' is often not learnt, and learners often 'learn' things which have not been taught at all. Learners often produce sentences such as: *I am student* or *My father is engineer* even though they have never been taught this, and even though their conscientious teacher is at pains to point out that the definite article is required here: *You are* **a** *student; Your father is* **an** *engineer.* Often learners persist in these errors for a long time, in spite of repeated correction.

This is frustrating for both learners and teachers, but the full picture is even more complicated than this. Learners soon reach a stage at which they produce accurately: *I am a student* when they are thinking carefully about the language; but when they are producing language spontaneously, or when their attention is drawn to another feature of the language, they continue to produce: *I am student.* There are, it seems, two kinds of learning. One of them has to do with learning to make sentences. Learners think hard about what they are doing and produce thoughtful, accurate samples of the language. The second kind of learning has to do with learning to produce language spontaneously, without conscious attention to detail. What learners produce spontaneously is often very different from what they produce when they are concentrating on making sentences.

We come up against this phenomenon time and time again in our classroom practice. We constantly observe instances where learners make errors which they are easily able to correct once they are pointed out. And we also observe, time and time again, that the same errors are repeated, even after they have been pointed out. This is one of the central puzzles in language teaching: how is it that learners can know something, in the sense that they are well aware of it when they are making sentences carefully and attentively, but at the same time not know it when they are producing language spontaneously?

In this chapter I will look first at my own experience in a class on question tags: why is it that these tags, which are relatively easy to explain, are so difficult for learners to master? I will then look at question forms in general: why do learners go on getting these wrong for so long even after they have understood the rules for question formation? The way learners go about learning question forms raises questions about learning in general – I will highlight some of these questions and speculate on possible explanations.

1.1 Some questions about tags

My first teaching job was at a secondary school in Ghana, West Africa. My Ghanaian students, who did not share a common first language, were learning English as a second language. They had not acquired

English as their first language at their mothers' knees. Most of them had their first contact with English in primary school, and by the time they reached secondary school nearly all of their lessons were taught through the medium of English. Their spoken English, however, was a dialect form which was very different from standard British English. They used this dialect not only in the classroom, but also when speaking to fellow students who came from another language group.

'Sensible' languages have a single form for question tags. French has *n'est-ce pas?*; Greek has δεν ειναι? (*dhen eeneh?*); Spanish uses *verdad?* or *no?* Unlike these sensible languages English has a wide range of question tags:

*We've met before, **haven't we?***
*You'll be there on time, **won't you?***
*They can do it, **can't they?***

But in the dialect of English used by my Ghanaian students there was only one tag, as in French and Greek:

*We've met before, **isn't it?***
*You'll be there on time, **isn't it?***
*They can do it, **isn't it?***

This tag is a form which is also often used by learners of English as a foreign language. It is even used by some native speakers of English – *We'll see you tomorrow, innit?*

Unfortunately my Ghanaian students were supposed to be learning standard British English. In their examinations they would be tested on standard British English – including the entire range of question tags. And, for some reason best known to themselves, examiners love to test question tags. I knew that my students would be tested in public examinations and that in those examinations, which in those days were in multiple-choice format, question tags would figure largely.

I was determined to eradicate their apparently serious error, and carefully prepared a lesson. This happened back in the 1960s, and, to someone trained in the 1990s, my lesson may have appeared to be old-fashioned in some respects, since it was based initially on grammatical explanation. It began with an explanation and demonstration showing how the auxiliary or modal verb was repeated in the tag, and how an affirmative clause had a negative tag. Then we looked at some sample sentences on the blackboard, until the students were able to supply tags consistently. I called out some statements and the students responded with the appropriate tag. I finished with one half of the class repeating a statement after me, and the other half of the class responding in chorus with the right tag.

> *We're learning English... **aren't we?***
> *We will have English next Monday... **won't we?***
> *We have English every Monday... **don't we?***

It all went beautifully. I felt all the warm satisfaction of someone who has achieved his lesson aims. There was one final stage. I asked the students to take out their exercise books so that they could write down a few sample tags to help them remember what they had learned. They all looked a little sheepish. Finally one of them, one of the brightest students in the class, put up his hand and explained the problem: *Please, sir, you've got our exercise books... **isn't it?*** My beautifully prepared and highly successful lesson vanished before my eyes. What my students seemed to have learnt turned out not to have been learnt, even by one of the brightest.

Please, sir, you've got our exercise books, isn't it?

In one sense I had done my job. I am sure that, when faced with multiple-choice questions, and given time to think, most of my students would be able to identify the correct tags. But most of them never incorporated these tags into their spontaneous speech. I soon learned that almost all Ghanaians, including those who were fluent, even eloquent in English, used only the all-purpose tag *isn't it?* – even if they could reproduce the complex system used by speakers of standard British English when asked to do so.

At the time I was simply puzzled and frustrated. I had spent a lot of time teaching something which was difficult and had little practical value. I had taught it so that it could be tested and so that my students might respond appropriately in a test. But it had certainly not become a part of their usable repertoire of English.

1.2 Some questions about questions

We know from research into second language learning that learners have to go through a series of stages before they are able to produce question forms consistently and accurately. This is something that teachers know from bitter experience. It takes a long time, for example, before learners spontaneously produce questions with the 'dummy auxiliary' *do*, as in: *What do you want?* Even sentences which they hear over and over again are distorted. On teacher-training courses I refer to this as the '*Please, teacher, what mean X?*-syndrome'. Learners may have been endlessly drilled in forms like *What do you want? Where do you live?* and so on. They will certainly have heard the phrase *What does X mean?* many, many times. But in class they consistently put up their hands and ask the question *Please, teacher, what mean X?*

Please, teacher, what mean ...?

In time, usually a long time, they get past this stage and begin to produce questions with *do* in the appropriate form, and the teacher breathes a sigh of relief at this evidence of real progress. But later we move on to reported questions: *Do you know **where they live**? Tell me **what you want.*** In these forms there is, of course, no dummy auxiliary *do*. Students are familiar with the forms ... *they live* and ... *you want*. There should be no real problem with putting these after a WH-word such as *what* or *where* to produce: *Tell me what you want* and *Do you know where they live?* But what happens? They regularly produce the forms: *Do you know where do they live? Tell me what do you want.* In a test on reported questions they may be able to produce the appropriate forms, but it takes some time, often a considerable time, before they eliminate the *do* auxiliary from their reported questions. This process is similar to that observed among L1 learners. The mastery of question forms might appear to be straightforward, but it involves a complex developmental process.

Why should this be the case? It may be that the forms *What do ...? What did ...?* and so on have become 'consolidated'. Once students have learned to use direct questions, then a WH-word like *what* or *where* automatically triggers an auxiliary, including the dummy auxiliary. What once came to them naturally – *Where I live? What you want?* – no longer comes naturally to them. The new forms – *Tell me what you want; Do you know where they live?* – are easily demonstrated, explained and understood, but they are not used spontaneously. To use them spontaneously it seems that learners first have to unlearn their old habits. They have to break the link between a WH-word and the auxiliary which they have acquired with such difficulty in the process of learning direct questions.

1.3 Some questions about learning

Some years ago, on an in-service teacher-training course, I asked teachers to make a list of the ten commonest mistakes made by learners. I asked one half of the group to list the most frequent errors in their first year classes, and the second group to list errors made in third year classes. When the lists were compared the teachers were horrified to see that seven of the mistakes they had listed occurred in **both** the first year **and** the third year. Third year students, like their first year counterparts, consistently produced forms like: *She want* ... instead of: *She wants* ... First and third year students seemed to have the same problems with articles, including the production of the forms: *I am student* and *You are teacher*, which I referred to above. Third year students still had problems with question forms, particularly the *do-* auxiliary, and so on.

This, of course, raised serious questions about what was happening in these classes. Had teachers really taken a full two years of teaching to eliminate only three mistakes? Were their third year students really not much better than their first year students? How could we account for this appalling failure?

Although the teachers accepted that they had been conspicuously unsuccessful in eradicating common errors, they still insisted that third year students had a much better command of English than first year students. They pointed out that third year students had a much wider vocabulary than the first years. They used English with greater fluency and confidence. Some of them were able to produce several consecutive sentences, albeit littered with errors. This was quite beyond their first year counterparts. The third years could understand and produce language that was quite beyond a first year student and, as part and parcel of this, they could make lots of mistakes that the first years could not even dream of.

The conclusion we reached was this: if it is the teacher's role to eliminate error, then these teachers had been remarkably unsuccessful – even though most of them were, by all reasonable standards, very good teachers. But if it is the teacher's role to help students develop enhanced performance and confidence, then all the teachers could claim genuine success. Their third year students spoke more English than their first year students, and they spoke it with greater fluency and confidence.

This, however, still left us looking for an explanation as to why the teachers' efforts to eliminate error had met with so little success. One teacher asked me if I had been any more successful in my days as a classroom teacher. Remembering my lesson on question tags, and countless other similar experiences, I had to admit that I had not. I had no simple answer to the question why some aspects of language are so resistant to teaching, and I certainly had no simple solution as to what might be done about this.

One possible explanation for this phenomenon is that learners are simply careless. They know that they should add *s* to the third person singular of the present simple tense, and they know how to form questions with the auxiliary *do*, but they are simply too careless to apply this knowledge when they are using the language spontaneously. But second language acquisition research, as well as our experience as teachers, tell us that these are stages that almost *all* learners go through. We can hardly dismiss *all* learners as careless. It seems much more likely that the processes we have described are a necessary part of learning, that learners have to go through a process which involves making mistakes before they can produce appropriate forms spontaneously and without conscious attention.

There is, then, plenty of evidence that learners do not move immediately from an understanding of new language forms to the spontaneous production of those forms. They go through a stage at which they can produce the form only when they are paying careful attention. They cannot produce the form when they are using language spontaneously, when they are thinking about getting meaning across rather than producing accurate sentences. In spontaneous language use there are conflicting priorities. The learners' main priority is to get their message across with appropriate speed and fluency; they may also be keen to produce language which is accurate – but speed and fluency conflict with accuracy.

1.4 Learning processes

It seems, then, that there is no direct and straightforward connection between teaching and learning. We cannot determine or predict what learners will make a part of their spontaneous language behaviour. However, our experience as teachers and the experience of the teachers in training reported above suggest that classroom instruction does help learners, and this is reinforced by second language acquisition research (see, for example, Long, 1983, 1988) which appears to show that learners develop more quickly and go on learning for longer if they are supported by instruction.

It is possible that teaching makes learners more aware of a particular form, it makes the form more noticeable. Until their attention is drawn to it, learners may not even notice the structure of *do*-questions. Perhaps they simply identify these forms as questions through their intonation patterns without paying attention to their form. Once the structure has been pointed out to them they begin to notice it when they come across it. Over time this repeated noticing enables them to incorporate the acceptable forms into their spontaneous language production. It is also possible that teaching helps learners form hypotheses about the language which they then go on to test and to refine. Yet another possibility is that classroom procedures encourage learners to think carefully about the language for themselves, and help to make them more independent learners.

It is worth looking at a number of processes which might contribute to learning, and following on from that we can go on to consider ways in which teachers might assist learning. Let us begin by postulating three language learning processes which I will refer to as **Recognition, System building** and **Exploration**. Let us look at these processes one by one.

Recognition: The first stage in learning probably involves recognising what it is that is to be learnt. Whether or not something is recognised is subject to a number of influences. It is subject, for example, to **salience**, how much it stands out from its background. This can be annoying for teachers, because strange and unusual words and phrases often stick in students' minds. On the other hand, syntactic markers, such as articles and auxiliary verbs, are far from salient. We need to draw attention to such items quite explicitly, and to encourage learners to look for them in future input.

Recognition takes place at a number of levels. We might, for example, encourage learners to recognise a general phenomenon, such as the behaviour of uncountable nouns in English, nouns which are not found in the plural nor with the indefinite article. We might do this at first by drawing attention to a number of frequently occurring nouns which refer to items of food and drink: *bread, food, rice, water* etc. Later we might go on to make the same point about other substances such as *oil, gas, iron* and *wood*. Once learners are aware that some nouns in English behave in this way they may immediately make links with similar nouns in their own language, and as a result go on to generalise that abstract ideas (*beauty, bravery, death* etc.) and activities (*help, travel, sleep* etc.) behave in the same way. If the learners' first language does not offer this kind of support, they may need more help with recognition. Even if their own language is similar to English in its general classification and treatment of uncountable nouns, the teacher might still usefully provide help with some very frequent nouns which are uncountable in English but not in most other languages, words like *advice, furniture, homework* and *equipment*.

Thus, teachers can help learners with recognition by explanation, by showing students how to recognise uncountable nouns. They can reinforce this by pointing out specific examples of these nouns as they occur in the language which learners experience in the classroom, and later by encouraging learners to identify these nouns for themselves. They can go on to exemplify and list uncountable nouns.

With some vocabulary items learning proceeds largely by recognition. If a word has an obvious referent in the outside world, it can be learnt as an individual item. I have an impressive restaurant vocabulary in Spanish even though my competence in Spanish conversation is very limited. I acquired my restaurant vocabulary mainly by studying restaurant menus and lists of words in a Spanish phrase book. As a result I can work my way through a menu and find what I want, even though I cannot engage a waiter in a productive discussion of how the food has been prepared. There are a number of lexical fields which lend themselves to this kind of learning, but we do need to be wary of rote learning. Even a simple word like *foot* can cause problems. For a speaker of Greek, for example, the word ποδι is the closest equivalent to *foot*, but ποδι refers not simply to the foot, but to the entire leg below the knee. This can occasionally cause problems for Greek learners of English as well as for English learners of Greek.

Depending on which is the student's first language, some grammatical items in English may also be assimilated without too much trouble once they have been recognised. Most European languages have words which are almost exact counterparts of the English direct and indirect articles, for example. Speakers of those languages can acquire the article system as if *the, a* and *an* were straightforward lexical items, without worrying about complex differences in use. For speakers of Greek, for example, the basic distinction is clear, but there are difficulties with proper names which in Greek always take a definite article. The way proper nouns are handled in English is inconsistent. In general we do not use the definite article with names but it is used with the names of seas and oceans, for example, although not with lakes. There is no logical reason why English should talk of *Lake Geneva* and *Lake Superior*, but insist on *the Atlantic Ocean* and *the North Sea*. French is similar to English in that it operates an inconsistent system, but the inconsistencies in French are different from those in English. For example French uses the definite article for the names of countries (*la France, la Grande Bretagne*), but not for towns or cities; it often uses the definite article for days of the week, but not for the months of the year. There is, therefore, a certain amount of 'tidying up' to do for all learners, but for many, including speakers of most European languages, the basic distinction between the definite and indefinite articles is straightforward, and the article system can be assimilated without too much difficulty.

Teachers can assist learners with recognition by providing lists of words organised into useful groups and by encouraging rote learning. They can identify grammatical systems which can usefully be transferred from the students' first language. As we have seen, one example for most European learners of English is the article system. In the same way, for French learners of English, the *going to* future can simply be transferred from the French.

System building: Language learning involves conscious processes which are familiar to all who have learnt a second language. Learners begin to form hypotheses about how grammatical systems work and teachers can help them do so. A good example is the relationship between continuous and simple tenses in English. In most elementary English courses learners begin by recognising the difference in meaning between the present simple and the present continuous. Without help and direction from the teacher it would be very difficult for learners to make the generalisation that the present simple is generally used for habitual actions or ongoing states:

I usually go to church on Sunday.
We live just outside Birmingham.

whereas the present continuous is generally used for something which is happening at the time of utterance:

*Wait a minute, I'm **listening** to the radio.*
*Dad's **watching** the football on TV.*

Without further help from the teacher it is even more difficult for learners to recognise that the present continuous can also be used for habitual actions or ongoing states if these actions or states are regarded as temporary:

*She's in her sixties but she's still **playing** tennis regularly.*
*We **are living** in Selly Oak for the time being.*

Teachers can provide useful rules of thumb to help learners work out the grammar, and they can support these rules with carefully chosen examples as well as by asking learners to find examples for themselves in the language they experience. They can supplement this by setting exercises which will require learners to apply the rules in order to produce language.

In the early stages of learning learners may practise routines which contribute to system building at a later stage. At the elementary level, for example, students may be introduced to a vocabulary building game which also incorporates insights into the use of the definite and indefinite articles in English. One such game, *What's in the bag?*, involves taking into the classroom a bag filled with objects that are familiar to the learners:

Teacher: *What do you think I've got in my bag?*
Student: *A pencil.*
Teacher: *Yes, I've got a pencil. Here it is.* (puts the pencil on her desk)
   Where is the pencil?
Student: *It's on the desk?*
Teacher: *Good. It's on the desk. What else have I got in my bag?*
Student: *A pen.*
Teacher: *Yes, I've got a pen ...*
etc.

As well as building vocabulary this game provides exposure to a number of useful phrases: *What have I got? I've got ... What else?*, and at least one useful pattern *N + is + prepositional phrase*. It also provides a number of possible insights into the use of the referential system in English: it introduces the indefinite article *a(n)*; it illustrates the use of the pronoun *it* to refer back to something which has been introduced; it shows the use of the definite article to refer to something specific.

However, if it is learnt at all, it is learnt only as a routine and leaves many questions unanswered. The fact that the teacher says: *It's a pencil* rather than: *It's the pencil* may appear to contradict the 'rule' that the first mention of a noun uses the indefinite article, while subsequent mentions use either the definite article or a pronoun like *it*. Why is the pencil described as being on *the desk*, rather than *a desk* ? A command of routines such as these does not mean that students have mastered these elements of the system; it simply provides them with samples of language which they can perhaps draw on as the system develops.

Although we have discussed words on the one hand and grammar on the other, it is often quite impossible to separate the two. This will become apparent as soon as we look at some of the words in English which are associated with complex grammatical patterns. The word *agreement* is a good example. In fact there are two words for *agreement*: there is a countable form of the word, which is found in sentences like:

We made an agreement to meet the following week.

while the uncountable *agreement* is found in sentences like:

We failed to reach agreement on the outstanding issues.

This uncountable *agreement* occurs in a number of fixed phrases such as *in agreement* or *by agreement*. In order to use this word effectively, a learner needs to know a good deal about the patterns in which it occurs. There are a number of collocational restrictions: we do not talk of *doing* an agreement; we normally *reach* or *come to* an agreement; we talk about *general agreement* or *broad agreement*, but not *wide agreement*. The word is also postmodified in particular ways: we talk about *agreement on* a particular issue, or *agreement on* a course of action; we frequently talk about *agreement to* do something; we say that there is *general agreement that* ... . Before learners can make productive use of the word *agreement* they need to be aware of these patterns, and of common collocations and collocational restrictions.

Knowing the meaning of the word and its first language equivalent or equivalents is a matter of recognition, and this provides an important starting point. But if learners are to make the word a useful part of their vocabulary, recognition can only be the first stage in a more complex learning process which involves system building. System building related to the word *agreement* links the word to other nouns formed from verbs. We not only talk about *an agreement to* do something – the words *decision, plan* and *arrangement* are used in exactly the same way. So nouns denoting the outcome of negotiation or planning are followed by the *to*-infinitive. Similarly nouns related to reporting verbs are often followed by a *that*-clause – nouns such as *belief, claim* and *suggestion*. We talk about *reaching* or *coming to agreement*. We also talk about reaching or coming to *an arrangement, a decision* or *a conclusion*. So the behaviour of a word like *agreement* is systematic. Learners will begin to use the word quickly and effectively if they are able to link it systematically to other words in the language.

Exploration: A lot of learning takes place by exploration. As they are exposed to language, learners find things out for themselves and begin to develop systems without even being aware that they are doing so. Foreign language learning in a natural environment involves a lot of exploration. If we are living in a foreign language environment we begin to make sense of the language we hear, and to develop grammatical systems without even thinking about it. We produce language because it **feels** right. There are at least two good reasons why discovery is an important and a necessary process, not only in the natural environment, but in classroom language learning too.

Learning a language is a huge task. Firstly, there is simply not enough time for a teacher to provide guidance on every aspect of language. As we pointed out above, the word *agreement* relates to a group of other words in a number of different ways. It belongs to various different networks. There are so many networks and so many words that we cannot help learners understand all of them. There is so much to learn that it cannot all be covered explicitly with rules and explanations.

Secondly, even if we wanted to, we cannot always provide learners with the guidance they need. For example, Hughes and McCarthy (1998) show how the generally accepted pedagogic rule, 'that the past perfect tense is used for an event that happened in a past time before another past time ...', enables learners to make well-formed sentences such as: *I spoke to Lisa Knox yesterday for the first time. I had met her 10 years ago but had not spoken to her*. But, as Hughes and McCarthy go on to point out, this rule does not show 'that the two sentences would be equally well formed if the second were in the past simple', although the emphasis would be different. What Hughes and McCarthy do not show is that a careful application of the rule would lead learners to produce some forms like: *I opened the door when the postman had knocked*, which are distinctly odd, if not ungrammatical. It is virtually impossible to frame a rule which will enable learners to make appropriate choices between the past simple and past perfect in these contexts. Hughes and McCarthy go on to draw the conclusion that:

> The rule therefore ... does not offer sufficiently precise guidelines to generate the choice when appropriate. In

> situations such as this our proposal is to look at the choices that real speakers and writers have made in real contexts and consider the contextual features that apparently motivated one choice or the other.
>
> (Hughes & McCarthy, 1988: 268)

This is an interesting proposal, but it is impossible to carry out. The distinctions are simply too subtle and complex to demonstrate and explain. Although my explicit grammar of English is much more complete than that of most learners, and although I have spent a good deal of my professional life working on grammatical description, I am quite unable to provide a satisfactory explanation why *I opened the door when the postman had knocked* is a most unlikely sentence of English whereas *I opened the door when the postman had gone* seems perfectly reasonable. This means that I am able to operate grammatical systems which are much more subtle than anything I am able to explain. In assessing whether something is or is not grammatical we often act on feel, and are quite unable to explain our intuitions. The sentence *I opened the door when the postman had knocked* is a case in point.

Much learning depends on something subtler than the conscious application of rules, even if those rules attempt to take account of contextual features. As learners are more exposed to language, they begin to refine the systems they have consciously built, and to develop systems that they are not even aware of. This is largely an unconscious process, but it is a process that can be sharpened and informed by instruction. We can provide learners with useful hints – like the rule about the past perfect cited by Hughes and McCarthy – but this is simply the beginning of a process of exploration. Learners must be encouraged to go on working with texts and gradually refining their own model of the verb system.

To stimulate the process of exploration we need to encourage learners to focus carefully on the wording of texts. To help with this, teachers can design consciousness-raising activities designed to encourage learners to search input for clues to assist language development, and to help them learn more independently. These activities can be quite straightforward, simply drawing learners' attention to text and requiring them to look carefully at the language they have processed. But one thing is certain: unless learners process language unconsciously to refine the systems they have built by conscious effort, they will not develop a model of the language which even begins to approach that of the native speaker.

I would like also to draw attention to a fourth element which I will call **rehearsal**. This is an activity rather than a process, and generally comes between recognition and system building.

Rehearsal: Learners work consciously to develop routines, and are assisted in this by teacher-led activities. Often a routine may consist of no more than a single utterance. Learners repeat and manipulate patterns and phrases which they believe will be particularly valuable: *Would you like ...? Would you mind ___ing ...? So do I.* etc. When learning a language in the outside world, we sometimes rehearse whole encounters. Before going to the shops and using a foreign language which I do not speak very well I go over possible encounters in my mind, trying to predict the language I will hear and the language I will need to produce.

Rehearsal seems to contribute to learning in the early stages. Teachers organise and orchestrate repetition of individual utterances on an individual and a class basis. They encourage learners to repeat samples of a form they want learners to master. Activities of this kind certainly seem to reinforce learners' motivation. They may assist recall and use, certainly for basic vocabulary, such as my Spanish menu items. It is much less likely to be the case with complex grammatical systems like the tense system. Paradoxically it does not seem to help a great deal with the terminal *-s* and with question forms, which would seem to be ideal candidates for this kind of learning. Current research simply does not tell us how this kind of controlled repetition contributes to learning, although this does not mean that we should ignore it entirely. If it is sensibly contextualised within various learning processes, it may well be useful. It does mean, however, that we should not make it the basis of a methodology. Learning is a complex developmental process; it is tempting to think that we can offer a quick fix, but it is a temptation which we should resist.

We have now looked at three main processes which contribute to learning. The first of these, **recognition**, can be directly assisted by teacher intervention, drawing students' attention to aspects of language form. The second process, **system building**, is a conscious process whereby learners try to work out rules, speculating on the systems of the language and how they relate to one another. This too can be assisted by teacher intervention: teachers can either provide input in a way which helps learners to formulate rules for themselves, or they can intervene by providing rules for learners. Finally we have **exploration**. This is an unconscious process whereby learners discover or refine the language for themselves. Teachers cannot assist this process by direct intervention, but they can devise activities which will encourage learners to look carefully at language in ways that are likely to prompt discovery.

We need, then, to design classroom activities which will promote recognition and conscious system building. We need also to design activities which will encourage learners to discover language for themselves, to explore the relationship between meaning and form. Activities appropriate to different learning processes will be illustrated throughout the following chapters. But, as we have shown, learning is of little use unless what is learnt becomes a part of the learner's spontaneous language production. We also need to provide learners with plenty of opportunities to use the language, so they can gradually begin to put into practice what they have learnt. Before we begin to consider language use in the classroom we will look briefly at how language is used in the outside world.

1.5 Some questions about language

Up to now in this chapter we have taken it more or less for granted that learning a language means learning to produce appropriate sentences in that language. This is certainly the traditional view of learning: success or failure is normally measured in terms of this ability to produce appropriate sentences. When our students produce accurate question tags, we feel we and they have succeeded. When they fail to do so, we feel that we have failed. Unfortunately, if we measure success in this way, then language programmes are usually characterised by failure rather than success. But there is another way of looking at language and language learning, and that way may lead us to a very different view of success and failure.

In 1975 Michael Halliday published a book describing how his young son, Nigel, learnt his first language, English. Normally we think of children as learning how to talk. When a child reaches the age of two, we say things like: *She can talk quite a lot now* or *She can say a lot of things now*. Halliday, however, looked at language in a rather different way. We can see this from the title of his book. He called it 'Learning How to **Mean**'. For Halliday the important thing about language is the capacity to mean. What a child has to acquire is the ability to interact with others in a way which produces desired outcomes. Clearly the ability to achieve meanings is related to the ability to make sentences, but they are not the same thing. By the age of two children are able to realise a range of meanings, but they rarely utter a sentence which would be considered grammatical in terms of the adult language system.

It is not always easy to work out what children want to mean. At an early age children communicate by putting words together and relying on someone else, usually their mother, to work out the meaning with the help of the context. At this stage children don't bother with the little words which are so frequent in the language of the adult speaker: articles (*the, a(n)*), prepositions (*in, on, at* and so on) and the forms of the verb *BE*. Such words are often called **structural** words as opposed to **lexical** words: nouns, adjectives, verbs and adverbs. A child will say, for example: *Dolly chair.* If this is accompanied by a pointing gesture, it probably means: *The doll is on that chair.* If it is accompanied by a gesture handing the doll to an adult, it may mean: *Please put the doll on a chair.* So the child puts together a string of lexical words supported by gesture and context, and depends on the adult's willingness to work out meanings and act on them.

Children rapidly add to their stock of words, and as they do so the grammar gradually develops. It is some time before they begin to build in structural words, and some time before they begin to use anything but a very rudimentary verb system. Nevertheless, in the early stages, children manage to communicate a lot, even though their language is very limited and consists mainly of strings of vocabulary items. As children grow older their developing intellectual capacity demands more and more complex meanings, making more and more demands on the child's grammar. The child responds by developing a grammar to meet the new demands.

We should be careful not to overestimate the similarities between first and second language learning. Unlike a child, the adult has reached a high level of intellectual development. An adult learner already speaks at least one language fluently and is able to use that language as a resource to help with the learning of a new language. In spite of this, few adults master a second language to anything like native speaker level, whereas almost all children successfully acquire their first language to the extent that they can speak it fluently and accurately. So there must be marked differences in the learning processes.

It seems, however, that learners acquiring language outside the classroom, where there is a premium on effective communication, will work like children acquiring their first language, and attempt to build up a meaning system. Like children they are content in the early stages of learning to rely on stringing words together, using a minimal grammar. One way the grammar develops is that learners begin to acquire new grammatical forms, which they could not previously use. But learners also have other ways of increasing their ability to mean.

The teaching process normally encourages learners to increase their stock of language by learning new words and patterns, but learners may also increase their capacity to mean by making better use of the language they already have. Thus, a learner who does not have adequate control of negative verbs forms, but who knows the word *no*, will produce forms like *I no want ...; I no like ...*, and so on. Resourceful learners will make use of their first language to create new forms even if these forms are not a part of standard English. A speaker of French who does not have control of the present perfect tense, for example, may use the present simple: *I already tell you this.* A third way of learning to mean is by generalising from what we know to generate something we don't know: a learner who does not know the past tense of the verb *run* will sensibly offer the form *runned.* A fourth way is by using alternative means of achieving a given end: a learner who does not have command of question forms may rely on intonation and a puzzled facial expression to mark questions. All of these are legitimate ways of extending the meaning system; they are all legitimate **meaning expansion strategies** and should be encouraged in the classroom.

But there is more to meaning than simply getting a basic meaning across – we need to get meanings across in a way that can be readily and easily processed by a listener. My Ghanaian students, for example, had a complex and efficient dialect of English which they used successfully and effectively in communicating with other Ghanaians from different language groups. But this system was sometimes enormously difficult to use for another speaker who did not share that particular dialect. My job was to offer them a form of English which would be more widely negotiable, which would be understand by an international community, a community which did not have access to the Ghanaian dialect.

We need to have a form of English which can be readily processed by a wide range of other users, an **internationally** negotiable meaning system. But there is a clash of priorities between teaching and learning. Learners of English at the intermediate level face a difficult choice. Should they produce English fluently so that they can take part in a conversation in a way which other speakers do not find irritatingly slow? If they choose to do this, they will certainly produce many grammatical errors and may, at times, make themselves difficult to understand.

The alternative – and this is the preferred alternative for many learners, particularly adult learners – is to concentrate on producing language with a high level of formal accuracy. This requires careful attention to the language they produce. As a result their production will probably be so slow and hesitant that other speakers may find it irritating and frustrating – and it will still be sprinkled with inaccuracies. Whether the emphasis is on acceptable speed and fluency, or on acceptable formal accuracy, depends on the circumstances of use and on the personality and age of the learner. It is not a simple question, and the answer will nearly always involve a compromise of some sort.

We also need a form of English which will enable us to present ourselves to other users of English in a favourable light. It is a fact of life that we make judgements of others on the basis of the language they use and the way they use it. I often refer to this problem as the 'Tarzan' problem. Tarzan was a popular character in the films of my youth. He was a man who had been raised by animals in the jungle, like Mowgli, the wolf child. He was entirely at home in the jungle. In every episode of his story he would face down lions and wrestle crocodiles with heroic panache. But his language was very limited – he would introduce himself by slapping his chest and proclaiming: *Me Tarzan*. Now if you have just disposed of a crocodile in heroic manner, this may be an entirely appropriate way to introduce yourself to the admiring onlookers, but if you want to make your way in polite society, you probably need a quite different form. At the very least you need to say: *Hi there. I'm Tarzan, the well-known king of the jungle*. Perhaps this is making too much of yourself. A more modest introduction would be: *Good afternoon. I don't think we've been introduced. I'm Tarzan. I live here in the jungle*. So we need a range of language forms which will enable us to choose whatever we see as appropriate to the circumstances and the way we wish to present ourselves.

I have a good friend called Fabienne, a French woman who is an expert in Old English. She can tell me things about the derivation of words in my own language which I find endlessly fascinating. Her English is rapid and fluent, but it is also quite obviously the English of a French speaker. Her accent is such that you need to hear only a single sentence to identify her as a French woman. She is entirely happy with this. She wants to be taken for what she is – a woman who is proud to be French, but who speaks remarkably good English. She has no desire to be taken for a native English speaker.

Decisions of this kind should be taken by learners themselves. What sort of English do they want to speak? Do they want to be able to speak English at a basic level, like Tarzan? Or do they want to speak English with a fluent command of a native-like grammar and vocabulary while retaining their non-Englishness, like Fabienne? Or do they want to be taken for a native speaker of English and sound entirely British or American or Australian or whatever? Language is a system of meanings, but the meanings it carries do more than tell people things and ask them to do things – these meanings also tell people about how we view ourselves and how we view them: these meanings 'make an impression' on people.

Sometimes learners will quite deliberately produce forms which they believe to be non-grammatical. In English there is a broad generalisation that longer is politer:

Open the door.
Please, open the door.
Would you open the door, please.
Please, would you mind opening the door?

The same phenomenon may exist in a learner's own language. Imagine then a learner who wants to be polite but who does not have access to the modal *would* and the phrase *would you mind*. Such a learner may well produce something like:

Please, I like you will open the door, please.

Politeness is achieved by the length of the request, but in order to achieve that length learners may quite deliberately produce language which they know to be ungrammatical.

So we can think of language as a meaning system, but we need to think of it as a negotiable meaning system, one that has to be used with a range of other speakers of the language. We also need to think of it as a system which allows us to present ourselves appropriately in a range of situations. And, finally, what we want is a system which enables us to present ourselves to others in a way which we find acceptable. But we need to recognise one important fact: the ability to mean is not **directly** related to the ability to produce accurate sentences in standard British or American English, or any other standardised form. Learners may accept the production of non-standard forms as the price they have to pay to enable them to speak rapidly and fluently. They may accept non-standard forms because they have no wish to be taken for a native speaker of English. Thus, we can speak of complementary purposes in producing language:

Basic message → **Concern for reader/listener** → **Presentation of self**

Learners are concerned first to get their message across with acceptable speed and fluency in real time. Secondly they will want to structure and mark their message in such a way as to make it readily comprehensible and acceptable to their reader or listener. Finally they will want to carry their message in a way that presents them as they wish to be seen. The language they produce will vary according to the circumstances in which it is produced and according to the learner's communicative priorities. Those familiar with Hallidayan functional grammar (see Halliday, 1978 and 1994) will recognise that these complementary purposes relate very closely to Halliday's metafunctions: **ideational, textual** and **interpersonal**.

Let us look at two extreme types of language use in the classroom and go on to consider the implications for learning. We will consider first

improvisation, where learners produce language with little or no time for preparation. We will then go on to look at a process I have labelled **consolidation,** where learners have time to produce a more considered version of a message.

- **Improvisation:** Sometimes language is produced with little time for preparation and in circumstances which make considerable demands on the learner's developing system. When this happens learners are obliged to improvise, to make the most of the language they have at their command. In improvisation learners are likely to be concerned principally with using language to get their basic message across. In the early stages of learning they will find it difficult to do this while simultaneously making allowances for their listener and the presentation of self.

  I have already suggested that at a very early stage learners will depend on stringing lexical items together to produce utterances like: *I student* or *Book on desk.* At the same time they will find a lexical means of encoding negation, for example, even if they have not yet encountered the full range of structural devices available in the target language to do this. They may simply include a marker of negation in the clause to produce sentences like: *I no see him* or *No get shoes.* In the same way they will produce questions not by inversion, but simply by intonation: *You like this? You are ready? Pen?* Instances of this sort of improvisation are well attested in the literature on second language acquisition. As the language develops and the demands on the learner increase they may call on the resources of their first language, like the French learner who produces: *I already tell you this.*

  It is very important for learners to have opportunities for improvisation in the classroom. This is particularly true at the elementary and intermediate levels. As soon as these learners begin to use the language outside the classroom they will be obliged to improvise. Unless they are willing to stretch their language resources in the classroom they will be quite unable to meet the communicative demands placed upon them outside. One of the most valuable skills elementary and intermediate learners can acquire is the ability to make a little language go a long way.

  There is a second reason why learners need to improvise: in the process of improvisation they will become aware of gaps in their knowledge of English. They will realise that there are meanings which they are unable to express. They will realise that there are other meanings which they are able to express only by going outside their grammatical knowledge, possibly by borrowing from the first language. These realisations will serve to make learners sensitive to input. They will begin to look for ways to supplement the gaps in their language which they have identified.

- **Consolidation:** Improvisation involves the application of the learner's system in unpredictable circumstances with little or no time for preparation. Consolidation is a different kind of procedure. If learners are given time to prepare for a language production activity, they will think carefully through what they want to say. They will want to go beyond the basic presentation of their message, to take account of the listeners and to present themselves in a favourable light. In order to do this they may ask for help from classmates and from their teacher. They may have recourse to reference books and possibly to texts which they have read and which express the ideas they are looking for.

  The value of consolidation activities is twofold. First learners will gradually be able to incorporate into their language items and patterns which they are aware of, but which they cannot command in spontaneous speech. Thus, language which is on the threshold of spontaneity may be incorporated into their performance. The second advantage is that in consolidation activities, learners will begin to build new systems into their performance in such a way that these systems can be called on as automatic routines rather than worked on consciously as part of the production process. They will, for example, gradually reach the stage where question forms become a part of their spontaneous repertoire, rather than items which are produced only when they are concentrating solely on form. They will begin to establish language routines which are essential to fluent performance. This is a process very similar to what Skehan (1998: 90) calls **relexicalisation**. If learners are to do this, they need plenty of opportunities to prepare for language use in meaningful situations.

In using language for communication in the classroom, then, learners need opportunities for improvisation, to get practice in making the most of their language and to identify gaps in their language. They also need consolidation activities to enable them to extend their usable language system and to build up useful routines. Activities like this are a part of most teachers' classroom repertoire. In Chapter 3 we will look at an approach to classroom learning which builds these activities into a coherent methodology.

1.6 Summary

I have suggested in this chapter that language learning is not simple and straightforward. Learners do not proceed from mastery of one form to mastery of the next until they have the whole system at their command. What most teachers have learnt from experience is that learners fail to learn a great deal of what they are supposed to learn, but that they also learn a great deal which they have not been taught. There is, however, evidence from research and from our classroom experience that instruction does help learners to approach their task more efficiently as they struggle with the complexities of language.

Most teaching strategies rely on the introduction of new language forms as the most efficient way forward. Because of this they rely on the presentation and practice of these new forms. But these new forms do not seem to be incorporated into the learner's language in a direct and straightforward way. If we accept this, it suggests that language learning is not simply a matter of acquiring new forms. As well as recognising new forms learners need to work consciously on building up the systems of the language. They also need encouragement to work with text in ways which will allow them to explore the language and develop spontaneously.

Language is most productively viewed as a system of meanings, rather than as a system of formal patterns. New meanings can be created by the application of a number of strategies, not simply by the acquisition of new forms. The application of these strategies often involves learners in producing forms which are not a part of the target language system. Learners need opportunities to develop these strategies by being asked to improvise with the language. This improvisation will also encourage them to identify gaps in their command of the language. Learners also need consolidation activities, opportunities to prepare for communicative activities. This will allow them to extend the repertoire of language available to them for communicative deployment. It will also enable them to build up language routines to provide a basis for fluency.

At any stage of learning all of these processes are likely to be involved. Some lexical and grammatical systems will be largely unknown, and will therefore be improvised. Some systems will be identified by the teacher and will be the focus of system building activities. Yet other systems will be discovered by the learners on their own initiative. This learning will enable learners to modify their improvised performance if they are given the time and the incentive to do so. As a result of consolidation activities learners will gradually attain spontaneous mastery by building consolidated routines into their spontaneous use.

The progression I am proposing can be shown like this:

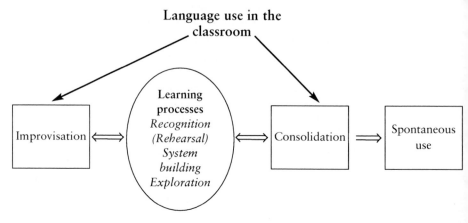

Fig. 1.1

Learners begin with a situation where they are unsure of the language and are therefore obliged to improvise. Through improvisation they identify gaps in their language knowledge which they will seek to fill. Learning activities focus on learning processes to provide input to fill these gaps as the language is refined and developed. This runs alongside learning processes which provide learners with access to a more and more complex model of the language. This more complex model is gradually incorporated into their language through consolidation activities, until it finally becomes a part of their spontaneous use. So language use in the classroom provides the context for language learning, and a preparation for spontaneous use outside the classroom.

In Section 1.2 we looked at the problems experienced by learners in developing *do*-questions, and later in developing indirect question forms. The way in which they develop *do*-questions suggests the following sequence of development:

- **Improvisation:** Learners simply 'make up' questions by adding WH-words to statements, or by using intonation as a question marker: *What you want?*
- **Recognition:** Learners recognise isolated *do*-question forms (*What do you want?*) and are able to recognise them as interrogative equivalents to affirmative sentences, but they do not see these forms as systematic. Perhaps they do not recognise that forms like *What you want?* are unacceptable, regarding them as alternative forms.

Perhaps they are unable to relate these questions systematically to corresponding affirmative forms. They do not understand the system of rules underlying this relationship.

- **System building:** Learners realise that almost all WH-questions involve inversion of the subject and an auxiliary verb (*What **are** you doing?*) or inversion of the subject and a modal verb (*What should we do?*). In the case of the present simple it is necessary to supply an auxiliary using the forms *do* and *does*, and in the case of the past simple the form *did*. This is part of their knowledge about language, but they are still unable to produce these forms spontaneously.
- **Consolidation:** Given more opportunities to use the language, learners begin to incorporate questions with inversion, including *do*-questions, in their production.
- **Spontaneous mastery:** Learners consistently produce *do*-questions without conscious effort.

But the development of *do*-questions also affects the learners' production of indirect questions:

- **Improvisation:** Learners have learnt to associate WH-words with auxiliary verbs, including *do*. They build up a routine where a WH-word is automatically followed by an auxiliary:

  He asked me what did I want.

  This is a stage which almost all learners go through.

- **Recognition:** Teachers encourage learners to recognise that there is no inversion or auxiliary *do* in reported questions:

  He asked me what I wanted.

  At the same time learners are beginning to recognise the forms which regularly introduce indirect questions (*ask, know, tell, wonder* etc.), but they are still unable to break the habit of linking WH-words with auxiliaries, including the auxiliary *do*.
- **System building:** In this case system building is fairly straightforward. It involves little more than recognising that there is no inversion in reported questions.
- **Consolidation:** Given more opportunities to use the language, learners begin to incorporate the sequence WH-word + subject + main verb (*Tell me **what** + **you** + **want.***) into their production.
- **Spontaneous mastery:** Finally learners consistently produce appropriate forms for indirect questions.

In both these sequences communicative activities involving improvisation and consolidation play a central part, allowing learners first to identify gaps in their language and later affording them time to incorporate the desired forms. I have suggested that **recognition** plays a part in the acquisition of both questions and reported questions, as it must in the learning of any item or system. I have also suggested that system building is an important part of *do*-questions. There is a rule-governed system which teachers can help learners to understand. There is little in the way of system building in the acquisition of reported questions. It is more a matter of reverting to previously established behaviour and simply adding *what* and *you want*.

In neither case have I suggested that exploration plays an important part in the learning process. In Section 1.5 we identified two reasons for exploration processes: firstly we cannot afford classroom time to cover all aspects of language. Secondly, some systems are too subtle for learners to acquire consciously. We have given the distinction between the past simple and the past perfect as an example. Learners must be encouraged to look at problematic items such as these in text, and gradually develop appropriate systems through a process of exploration. Questions and reported questions, however, are important enough to justify class time, and it is possible for teachers to provide adequate support for them to be learnt consciously. This demonstrates an important principle: different learning processes will predominate in solving different learning problems. As we saw in Section 1.4, discovery plays a necessary role in the acquisition of the tense system, which involves distinctions that are too subtle to explain. But discovery is not a necessary part of learning question forms which can be explained and demonstrated with relative ease.

The question we need to ask is how instruction can most efficiently support these processes. The teaching strategies we adopt will depend on what is being learnt, but whatever strategy we adopt we should be aware that learners all have their own agenda and their own priorities. At some stages, particularly in the early stages, their priority may be the development of a basic meaning system with little attention to accuracy. Other learners may have different priorities and be concerned with keeping to simple, safe and accurate utterances. As their systems develop, so learners are likely to increase the demands they make on themselves. In line with the sequence outlined above:

Basic message → Concern for reader/listener → Presentation of self

they are likely to look for forms of the language which are more widely negotiable and which make a better impression. All this is part of meaning. If teachers support the learning processes outlined above, it seems reasonable to suppose that the developmental process will be driven by the learner's desire to mean, rather than by the teacher's desire to impose new language forms on learners.

In the next chapter we will look at a methodology which incorporates the learning processes and the communicative processes we have looked at here.

2 Grammar and lexis and learning

In this chapter we will look at grammar and lexis, or vocabulary, and at the relationship between the two. I used to think that these were quite separate, that grammar was about sentences and lexis was about words. I thought that learners first learnt how to make grammatical sentences and, as they did this, they learnt to insert the words they had learnt in order to make more and more sentences. But research, particularly over the last fifteen years or so, is beginning to demonstrate more and more clearly that the relationship between grammar and lexis is much closer than this: in making sentences we may start with the grammar, but the final shape of a sentence is determined by the words which make up the sentence. Let us take a simple example. These are both likely sentences of English:

I laughed.
She bought it.

But the following are not likely sentences of English:

I put.
She put it.

The verb *put* is incomplete unless it is followed by both a direct object, such as *it*, and also an adverbial of place like *here* or *away*:

I put it on the shelf.
She put it away.

Taking three different verbs, *laugh, buy* and *put*, as starting points results in sentences which are quite different in structure.

If you look back to the first sentence of this chapter you will see that the word *relationship* is followed by *between*. This again shows that once you see a particular word it is often possible to predict what will follow. As soon as you see *We will look at ... the relationship*, you know that what follows must be the word *between* and then a list of the things that are related. If these things have not already been mentioned, you will have a phrase with the words *between ... and ...*, a phrase like *the relationship **between** grammar **and** lexis*. If, however, the things related have already been listed, you will have a word or phrase which refers back to them, such as *the relationship between **them*** or, as in the first sentence above, *the relationship between **the two***. So once you have chosen the word *relationship* you have also chosen the way the sentence will develop. The lexis and the grammar, the words and the sentence, proceed hand-in-hand.

We can begin by looking at the broad grammatical framework within which words operate, then we will go on to see how the shape of a grammatical sentence is determined by the words that it contains. As we do this we will have to simplify things a bit, but we will go on to look at things more fully in later chapters.

2.1 The grammar of structure

Structure is here employed to mean the way items – words and phrases – are sequenced to make up larger units. In an English clause, for example, we typically find a noun as the subject followed by a verb, followed by another noun, the object, so that the clause has the structure **subject** → **verb** → **object**. In Japanese, however, a clause typically has the structure **subject** → **object** → **verb**. Clause structure in Japanese is different from that in English – the elements come in a different order. There are also differences in the way noun phrases are structured; in English, adjectives come in front of the noun; in Japanese, they come after the noun. So English and Japanese have marked differences in structure: their grammatical elements are organised in very different ways.

2.1.1 The structure of the clause

We can begin by thinking, in very general terms, about how clauses are made up. We describe the structure of a clause by listing the elements which make up that clause. The clauses listed above, for example, would be described as follows:

> *I / laughed.* (noun + verb or N + V)
> *She / bought / a dress.* (noun + verb + noun, or N + V + N)
> *The little boy / put / it / on the shelf.* (N + V + N + Adv.)

I am using the term **adverbial** to refer to what some grammars describe as adverbs, adverbial phrases and prepositional phrases. In the sentence:

> *He promised <u>faithfully</u> to do the job <u>after lunch</u>, and to complete it <u>as quickly as possible</u>.*

the three underlined elements would be regarded as adverbials. Using abbreviations for noun (N), verb (V), adverbial (Adv.), and adjective (Adj.), we can set out very general rules to describe the structure of the English clause:

a. The basic structure of the clause is N + V (+ ?). This means that the first element in the clause is a noun or a noun equivalent such as a pronoun (*I, you, she, it, they*) or a noun phrase (*My old friend, the man in the moon* etc.). This is followed by a verb which *may* be followed by something else (represented above by (+ ?)) depending on the nature of the verb. Examples are:

> *Everybody / laughed.* (N + V)
> *We all / enjoyed / the party.* (N + V + N)
> *The old lady / put / her bags / in the car.* (N + V + N + Adv.)
> *This / made / my friend / angry.* (N + V + N + Adj.)

In all these cases the continuation of the clause after the verb is determined by the ***meaning*** of the verb, not by abstract grammatical considerations. It makes no sense, for example, to say: *The old lady put* or *The old lady put her bags;* to make sense of the verb *put* we need the full clause: *The old lady put her bags in the car.* The meaning of the verb determines what will follow it. We have given only four examples, but there are a large number of possible patterns after the verb (see Task 2.1).

b. The first noun phrase in the clause functions as the subject of the verb. Again this is a powerful general rule to which there are very few exceptions.

c. All English clauses must have a word or phrase which acts as grammatical subject. In some languages a verb can function without a subject. In Italian, for example, the subject can be 'hidden' in the verb, to give a clause such as *ti amo*, meaning *I love you*. Here *ti* means *you* and *amo* means *I love*. Although there is a word for *I* in Italian (*io*), it is not very common, being used only for emphasis. Languages like Italian are sometimes known as pro-drop (for pronoun-drop) languages, because when the subject of the clause is a pronoun, it can be dropped, or left out. The term pro-drop is perhaps an unfortunate one because it defines other languages in terms of the way they deviate from English. In English we must have a subject. If there is no obvious subject we need to supply a 'dummy' subject, usually *it* or *there*, as in:

> *It's raining.*
> *There is no time to waste.*

This feature of English can cause problems for learners whose native language is a pro-drop language (see Task 2.2).

Task 2.1:

Look at the sentence beginnings numbered 1–5 below. Can you match them with the completions, numbered a–e? Can you say what it was that enabled you to complete the task successfully?

1. Everybody stopped   a) to go home.
2. We wanted   b) him angry.
3. Don't try to prevent me   c) where he is.
4. I wonder   d) working.
5. It made   e) from going.

Commentary on Task 2.1:

The correct answers are: 1 d; 2 a; 3 e; 4 c; 5 b.
You were able to complete the task because you know what pattern to expect after each verb. The verb *stop* is normally followed by the -*ing*-form of the verb. *Want* is followed either by a noun (*We wanted help*) or, as in this example, by a verb with the *to*-infinitive. *Prevent* followed by a noun is normally followed by *from* and the -*ing*-form of the verb. *Wonder* is followed by either *if* or a question word and then a clause. *Make*, meaning *force* or *compel*, is followed by a noun and then by an adjective, as here, or by the base form of the verb, as in *It made everyone laugh*.

As you read the first part (1–5) of each clause, your knowledge of the verb led you to predict what would follow. You were then able to check your prediction against the possible completions (a–e). What enabled you to do the task, therefore, was your knowledge of words and the patterns which follow them.

Task 2.2:

Complete the following sentences by putting *it* or *there* in the appropriate place. When do we use *there* as a 'dummy subject', and when do we use *it*?

Try translating these sentences into another language. If you need to include a word as the subject, such as *it* or *there*, then the language you have chosen is like English – you must have a word functioning as subject. If there is no need to supply a word as subject, then you are using a pro-drop language, one which does not always have a word as subject. Referential pronouns (*I, you, he*, etc.) are optional (often emphatic) in pro-drop languages, but dummy pronouns simply do not exist.

1. I'm tired. Is nearly midnight.
2. Be careful. Has been an accident.
3. Is some money in the drawer.
4. Is dangerous to drive too fast.

Commentary on Task 2.2:

The correct answers are:

1. I'm tired. **It** is nearly midnight.
2. Be careful. **There** has been an accident.
3. **There** is some money in the drawer.
4. **It** is dangerous to drive too fast.

Normally we use *there* when we are talking about the existence or occurrence of something (*an accident*) or when we are talking about the location of something (*in the drawer*). Otherwise we normally use *it*. Note that in a sentence like: *I've found your purse: it was in the kitchen*, the word *it* is not a dummy subject; it is a pronoun standing in place of *your purse*.

I don't know which language you used for your translation, but the following languages are pro-drop: Italian; Japanese; Korean; Portuguese; Spanish. The following are not: French; German.

There is, of course, a lot more to the structure of the English clause. As well as the adverbials we have seen so far, it may include adverbials found in other positions in the clause. We have clauses like:

Naturally / we all / enjoyed / the party. (Adv. + N + V + N)
It / always / rains / on Sunday. (N + Adv. + V + Adv.)

The positioning of these adverbials in the clause can be quite complicated. Adverbials which say something about the whole clause, such as *naturally* or *surprisingly*, usually come at the beginning of the clause. But adverbs of degree, for example, normally come at the end of a clause:

*I enjoyed the party **very much**.*

These adverbs of degree can be found before the verb:

*I **very much** enjoyed the party.*

but not between the verb and its object:

*I enjoyed very much the party[1].

or at the beginning of the clause:

*Very much I enjoyed the party.

We can provide very general rules for the basic structure of the clause, but once we go beyond that basis, the structure will depend on the words we add to the clause. We can, then, provide firm guidelines for the structure of the clause. And we can provide equally firm guidelines for the elements which make up the clause – the noun phrase and the verb phrase.

2.1.2 The noun phrase

The simplest noun phrase consists of a single word, a noun or pronoun (*I, you, children, information*). Most noun phrases are introduced by a determiner. The most frequent determiners are articles (*the, a(n)*), possessives (*my, your, our, their*) and demonstratives (*this, that, these, those*). After the determiner we may see one adjective or two, extremely rarely more than two. Then comes the noun. The basic structure of the noun phrase, then, is (determiner) + (adjective(s)) + noun, in that order. The brackets here mark optional elements in the clause, so the description:

(determiner) + (adjective(s)) + noun

means that any noun phrase must have a noun or pronoun in it, and that noun or pronoun may or may not be preceded by a determiner and one or more adjectives, in that order. The ordering of the noun phrase is fixed and unalterable. So that: *that big black cat* is grammatical, whereas: **that cat big black* is not. Once we go beyond this basic description, the noun phrase becomes very complicated indeed, with further items, quantifiers and partitives, coming in front of the noun, and yet other items, such as prepositional phrases, coming after the noun as postmodifiers. The noun phrase *both of those books on the desk* has the structure:

quantifier (*both of*) + determiner (*those*) + noun (*books*) + postmodifier (*on the desk*).

[1]The asterisk * is used to mark a clause or sentence which is considered ungrammatical.

It seems that the basic ordering of elements in the noun phrase is acquired fairly readily by learners, as errors in this aspect of structure are relatively infrequent. But, unless they are given guidance and encouragement, learners often fail to take full advantage of the potential of the noun phrase, particularly with regard to postmodification. We will look at these complex structures in more detail in Chapter 4 (The grammar of structure).

2.1.3 The verb phrase

The structure of the verb phrase is entirely predictable. The forms *I am going*; *I have gone* and *I have been going* are grammatical. Any variations, such as *I going am* or *I been going have,* are ungrammatical. We will look at this in detail in Chapter 5.

2.2 The grammar of orientation

In teaching a language we always spend a good deal of time on the tense system, and also on the articles and other determiners such as *some* and *any*. These systems are central to the language because they show how the things we are speaking or writing about are related to the real world and to other elements in the text. Given the elements in a clause *wife – work – garden – weekend* we know what the clause is about but we are unable to find any 'orientation' – we cannot identify exactly who the message is about; whether it refers to past, present or future time; whether it refers to a particular wife and garden or to wives and gardens in general. But given the clause *my wife works in the garden most weekends,* you can identify the wife as the wife of the speaker, and the garden as their garden. The tense of the verb tells you that the statement is a general statement relevant to present time. This is reinforced by the adverbial phrase consisting of the general determiner, *most,* and the noun *weekends.*

The function of the tense system is exactly this: to enable us to orient ourselves to the elements in the proposition and to relate them to one another, particularly in terms of time. The past tense, for example, is used to refer to something which occurred at a particular time in the past. The use of the present perfect tense asserts that the action of the verb has some relevance to the present or future.

Another kind of orientation has to do with the organisation of information in text.

Task 2.3:

Is this text grammatical? Is it acceptable as a text? Can you rewrite it to make it more readable? Can you give reasons for the way you have rewritten it?

There is a new castle situated on a hill high above the town. Sir Robert Fitzwilliam built it in the twelfth century. Raiders from Scotland attacked it regularly over the next two hundred years without success. Cromwell finally captured it in 1645 and destroyed it. Once Cromwell had taken the castle he set about subduing the surrounding countryside...

Commentary on Task 2.3:

The text is grammatical in the sense that all the sentences are grammatical. I am not sure that it is acceptable as text – it is certainly rather an odd text. It could usefully be rewritten as follows:

1. There is a new castle situated on a hill high above the town. 2. It was built in the twelfth century by Sir Robert Fitzwilliam. 3. Over the next two hundred years it was regularly attacked without success by raiders from Scotland.

4. It was Cromwell who finally captured and destroyed the castle in 1645. 5. Once Cromwell had taken the castle he set about subduing the surrounding countryside...

The usual way of organising information in the clause is to move from given to new. In the first clause of the original text, *the castle* is the theme, the established or given unit. But the second sentence begins not with the established theme, *the castle*, but with *Sir Robert Fitzwilliam*. The next sentence begins with another new theme, *raiders from Scotland*.

In my rewritten version, *the castle* is the theme in the first sentence, and this is picked up at the beginning of the second sentence with the pronoun *It*, referring to *the castle*. The next sentence picks up the idea of chronology and opens with *Over the next two hundred years*, which is followed by the word *it*, again picking up the castle as theme. In the next sentence I have brought in a change of theme and switched the focus to *Cromwell*. I have done this because *Cromwell* is going to be the theme of the next section of text. I have marked this switch of theme in two ways – by a paragraph break and also with the phrase *It was Cromwell who ...*

There are a number of devices which mark information as given or new. The pronoun, *it*, in sentences 2 and 3 makes us look for an item, *the castle,* which has already been identified in the text. In sentences 4 and 5 there is a reference to *the castle.* The definite article informs us that *the castle* is a given item, that it can be identified from the text or context. If sentence 5 read *Once Cromwell had taken a castle he set about subduing the surrounding countryside,* this would change the meaning. It would be a comment not about this particular castle but about Cromwell's general practice on these occasions.

As you see from Task 2.3 the passive voice is one of the devices we have for organising information in the clause. Since word order in English is fixed, the first noun in the sentence is almost always the subject. So we need to organise the clause in such a way that the grammatical subject of the clause and the theme are one and the same. One way of doing this is the passive voice. We also need devices to mark a change of theme. One such device is known as **clefting**. A cleft sentence is one which begins with the words *It was* —— *who/which* .... In the spoken language, of course, we make constant use of intonation to help achieve the same ends.

We also have elements in the text in our commentary above, such as the definite article and the pronoun *it*, which enable us to identify these elements as part of shared knowledge. Like the grammar of structure these referential elements of the grammatical system are highly systematic. We can make useful generalisations about them, but they can only be studied in context, since their function and meaning is necessarily related to context. These, together with devices such as the passive and clefting, enable us to build up text which is coherent and reader-friendly or listener-friendly.

Unfortunately it takes learners a very long time to master these systems, or at least those elements of it which do not correspond closely to their own language. The tense system too is notoriously difficult. At first sight the systems of orientation would seem to justify the huge amount of classroom time spent on them. They appear to be teachable in that it is possible to provide useful general rules covering these systems. But the results do not seem to repay the large amounts of time spent teaching them. We saw in the first chapter that learners go through a long period in which something is known consciously, but is not part of spontaneous language production. This seems to be particularly true of the systems of orientation.

As we shall see later, we can help learners with orientation by making useful generalisations. But they will also need a good deal of exposure to language if they are to develop the grammar of orientation, and they will learn more efficiently from that exposure if they are encouraged to explore for themselves the language to which they are exposed.

2.3 Pattern grammar

We have already seen how verbs like *stop, want, prevent, wonder* and *make* predict what will follow in the clause. When we use or hear one of these words, we have a good idea of the shape of what follows. And we saw at the beginning of this chapter that other words are also found in predictable patterns. The noun *relationship*, for example, is found in the pattern N (*relationship*) *between* N *and* N. Other nouns which are commonly found with this pattern are *agreement, quarrel* and *fight*. In this section we will look at a few other words and the patterns associated with them.

There are a number of common adjectives in English which are frequently followed by the *to*-infinitive and which typically feature in the frame: It + BE + Adj. + *to* + Verb. This means *It*, followed by part of the verb *to be*, followed by an adjective, followed by the *to*-infinitive:

It	BE	Adj.	*to*-infinitive
It	*is*	*nice*	*to meet you.*

Here are some examples:

1. It'd be very **difficult to** go through your working life ... living up to the image that you gave at your interview, if it isn't you.

2. I've found in interviews that it's actually **better to** say, I'd like a moment to think about that. I hadn't thought of that before. I'd like a minute – to digest the information and think of an answer.

3. It's **easy to** say 'Have confidence in yourself', but not so **easy** to achieve.

4. It's **polite to** knock before you enter an office if the door is closed.

5. It's *important to* create a good impression at the interview.

6. He said it's very *unusual to* find a well at the top of a hill. And if there's water up there, near the summit, then there's almost certainly even more water down in the valley.

7. Although it is *possible* for certain individuals *to* live to unexpectedly great ages, most crocodiles and alligators live for about 30 years.

8. This would be the twofold effect of getting the job done cheaply and making it *safe* for the local people *to* cross the river.

If we look at these adjectives, we see that they are not a random selection. They all function as an evaluation of some sort and can be divided into groups according to meaning:

Group 1: GOOD/BAD: *better; polite.*
Group 2: EASY/DIFFICULT: *easy; difficult; possible.*
Group 3: USUAL/UNUSUAL: *unusual.*
Group 4: WISE/FOOLISH: *important; safe.*

It is possible to identify other adjectives commonly found with this pattern and allocate them to the same groups: *nice, interesting, fashionable, impossible, simple, rare, usual, necessary, essential, silly, dangerous* etc. In some cases you might see a word as fitting in more than one group. The word *fashionable*, for example, may be seen as either GOOD/BAD or USUAL/UNUSUAL, depending on the context. But the principle is clear; words which share a given pattern are likely to share meaning and function (see Francis, Hunston and Manning, 1997). In this case the function is evaluation, and the adjectives can, as we have seen, be allocated to groups according to their meaning.

Task 2.4:
Think of the meanings of the words *nice, interesting, fashionable, impossible, simple, rare, usual, necessary, silly, dangerous, rude, risky, essential.* Can you sort these words into the groups: GOOD/BAD; EASY/DIFFICULT; USUAL/UNUSUAL; WISE/FOOLISH?

> **Key to Task 2.4:**
> GOOD/BAD: *nice, interesting, (fashionable), rude.*
> EASY/DIFFICULT: *impossible, simple.*
> USUAL/UNUSUAL: *(fashionable), rare, usual.*
> WISE/FOOLISH: *necessary, silly, dangerous, risky, essential.*

In our discussion of the grammar of structure we noted that 'the continuation of the clause after the verb is determined by the **meaning** of the verb, not by grammatical considerations'. There is, for example, a group of verbs called **double object verbs,** which are followed by two nouns:

> *He / gave / me / a bit of a surprise.*
> *I / sent / you / a message.*
> *She / brought / me / a cup of tea.*
> *I / will tell / them / a bedtime story.*

We can group these words into the following groups:

GROUP 1: GIVE/SEND: *give, offer, hand, pay* etc.
GROUP 2: BRING: *bring, get, buy, fetch* etc.
GROUP 3: ASK/TELL: *ask, tell, read, teach* etc.

Unfortunately the behaviour of words is not entirely predictable. A learner who has formed the generalisation that verbs of *giving* and *sending* are followed by N + N and who then comes across another word with the same meaning, the verb *present* for example, would reasonably predict the following sentence:

> *They presented her a magnificent bouquet of flowers.*

But this is an overgeneralisation resulting in an error. The usual form is:

> *They presented her **with** a magnificent bouquet of flowers.*

The error is an intelligent one, and one which shows signs of language development. It shows that the learner is making appropriate generalisations about verbs of giving and sending. Unfortunately the learner does not yet associate the appropriate pattern with the verb *present.* It is also an 'acceptable' error. Any competent speaker of English will readily recognise what is happening when someone says: *I presented her a magnificent bouquet,* and will have no trouble in processing the message. But this example does show that, in order to refine the association between words and patterns, learners need lots of exposure and need to be constantly on the lookout for these associations.

Nouns too fit into patterns. If we take, for example, the pattern:

Noun + *of* + ...V-*ing* (Noun followed by *of* followed by a verb ending in -*ing*)

we can think of phrases like *the possibility of, the idea of, dislike of* ... and so on; there is a class of words which are normally found with this pattern. We can break these down into sub-classes according to meaning. Together with *possibility* we would find other words to do with possibility or chance: words like *chance, danger, probability* and *likelihood*. Together with *dislike* we would find other words to do with liking and disliking: *love, hatred* and *fear*.

The important thing here is that words relate to patterns and that we can often predict the relationship between word meaning and pattern. If, for example, learners come across the word *risk*, meaning danger, as in: *You can reduce the risk of heart disease by exercising regularly*, they may then be able to use the word with the pattern *of* + V-*ing* as in: *If you smoke heavily there is a risk of developing lung cancer.*

Language users have, then, a knowledge of a vast array of language patterns and of the words associated with those patterns. Learners must gradually identify the patterns of English and relate them to the words in the language. This is an immense undertaking. We cannot present our learners with a list of all the patterns of English and of the words associated with each pattern. We can, however, make learners aware that this is an important feature of the language, and we can give them useful guidelines and strategies to help them. In order to do this we must evolve an appropriate teaching strategy. In terms of the learning processes outlined in Section 1.5, this suggests that we need to work through recognition, system building and exploration. Learners need first to recognise the general importance of patterns in language and to recognise specific patterns. Secondly, as they recognise each pattern, they need to be encouraged to systematise it by making generalisations about the meanings of the words involved in those patterns. Finally, they need to explore the language they experience to refine their knowledge of the pattern by extending their repertoire of words using the pattern, and by identifying words such as the verb *present* which do not fit the overall generalisation.

2.4 Class

We have shown in the previous section that words relate to patterns. We can think of words which relate to the same pattern as belonging to the same group or **class**. We looked, for example, at the class of double object verbs, and the class of evaluative adjectives found with *It + BE + Adj. + to ...*, and the class of nouns followed by *of + -ing*. We need to encourage learners to identify classes of words and relate them to the patterns in which they occur.

There are other classes of word which relate to the grammar of structure. We looked earlier at adverbs of degree which usually come at the end of the clause but are not found immediately after the verb. There is a small, but interesting class of adverbs sometimes called broad negative adverbs (*barely, hardly, rarely, scarcely* and *seldom*) which are normally found in front of the verb (for a list see Sinclair, 1990):

> *I could hardly believe my eyes.*
> *You seldom see him nowadays.*

But if the verb is the simple present or simple past tense of the verb *BE*, the adverb comes after the verb:

> *She is barely six months old.*
> *The office was hardly ever empty.*

At an advanced level learners may need to know that these adverbs can come at the beginning of a clause, but that they have drastic effects when they do: the verb and the auxiliary are inverted:

> *Seldom have I seen such incompetence.*
> *Hardly had we reached safety when the avalanche struck.*

or an auxiliary *DO* must be supplied:

> *Rarely do you find such an abundance of animals as in this area.*

We will have to make teaching decisions at each stage about how much learners need to know about a class of words. At an intermediate stage they need to be aware that broad negative adverbs come before the verb or after the verb *BE*. These words occur very frequently in these positions, only rarely are they found at the beginning of the clause. For this reason we may postpone giving this information until students have reached an advanced level.

Finally there are classes of word which relate to the grammar of orientation. One such group is **uncountable nouns** such as *information, health, water, furniture* and *luggage*. These uncountable nouns have no plural form and are not found with the indefinite article:

> *I heard some interesting **informations** this morning.*
> *She was struggling with **a heavy luggage.***

Another such group are stative verbs like *understand, believe* and *belong*, which are hardly ever found in the continuous tenses. It is most unusual to come across sentences like:

> *That book **is belonging** to me.*
> *I **am not understanding** what you say.*

The picture which begins to emerge is as follows: we have a set of broad generalisations about the language relating to its overall structure and the grammatical devices which link the message to the real world. But these broad generalisations provide no more than a template, a set of highly abstract guidelines as to what might be done with the language. As soon as we begin to select the words which will realise the framework then pattern grammar takes over. The way the structure is realised depends very much on the words which realise the structure. So we begin with the idea of basic clause structure: N + V + ?. As soon as we select, let us say, the verb *give*, then we predict that the clause structure is likely to be: N + V + N + N. We may want to modify the message by adding an adverbial. In this case the structure will depend on the adverbial we choose. If, for example, we choose an adverb of frequency, say the word *usually*, then the most likely structure is N + Adv. + N + N. Thus, a clause like *My father usually gave me money for my birthday*, draws initially on the basic clause structure N + V + ?, but is, in a much more real sense, the product of the words which make up the clause.

There are, therefore, classes of word which relate to all aspects of grammar: pattern, structure and orientation. Once we see language from this perspective then we can see that lexis and the behaviour and patterning of individual words are enormously important. And, if we accept this, then the concept of class becomes central both to language description and to language learning. It is this concept of class which provides a link between grammar and lexis. When we learn words we also need to learn about their behaviour, the way they pattern with other words.

What learners are doing in working out the language is observing patternings, observing which words relate to these patternings, allocating those words to classes according to their meaning, and going on to make hypotheses about the behaviour of other words on the basis of their observations. In putting together clauses and sentences we draw on a broad grammatical outline, but much more on the behaviour of individual words.

The concept of class offers an important organising principle for instructional activities. Once learners have recognised certain exemplars of the class of double object verbs, for example, we need to list the most frequent double object verbs. This will serve the immediate objective of allowing learners to build these verbs into their system, and will also provide them with guidelines for the recognition of other double object verbs as part of the exploration process.

Now that we have established this link between grammar and lexis we can go on to look more closely at the idea of lexis and what it might incorporate.

2.5 Lexical phrases and frames

Much of the language we produce is made up not of individual words, but of strings of words which we carry around with us as fixed phrases. If I offer you the words *as a matter of ...*, and ask you to predict the word which follows, you will almost certainly nominate the word *fact*. As an experienced user of English you carry in your mind the phrase *as a matter of fact* as a fixed unit. Of course it is possible to find other words to complete the phrase. For example, we often say *as a matter of course*, and sometimes *as a matter of urgency*.

We do not work out the grammatical structure of a phrase like *as a matter of fact*. It is called to mind as a single unit. There are many other phrases, thousands of them, which we use so frequently that they come to us as single units: *Would you like ...?, It's up to you, What's the matter?, What a surprise!, You can if you want ...*. Indeed, if we were not able to organise and store language as chunks, we might not be able to operate as quickly and efficiently as we need to in everyday spoken communication:

> The user ... operates with a more lexical unit of analysis, and achieves communication in real time not by the complexities of producing utterances on the basis of a rule system, constructing anew each time, but instead draws on ready-made elements and chunks, without the need to construct each chunk independently and to lose time planning internal organisation.
>
> (Skehan, 1992: 186)

What Skehan is saying here is that if we had to compose each message anew we would not be able to produce language rapidly and fluently. We simply don't have time to build up messages anew every time, building up sentences by applying grammatical rules. The only way we can produce language rapidly and fluently is by building up routines and relying on 'ready-made elements and chunks'. The same applies to patterns. When we use the word *relationship* we go on to produce the word *between* in an appropriate context. The word *relationship* does not come to mind on its own, it comes associated with the appropriate pattern ready to be used instantly.

There is another interesting feature of lexical phrases. We might think that any sentence which is grammatical must be a part of the language. But this is not the case. If this were so we would be able to put into a given slot any word which is grammatical and which makes sense. If we can say *as a matter of fact* or *as a matter of course*, we ought to be able to say *as a matter of opinion*. But the phrase *as a matter of opinion* hardly ever occurs, even though *it's a matter of opinion* and *that's a matter of opinion* are quite common. Instead of *as a matter of opinion* we use the phrase *in my opinion* to cover the same meaning.

We can't, then, compose any grammatical sentence and expect our listeners to process it quickly and easily. Let us take two obvious examples. The sentence *It's forty-seven past two* is entirely grammatical and has a clear meaning. But we simply don't say things like that. We would say: *It's two forty-seven* or *It's thirteen minutes to three* or, if we are not too worried about precise accuracy, *It's quarter to three*. Similarly, in giving a phone number, I would not say *seventy-two, thirty-two, twenty-three*. British speakers of English would not expect this kind of formulation and would find it difficult to process – even though this is the way telephone numbers are grouped in French and a number of other languages. In British English we use the form *seven two three, two two three*, or *seven two three, double two three*.

Efficient communication is, then, not simply a matter of making any grammatical sentence. It depends on having a stock of fixed phrases which we can string together rapidly and efficiently, phrases like *as a matter of fact, it's up to you* or *what's the matter*. It is also a matter of recognising and producing familiar forms of speech which can be readily processed – *quarter to three* rather than *forty-seven past two*, or *in my opinion* rather than *as a matter of opinion*.

Sometimes the phrases we produce in this way are completely fixed, functioning in the same way as single words. We have, for example, phrases like *by and large* or *spick and span*. There is no other way of completing the frame *by and ...* or *spick and ...* . More often the phrases we use are variable, but the variation is restricted. The example we have given here is *as a matter of fact*. This allows *as a matter of course* or *as a matter of urgency*, but not *as a matter of opinion*. Similarly a phrase like *Watch your step* allows the variation *Mind your step* but not *Mind your steps* or *Watch your pace*.

We also have frames which allow considerable variation. These would include things like *Would you mind ...?* or *Have you ever ...?* which allow a whole range of possible completions. Similarly in telling the time we have the frame *... minutes to ...*, where the first slot allows any number up to twenty-nine and the second slot any number up to twelve.

Frames can be highly productive and we can encourage rapid accumulation by highlighting what Sinclair (1990) calls productive features. Productive features enable learners to 'make individual choices, with no serious risk of error', and thereby 'give scope for creativity and innovation'. Examples in Sinclair (1990) include the frame *from a(n)* Adj. *point of view*. This frame can be used to limit or focus a statement:

*Everything looks good **from a financial point of view**.*
*That would be a risky decision **from a political point of view**.*

The same applies to the frame *in* Adj. *terms*:

*Everything looks good **in financial terms**.*
*That would be a risky decision **in political terms**.*

Phrases and frames such as these are very much like vocabulary items. We do not compose them afresh each time we use them, any more than we compose afresh the word *unhappiness* from the parts *un-*, *happy* and *-ness*. We carry them around as units, and slot them into the message like single items. It follows, then, that there are good reasons why we should think of these frames and phrases as lexical items rather than being assembled grammatically. Just as we know a stock of words which we can produce and insert in the appropriate place at the appropriate time, so we have a stock of frames and phrases which we treat in very much the same way.

In providing instructional support we need first to establish general recognition by making learners aware of the importance of lexical phrases and encouraging them to look for these phrases in future input. Secondly, we need to identify phrases which are particularly frequent and find ways of classifying these to facilitate recall and use.

2.6 Collocation

We say that words 'collocate' if they occur together more frequently than one would expect. Sometimes this happens because the words are simply likely to be found in the same context. This would be the case with the words *dog* and *tail*, for example. And we could predict a number of other words which collocate with *dog*: *bone, bite, cat* and *kennel*, for example. In the same way, the word *drink* collocates with *beer, wine, lemonade* and *water*. From the learner's point of view these collocations are accidental and easily learnt. If a learner knows the word for *drink* and the word for *beer* then these two words are certainly likely to crop up together more than the words *beer* and *dog*, for example.

There are, however, other collocations which do need to be learnt. Someone who knows the word *strong* and the word *tea*, for example, may not know that these two words frequently go together in English – that we talk about *strong tea* and *weak tea*. Someone who knows the word *sour* and the word *milk* may not know that these two words go together, that we talk about milk *going sour* rather than milk *getting old* or *going bitter*. Along with collocations we have collocational restrictions. We talk about *strong tea* and *weak tea*, but if we are talking about cheese we use the words *strong* and *mild*. We do not describe cheese as *weak*, and we do not describe tea as *mild*. So another aspect of lexical knowledge is knowing which words go together even if it may not be possible to predict this association from the general meanings of the words. We also need to know which words do **not** go together, such as *mild* and *tea*, even though one might sensibly predict that they will go together.

Again we need to encourage recognition of the general phenomenon of collocation. This may be done by providing useful exemplars and also by encouraging learners to think about the importance of collocation in their own language. We might reinforce this by looking at collocations with frequent words like *strong*. Learners might, for example, be invited to interpret phrases like *strong drink, strong language*, and *strong winds*.

2.7 Words

Pattern grammar, lexical phrases and collocation have one thing in common: they all show us that words exist in company with other words and related concepts. We cannot learn to use a word unless we learn the patterns and phrases in which it occurs and the words with which it is associated. There is no point in knowing the word *give* unless we can put it in the pattern V + N + N. If we are going to make effective use of the word *usually*, we need to know that it commonly comes in front of the verb. If we are to use words like *nice* and *easy* to evaluate, we need to associate them with the pattern *It + BE* + Adj. + *to* + V. If we are going to talk about tea, we need to be able to describe it as *strong* or *weak*. If we are going to talk about dogs, we will need words like *bone, bite, kennel, tail* and *wag.*

It seems that, for competent speakers of the language, words act as triggers. As soon as a word is called to mind a host of associations come with it. We are instantly aware of other words which are likely to occur around it. We may also be aware of the way the structure of the clause is likely to develop, or what sort of pattern is likely to follow. We quoted Skehan above to show that the only way we can produce language fluently is by relying on ready-made elements or chunks. In the same way, if we are to operate fluently, we need to be able to recall with a word an array of associated knowledge. Fluent language use depends not simply on knowing a lot of words, but also on knowing a lot about a lot of words.

Of course we need to list words under lexis. But at the same time we need to recognise that recognising a word is not enough for language use. We need also to know the words with which it associates and the patterns, frames and phrases in which it occurs.

2.8 Summary

The model of description we have outlined above is summarised in Fig. 2.1. This summary shows the importance of the interlevel, **class**, which looks back to structure, orientation and pattern, and forward to words and phrases. We can relate this to the learning processes outlined in Section 1.4:

- **Recognition:** Learners notice a pattern of behaviour, for example that the adjective *easy* is used to evaluate in the pattern *It + BE + easy + to + Verb.*
- **System building:** Once the pattern has been recognised, other adjectives which behave in the same way can be identified and classified (e.g. *difficult, nice, unusual*), and learners can begin to identify categories of meaning (GOOD/BAD; EASY/DIFFICULT; USUAL/UNUSUAL) which account for these words.
- **Exploration:** It is impossible to identify for the learner all the words which occur with a particular pattern. As learners are exposed to further text, however, they will begin to recognise other words likely to be found with the same pattern.

We can help learners with this process by highlighting the patterns, by helping to list other words commonly found in the same pattern and by

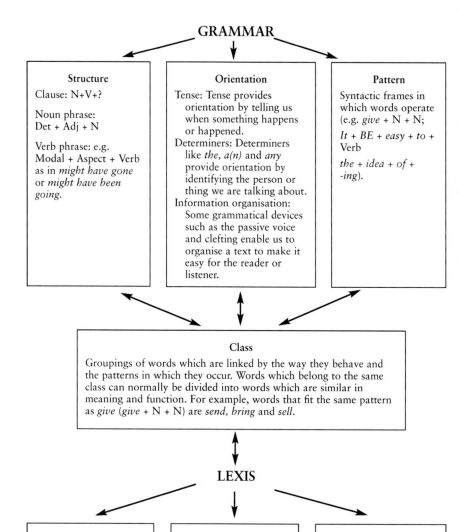

GRAMMAR

Structure

Clause: N+V+?

Noun phrase:
Det + Adj + N

Verb phrase: e.g.
Modal + Aspect + Verb
as in *might have gone*
or *might have been
going.*

Orientation

Tense: Tense provides
  orientation by telling us
  when something happens
  or happened.
Determiners: Determiners
  like *the, a(n)* and *any*
  provide orientation by
  identifying the person or
  thing we are talking about.
Information organisation:
  Some grammatical devices
  such as the passive voice
  and clefting enable us to
  organise a text to make it
  easy for the reader or
  listener.

Pattern

Syntactic frames in
which words operate
(e.g. *give* + N + N;
It + *BE* + *easy* + *to* +
Verb
the + *idea* + *of* +
-ing).

Class

Groupings of words which are linked by the way they behave and
the patterns in which they occur. Words which belong to the same
class can normally be divided into words which are similar in
meaning and function. For example, words that fit the same pattern
as *give* (*give* + N + N) are *send, bring* and *sell*.

LEXIS

Lexical phrases/frames

Items made up of more
than one word, but
which are carried in the
memory in the same
way as individual words
(e.g. *as a matter of fact*).
Some of these items are
frames with gaps filled
by variable items (e.g.
*ten / a quarter / twenty
to one / two / three*
etc.).

Collocation

Words which are likely
to occur together are
said to 'collocate'. Some
of these collocations,
like *dog* and *kennel*, are
predictable. Some of
them, like *weak* and *tea*,
have to be learnt. These
words are closely related
in the mind so that a
word 'triggers' its
associated collocates.

Words

In theory it is possible to
list the individual words
that a person knows. In
fact words are not
known individually.
Each one is linked to a
range of associated
words and patterns.

Fig. 2.1 Grammar and lexis

48

encouraging them to explore input and allocate these words to categories of meaning. The same applies to double object verbs, countable and uncountable nouns, and many other classes.

The same processes will apply to tense forms. A learner may begin by recognising the present continuous form and noting that it is used for actions taking place at the time of utterance. At first the relationship between the present continuous simple and the present simple will be unclear. Gradually the teacher will help learners to build up a system which incorporates both forms. At the same time learners will be encouraged to take note of the use of the forms in text and refine the system.

But different aspects of the grammar demand different learning processes and different instructional strategies. The grammar of structure, for example, is very much rule governed and instruction can provide a lot of support for system building. We can isolate the structure of the noun phrase, for example, and provide a fairly comprehensive list of quantifiers and partitives (see Sections 4.2.1 and 4.2.2 below). We can go on to provide opportunities to practise these items with a minimal context.

We have seen that these learning processes will be supplemented with opportunities to use language. Some of these language use activities will place an emphasis on improvisation, allowing learners to develop language which they can use effectively outside the classroom, and encouraging them to recognise gaps in their knowledge. Other language use activities will emphasise consolidation, allowing learners to incorporate new or refined systems into their language, and enabling them to build up routines which provide the basis for fluency.

3 Developing a teaching strategy

In the last chapter we outlined a model to show the relationship between grammar and lexis. As teachers we often see language learning as solving a succession of grammatical problems. We see grammar as coming first and as providing the framework in which lexis can operate. We have to solve the grammatical problems before we can put the vocabulary to work. In theory this is an entirely reasonable way to operate. But as we saw in our discussion in the first chapter things do not seem to work out that way. Learners do not solve one problem, such as the formation of *do*-questions, incorporate this into their language and then move on to the next stage. They still fail to use *do*-questions consistently, long after they have worked out the problem of how to produce them consciously.

Since this model does not seem to accord with the way language learning develops, perhaps we should consider another possibility. In Section 1.5 I suggested that learning to use language involves improvisation. In the early stages of learning learners improvise by stringing words and phrases together to communicate. As they learn more and more words the messages they want to communicate become more and more complex. If they are to make their meaning clear, they need to build in more and more the grammar of orientation. And if they want to use language efficiently, they need to build up patterns and phrases which they can call to mind rapidly and spontaneously. If we take this view, then, instead of a process in which learners first learn how to make grammatical sentences and subsequently learn to put in the words they have learnt, we have a process in which learners begin by stringing words together and gradually learn to be more precise in their orientation, and to be more rapid and efficient in their recall and use of patterns and phrases.

In a discussion of the importance of lexical phrases in language Widdowson makes this point:

> ... communicative competence is not a matter of knowing rules for the composition of sentences ... It is much more a matter of knowing a stock of partially pre-assembled patterns,

formulaic frameworks, and a kit of rules, so to speak, and being able to apply the rules to make whatever adjustments are necessary according to contextual demands. Communicative competence in this view is essentially a matter of adaptation, and rules are not generative but regulative and subservient.

(Widdowson, 1989: 135)

By communicative competence Widdowson means, among other things, the ability to produce language spontaneously and rapidly. On the one hand we have **a stock of partially pre-assembled patterns** and **formulaic frameworks**. On the other hand we have **a kit of rules**. The driving force in language use is the assembly of a message. The message is composed of lexical items, in the wider sense of lexis which we established above, which includes frames, phrases and collocation. The kit of rules enables us to adjust the message. It enables us to orient the message relating it more precisely to the outside world. It enables us to make the structural adjustments which mark a clause as affirmative, negative or interrogative, or to switch from talking about the past to talking about the present. It enables us to fit the clause into its surrounding context to provide a smooth flow of information. So the kit of rules – the grammar of structure and orientation – is important, but it is subsidiary to the need and desire to communicate. What Widdowson says here implies that there will be a primary concern with stringing elements together and the grammar, the 'kit of rules', will be **regulative and subservient.**

It seems, then, that the basic element in an effective teaching strategy might be to encourage and enable learners to do what they can with the language they have at their disposal, to make messages and deliver them with some fluency, even if the language used is highly inaccurate. As learners build up a communicative capacity we can encourage them more and more to pay attention to the forms of language they produce. We begin by stimulating language use and gradually help learners to shape that language so that it conforms more closely to the target forms.

This suggests two major questions. Firstly, how do we help classroom learners to develop a communicative capacity? Secondly, how do we encourage them to pay attention to form? This second question might usefully be broken down into a number of subsidiary questions: How do we encourage learners to pay attention to form so as to assist recognition? How do we help learners to assign words to classes so as to build up patterns? How do we help them to nest one pattern within another so they can produce complex noun phrases and clauses? How do we help them to grapple with the complexities of orientation?

3.1 Tasks and communicative purpose

In Section 1.5 we looked at activities which focus on improvisation and consolidation. We described these as activities involving language use. We will begin this section by looking more closely at what is involved in using language to achieve a communicative purpose in the classroom. We will then go on to look at a cycle of activities which aims to encourage learners to use language in order to develop a communicative capacity.

Brazil (1995) emphasises that in processing language we are driven by the need to communicate. Grammarians are interested in the construction of sentences. They assume that:

> ... the mechanism whereby words are assembled to make larger units will be revealed to us if we begin by thinking of speakers as aiming, in everything they do linguistically, at the production of objects called 'sentences'.   (Brazil, 1995: 2)

In using language, however, our purpose is not the production of sentences but the construction of meanings. Brazil argues that:

> ... the mechanism whereby words are assembled to make larger units will be revealed to us if we begin by thinking of speakers as pursuing some useful communicative purpose and as aiming, at any one time, at the successful accomplishment of that purpose.   (1995: 2)

In our concern with the gap between knowledge and use we drew attention to a **learning paradox**. We asked how it was possible that learners could know something in the sense of being able to manipulate language forms appropriately when they were paying conscious attention, and at the same time fail to produce these forms as part of their spontaneous language production. If we follow Brazil's lead we might argue that the two processes, producing sentences and achieving a communicative purpose, are quite different processes. Learners who are concerned to produce messages to convey meanings rapidly and efficiently will adopt quite different strategies from those involved in constructing sentences.

Willis and Willis (2000) define a task as follows:

> Central to the notion of 'task' is the exchange of meanings. J. Willis (1996) defines a task as an activity 'where ... language is used by the learner for a communicative purpose (goal) in order to achieve an outcome'. One obvious outcome is the exchange of information in spoken or written form. But there

are other possible outcomes to which the exchange of information may be contributory but subsidiary. We may ask learners to exchange and carry out instructions or to solve a problem or to entertain one another with anecdotes, spoken or written. We may ask them to interpret and summarise a written or spoken text in order to fill an information gap. All of these activities have a goal which is independent of the language used to achieve that goal. (2000: 173)

The notion of language used to achieve an outcome is very much in line with Brazil's notion of speakers as pursuing some useful communicative purpose and as aiming, at any one time, at the successful accomplishment of that purpose. Let us exemplify this by looking at a task cycle based on a written text (for a detailed description see J. Willis, 1996).

3.1.1 Task: Language use

Teaching Activity 3.1:

You are going to read a newspaper article about someone trying to rob a shop. Here are some ideas to help you with the story:

The characters: a shopkeeper; her two children; a man; an eight-year-old boy; the police

The setting: a corner shop in Ashton-under-Lyme, near Manchester

The props: a balaclava; a plastic carrier bag; a pistol

This is what they said

Work in groups and guess what happened in the story. Compare your ideas with others in your group. Try to include all the things shown above in your story.

Commentary on Teaching Activity 3.1:

As we shall see, this is the first of a three-phase task cycle. We will call this first phase *the task phase*. It involves students in an exchange of meanings as they try to predict the story. The outcome of the activity is the story, but there will be a lot of language used in working towards the story. There will certainly be a lot of improvisation in the language used. Learners are producing language spontaneously and at times will be stretched beyond the language they can use with confidence.

Task 3.1:

How would you do the teaching activity above? Would your intermediate students be able to do this task? What help would they need? What sort of language would they use? Would there be many mistakes?

Commentary on Task 3.1:

Intermediate students would probably be able to do this task, but only with the right kind of help from their teacher. You would probably need to give the following support and help:

- You would need to make sure that they understood what was expected of them. To do this you might ask them for a few ideas and help them begin the story. For example:
    Teacher: OK. You need to say who was in the shop – probably the shopkeeper and her children. And who do you think came into the shop?
    Student: The eight-year-old boy.
    Teacher: Yes, it might have been the boy, or ...?
    Student: The man.
    Teacher: Yes, it might have been the man. The shopkeeper says: "As I gave him his change a man came in." Who was 'he'? Who got the change?
    Student: The boy.
    Teacher: Yes, it must have been the boy. So it seems the boy was in the shop when the man came in. OK, can you work out the rest of the story?

- We have argued that the basis of communication is lexical. You would therefore need to give students some help with lexis. Before you even look at the task it might be worth doing a review and introduction of lexis along these lines:

    Which of these words would you expect to find in a newspaper article about a robbery? Use your dictionary to help you choose five words:

    Aeroplane; alarm; balaclava; bank; destination; firearm; flight; fly; house; mask; passport; pistol; point; police; reserve; shoot; shop; thief; ticket; timetable; travel.

    Here you have a number of words to do with robbery, and a number of other words which act as distracters. In this example all the distracters are to do with travel. You could choose distracters from any field which students have recently studied. This exercise would provide opportunities for learners to come to terms with some of the new words they might need for the task. They will also come across words which will be used in the reading text at a later stage, such as *balaclava*, an old-fashioned word for a ski-mask.

- You may feel that you need to give help with grammar, by reviewing the past tense, for example. I don't think that this is really necessary, however. Students will understand that the events take place in the past, even if there are mistakes with past tenses. Provided you give students the lexis they need they can manage with the grammar they already have.

- Working in groups, students are likely to use very informal language with many mistakes. It is not easy for them to work on a problem and put their thoughts into words at the same time. They are grappling with meaning and so they don't have enough time or spare mental capacity to pay much attention to form. This doesn't matter when they are working in small groups and everyone else in the group is working in the same way.

3.1.2 Task, planning and report: From improvisation to consolidation

So far we have worked with students to provide them with the necessary lexis. Students have then worked in groups to put together a story. At the next stage of the task cycle they are asked to prepare to tell the story to the class as a whole:

Teaching Activity 3.2:
Once you have decided on your story, write down a few notes to help you tell your story to the class. Do not write more than ten words. Now get ready to tell your story.

Willis (1996) calls these phases of the task cycle the **planning** and **report** phases. Here the students work in groups to prepare a spokesman to tell the story to the whole class on behalf of the group (**planning**) and then the spokesman goes on to tell the story (**report**).

Task 3.2:

During the first phase of the task cycle the students had little concern for accuracy. What do you think will happen in these two phases?

Commentary on Task 3.2:

These phases of the task cycle are quite different. Students know that the **report** phase will be, in a sense, a **public performance**. The spokesman for the group will be talking to the class as a whole, not in the privacy of a small group who are all working together. They have already decided on their story so they have time to think about how the story will be worded. In other words they have both a reason to think about form and also the time to do so. In Section 1.5 we looked at the learner's purposes in producing language:

Basic message → Concern for reader/listener → Presentation of self

During the first phase of the task cycle the primary concern is with basic meaning. In the preparation and report phases the priority shifts to a concern for the listener and a concern with the presentation of self. Learners will take time to phrase their message carefully, moving towards what they believe to be accurate in terms of English. Although this involves a focus on form, I prefer to think of it as a focus on language **development**. I see a focus on form as teacher-initiated and teacher-led, while a focus on development is student-initiated and student-led. At this stage of the task cycle students will be adapting their language in ways which make sense to them, not in ways that are imposed on them by the teacher. They will not be concerned only with accuracy, they will also want to retain forms of the language that they can produce with speed and fluency. This is, then, what we described earlier in Section 1.5 as a consolidation activity.

At the next stage of the task cycle speakers from the groups take turns to tell a story. As we saw in the Commentary on Task 3.2 students will try here to use the resources of the language not only to get a message across, but also to take account of the needs of their listeners and to present themselves in a favourable light. As the story is told, other groups listen carefully to see how the story differs from their own version. This is a listening task. In this case the outcome is a list of the differences between two stories.

Finally students read a newspaper article and find out which of the group versions came closest to the newspaper story. Again this is a task. The reading has an outcome – the comparison between the newspaper story and the stories they have heard, and a judgement based on that comparison.

PISTOL-PACKING EIGHT-YEAR-OLD TRIES TO ROB CORNER SWEET SHOP

POLICE were last night searching for an eight-year-old boy who attempted to hold up a sweet shop with a pistol, *writes David Ward.*

The boy, wearing a balaclava, threw a carrier bag at the shopkeeper at the corner store in Ashton-under-Lyme, Greater Manchester, and ordered her to fill it up.

"I don't know whether he wanted me to fill the bag with sweets or money," said the woman, who does not wish to be named. "It didn't appear to be a toy gun to me. I was not sure whether it was real or not, but it didn't look like the toys my little boy has."

The boy went into the shop and bought some Smarties for 25p. "He gave me a 50p piece and as I gave him his change a man came in. He waited until the man went. Then he threw a plastic carrier bag at me, pointed a gun at me and said: 'Put everything in'." He fled when the woman, who had her two children with her, pressed an alarm.

The boy is described as 3ft 6in tall, dressed in jeans and a dark coat.

A police spokesman said, "We are taking this very seriously, as we would any robbery involving a firearm, fake or not."

(From: The Guardian, *22 February, 1994)*

At this stage learners have spent a good deal of time working with this text and the meanings that it encodes. They have produced their own version of the story and at the planning stage they reviewed this with a focus on development, on making the best possible use of their language resources. They will read the text with real attention to meaning, since by now they really want to know how the story turns out. There may also be elements of recognition and exploration as learners engage in reading. Since they have already attempted to engage in these meanings for themselves they will be sensitive to the way the meanings are expressed in the text. So the task cycle is as follows:

Preparation: Vocabulary input

Task: Predicting a story (improvised language use with a focus on basic meaning)

Planning: Preparing to tell a story to the class (a consolidation activity which involves language development with a focus on aspects of form regarded as relevant by the learners)

Report: Telling the story to the class (another consolidation activity with a focus on form to take account of listeners and of presentation of self)

Reading: This particular task leads into the study of a text. Learners will be involved in reading with a communicative purpose, namely to check whose version of the story is closest to the original. This may also involve learning processes of recognition and exploration.

3.2 Language focus and learning processes

Communicative activities leading from improvisation to consolidation provide a context for learning to use language. Within this context we need to provide a focus on language to promote language learning. Let us look at a number of possible language focus exercises and see how these relate to the language learning processes of recognition, system building and exploration. Let us assume that learners have been through the **Task** → **Planning** → **Report** sequence. They are now familiar with the text and what it means. They may still have some questions in their minds, but they are sufficiently well prepared to go on to look in detail at some aspects of the language of the text.

Teaching Activity 3.3:

In the headline there is one phrase using *to: Eight-year-old **tries to rob** corner sweet shop*. Can you pick out five other phrases with *to*? Rewrite these phrases using the following words: *seem; told; tried; want; wanted.*

Commentary on Teaching Activity 3.3:

The phrases are: **attempted to** *hold up*; **ordered her to** *fill it up*; **wanted me to** *fill the bag*; *does not **wish to** be named; didn't **appear to** be a toy gun.*

This activity promotes *recognition*. It focuses on the form of the *to*-infinitive and highlights five words (*attempt, order, want, wish, appear*) associated with this form.

The second part of the activity, the rewriting, begins to promote system building, encouraging students to think about the meanings of verbs associated with the pattern.

Teaching Activity 3.4:

Look at these two patterns:

Pattern 1: An eight-year-old *attempted to* hold up a sweet shop. (Verb + *to*)

It didn't *appear to* be a toy gun.

Pattern 2: He *ordered **her** to* fill it up. (Verb + N + *to*)

He *wanted **me** to* fill the bag.

Look at the following sentences. How many are Pattern 1? How many are Pattern 2?

1. I'd like to go home now.
2. I'd like you to go home now.
3. I didn't expect him to be here.
4. I didn't expect to see you here.
5. There doesn't seem to be anybody at home.
6. They wanted to ask me a few questions.
7. Did you remember to lock the door?
8. Who told you to do that?
9. Try to remember as many words as you can.
10. Don't forget to telephone.

Commentary on Teaching Activity 3.4:

Pattern 1 is found in sentences 1, 4, 5, 6, 7, 9, 10. Pattern 2 is found in 2, 3, 8. Again the primary focus is on the recognition of patterns. There are two distinct patterns here which need to be recognised separately.

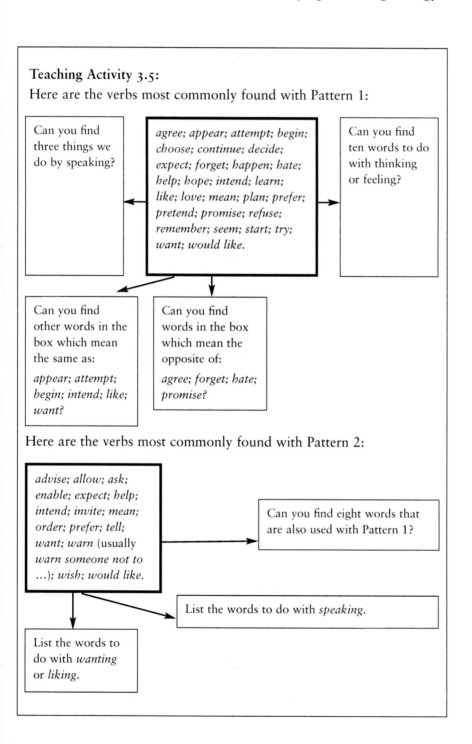

Teaching Activity 3.5:
Here are the verbs most commonly found with Pattern 1:

Can you find three things we do by speaking?

agree; appear; attempt; begin; choose; continue; decide; expect; forget; happen; hate; help; hope; intend; learn; like; love; mean; plan; prefer; pretend; promise; refuse; remember; seem; start; try; want; would like.

Can you find ten words to do with thinking or feeling?

Can you find other words in the box which mean the same as:

appear; attempt; begin; intend; like; want?

Can you find words in the box which mean the opposite of:

agree; forget; hate; promise?

Here are the verbs most commonly found with Pattern 2:

advise; allow; ask; enable; expect; help; intend; invite; mean; order; prefer; tell; want; warn (usually warn someone not to ...); wish; would like.

Can you find eight words that are also used with Pattern 1?

List the words to do with *speaking.*

List the words to do with *wanting* or *liking.*

Commentary on Teaching Activity 3.5:

The focus shifts here from recognition to system building. Two patterns have been recognised. Learners now have to build a system around them, working out the classes of word which feature in the two patterns. This system building activity paves the way for exploration. Once learners have an idea of the classes of verbs that are followed by one of the target patterns they can look out in future for verbs used in this way, and add them to their store. At the same time they can begin to use with this pattern words which are already in their lexical store and which fit into one of these meaning categories.

We might consider how these exercises would be put together. It would probably not be productive to carry out three consecutive exercises on the same grammatical item. Learners may well find it difficult to maintain their concentration. The third activity in particular is one which demands a good deal of time and thought. There is a good case, therefore, for setting Activity 3.5 as homework and allowing learners to work on it together or to use dictionaries to help them.

Teaching Activity 3.6:

Can you remember the last three paragraphs of the text? See if you can restore them by filling the gaps, where necessary, without looking at the original text:

___ boy went into ___ shop and bought ____ Smarties for 25p. "___ gave me a 50p piece and as ___ gave ___ ___ change ___ man came in. ___ waited until ___ man went. Then ___ threw ___ plastic carrier bag at ___, pointed ___ gun at ___ and said: 'Put everything in'." ___ fled when ___ woman, who had ___ two children with ___, pressed ___ alarm.

___ boy is described as 3ft 6in tall, dressed in jeans and ___ dark coat.

___ police spokesman said, "___ are taking ___ very seriously, as we would ___ robbery involving ___ firearm, fake or not."

Commentary on Teaching Activity 3.6:

This is a very simple activity which at first sight involves nothing more than recall of the text. You will almost certainly find that you can do this exercise without too much trouble. It is not simply because you can recall the text that you can do the exercise, but because you have a thorough command of the referential systems of English. Learners will certainly be unable to recall the text in sufficient detail to do the whole activity from memory. In doing the exercises they too will have to draw on their command of referential systems, focusing on words like *the, I, him* and *his*. There will be a good deal of speculation as they do this, and some discussion if the activity is carried out in groups as it almost certainly should be.

The activity focuses on system building and moves on to exploration. It involves system building where a learner applies a rule in order to fill a gap, either with the original word or with an acceptable alternative. The activity involves exploration where a learner is obliged to rely on recall of the appropriate form or where they are unsure of the answer and are obliged to check against the original text.

Another way of encouraging system building and exploration is through **progressive deletion**. The teacher writes down a target sentence and asks a student to read it aloud.

Teaching Activity 3.7:
1. Choose a sentence, for example, *A police spokesman said, "We are taking this very seriously, as we would any robbery involving a firearm, fake or not."*
2. Write up the sentence on the board and ask one or two students to read it out loud.
3. Rub out one or two words replacing them with dashes corresponding to the number of letters in the words:

    A police spokesman said, "We are - - - - - - this very seriously, as we would any - - - - - - - involving a firearm, fake or not."
4. Another student is then asked to read out the full sentence, including the words which have been erased.
5. Erase more words:

    A police spokesman said, "We are - - - - - - this very - - - - - - - - -, as we - - - - - any - - - - - - - involving a firearm, - - - - or - - -."

Again a student is asked to reconstruct and read out the full sentence.

6. This process continues until the students are asked to recall from a framework which consists simply of a series of dashes.

Commentary on Teaching Activity 3.7:

As a classroom technique progressive deletion has a number of advantages. It is possible to select a sentence which provides a valuable context for a number of useful items, in this case the use of the very frequent lexical items *any, involving* and *would*, the phrase *... or not* and the phrase *taking seriously*. After each deletion learners can be asked to work on recall in groups. This encourages them to consider and discuss the possibilities, opening their minds to alternative possibilities. The level of difficulty of the activity can be precisely controlled. It can be made easier or more difficult by varying the length of the target sentence, or by increasing the number of readings after each deletion. Most important of all, however, is the fact that learners find the activity challenging and engaging.

There can, of course, be no guarantee that recall activities will lead directly to learning, but they will highlight items in a way which encourages recognition and exploration. If, for example, students come across future hypothetical uses of the modal *would*, then the phrase *as we would any robbery involving a firearm* may provide a useful starting point. In order to recall a sentence consisting of twenty words learners will need to make sense of its structure and wording. In order to do this they are obliged to rely on previous learning to provide conscious insights (system building) and identification of new patterns (recognition and exploration).

Teaching Activity 3.8:

Look at the following words. Can you use these words as a starting point to recall the first two sentences?

Police last night search eight-year-old boy attempt hold up sweet shop pistol. Boy wear balaclava throw carrier bag shopkeeper corner store Ashton-under-Lyme Greater Manchester order her fill up.

Commentary on Teaching Activity 3.8:

This is the kind of activity which is sometimes called **grammaticisation**. If we accept that learners generally begin with a lexical form of expression and move gradually towards fully grammatical utterances, then an activity of this kind has an obvious value in that it mirrors the development process.

We have looked at a number of activities which will contribute to learning. If a lesson is to be successful and memorable, however, it is important to motivate learners. One way of doing this is to provide a sharp focus on the major learning items in the lesson. You can do this by giving a review of the lesson, summarising what has been 'learnt', or at least what lexical and grammatical forms have been highlighted.

Teaching Activity 3.9:

Write down ten words and five phrases from this unit which will be useful to you. Compare your list with those compiled by others in your group.

Another way of doing this is to provide an opportunity for controlled practice at the end of the teaching cycle.

Teaching Activity 3.10:

Choose *either*

- three things you *want / would like* to do over the next year.

or

- three things you *hope / intend / plan* to do in the next month.

Write down the three things in your book. Close your book and see how many of the things you can remember and tell to the class.

Choose *either*

- three things your teacher doesn't *allow* you to do in class.

or

- three things a computer *enables* you to do.

or

- three things you *would like* someone to give you.

Write these three things in your book. Close your book and see how many of the things you can remember and tell to the class.

Commentary on Teaching Activity 3.10:

This is the sort of activity which often comes at the beginning of a lesson. It isolates a particular structure and encourages learners to use it under controlled circumstances. It is the kind of activity we referred to at the end of the first chapter as *rehearsal*. If learners have already understood the pattern and the way it works, this rehearsal will help them to consolidate a number of phrases which are likely to be of use to them outside the classroom. But there can be no guarantee that they will master the items at this stage.

Activities like Teaching Activities 3.9 and 3.10, which summarise what has been covered in the lesson, are important ways of packaging a lesson. They provide a summary of learning opportunities which helps to motivate students.

3.2.1 Summary

We are now in a position to relate learning processes to the model of grammar set up in the last chapter. Roughly speaking we can take the elements in our model of language outlined in the last chapter and arrange them in a cline from those elements which are readily accessible to accumulation, through those which involve problem solving, to elements which must depend on exploration.

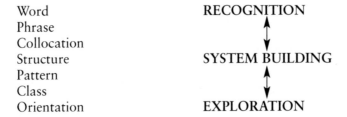

Word	RECOGNITION
Phrase	
Collocation	
Structure	SYSTEM BUILDING
Pattern	
Class	
Orientation	EXPLORATION

The elements at the top of the scale are those which can be recognised by learners and committed to memory. Extreme examples would be words like *cat* and *dog* which have referents in the outside world and usually have recognisable and reliable first language equivalents. Those towards the bottom of the scale need long exposure and constant teacher support. Examples are the use of the past simple and present perfect tenses, and the use of the definite and indefinite articles. Elements at the top can be readily demonstrated or explained out of context. Those towards the bottom are complex, often too complex, to demonstrate or explain fully, and need to be studied in text. Control of these features of language will only come after continued exposure.

The scale therefore offers a guide to learnability. We can expect students to learn word lists and fixed phrases. As teachers we can make things easier by helping them to organise their learning, and by making links to other areas of language. When it comes to patterns and frames we can first make them aware of the role played by these features of language. We can then help them to recognise patterns and relate them to words and meanings. Again we are offering valuable support in helping to define what it is that is to be learnt. With orientation we can only provide guidelines and exposure. Beyond this, learning will be an unconscious and gradual process. It will be a process of exploration.

3.2.2 Controlled practice

There are, I think, three advantages to controlled practice when it comes **after** rather than **before** a task. The first is that it highlights what has been 'learnt'. In fact, it highlights what **appears** to have been learnt. We can never guarantee that learning will take place no matter how appropriate the learning activities employed. But learners like to have a summary of what has been covered in a given lesson. A short, sharp burst of controlled practice is a quick way of giving such a summary. At the end of a lesson based on Text 1, for example, we might ask students to carry out an exercise like the one shown in Teaching Activity 3.10 above.

The second advantage of this process is that it enables students to produce and learn forms which they can see as relevant to their own lives. They can begin to personalise language in a way that enhances motivation. Finally, as students display the sentences they have written down, the teacher can use these as the basis for controlled practice, concentrating on pronunciation and intonation. The fact that learners practise these forms may help to build up motor fluency. By this I mean the ability learners need to develop to get their tongues round new sounds, words and phrases, so that they have sufficient control of pronunciation to produce these forms rapidly, something which is particularly important at the beginner stage. But there can, of course, be no guarantee that these phrases will immediately become a part of the learner's spontaneous repertoire.

3.3 Summary

We have outlined a teaching sequence which begins with a communicative task, and have argued that a procedure which begins with a focus on form will not actually help learners to communicate effectively and will mean that they are concerned with form rather than meaning, with constructing sentences rather than achieving a communicative objective. We have stressed the importance of language development. This involves processes in which learners have time to recast a message. It means they will pay more attention to the forms they use, encouraging them to go beyond their basic message and to take careful account of their reader or listener as well as of the way they are presenting themselves (Basic message → Concern for reader/listener → Presentation of self). The important feature of these language development activities is that learners will not be concerned simply to produce accurate forms, they will make decisions which enable them to use forms they can produce with speed and fluency.

We then went on to look at appropriate language learning activities. Some activities might be described as recognition and accumulation activities. These might involve rote learning of word lists, for example. We also need system building activities. An example of a system building activity would be when students work to categorise words associated with a particular pattern. This is a problem with a finite solution, and teachers can provide clear guidance towards a solution. Finally we need to take account of exploration activities. These activities relate particularly to the learning of orientation. Orientation is so complex that it cannot be explained satisfactorily by a set of rules. The best a teacher can do is offer learners some rule-of-thumb guidelines, and then encourage learners to work out the systems for themselves. Work on orientation must relate to text, since orientation has no meaning apart from text, and students must be given opportunities through communicative activities and language development activities to test their developing systems.

I stressed the need to look carefully not only at exercises but also at learning processes. I suggested that some rote learning activities might actually involve problem solving, and concluded that we need to consider not only the outcome of an activity, but also the learning processes involved. Finally, we looked at a role for summarising activities to highlight what has been learnt, to enable learners to work with words, phrases and sentences relevant to their own lives.

In the next few chapters we will go on to look at the grammar of structure and orientation, and at pattern and class, and we will suggest what kind of learning activity is appropriate to these areas of the grammar.

4 The grammar of structure

We established in Section 2.1 that structure refers to the way items – words and phrases – are sequenced to make up larger units. Words are built up to make phrases but, as we saw, the ordering is not random: *the black cat* is a possible ordering, *cat the black* is not. Words and phrases build up into clauses, but again the ordering is not random: *I am studying grammar* is possible, but *Grammar am studying I* is not. Clauses can be built up in turn to make sentences. In the text we looked at in Chapter 3 we found the following sentence: *He gave me a 50p piece and as I gave him his change a man came in.* This sentence is made up of three clauses:

1. *He gave me a 50p piece.*
2. *I gave him his change.*
3. *A man came in.*

Clauses 1 and 3 are joined by the conjunction *and*: *He gave me a 50p coin and a man came in.* Clause 2 is inserted between these two clauses, introduced by the subordinating conjunction *as*. So a sentence may be built up from two or more clauses. In this chapter we are concerned with the structure of these component clauses.

4.1 Clauses: Structure and pattern

In Section 2.1 I set out three rules which I claimed accounted for the structure of the English clause:

- The basic structure of the clause is N + V + ?. The continuation of the clause after the verb is determined by the meaning of the verb, not by abstract grammatical considerations.
- The first noun phrase in the clause functions as the subject of the clause.
- All English clauses must have a word or phrase acting as subject.

Thus we have an initiating structure N + V and what occurs after that will depend on the meaning of the V and therefore on the pattern which follows it. Whatever follows will, however, still conform to the basic N + V + ? structure. This was illustrated with the following examples:

I / laughed. (N + V)
She / bought / a dress. (N + V + N)
I / will put / it / away. (N + V + N + Adv.)

In addition to these basic elements of structure we also have **circumstances**, or **circumstantial elements**, which are optional rather than necessary elements. So the clause, *I enjoyed the film* is complete in itself, but it could be extended by adding one or more circumstantial elements: *I (thoroughly) enjoyed the film (last night)*.

Let us imagine a sentence beginning with the words *Computers enable ....* How would you predict this sentence will develop? To complete the meaning of *enable* we need to know who is enabled, and what they are enabled to do. In order to fulfil these requirements the verb *enable* is always followed by the pattern N + *to*-infinitive.

Let us imagine the sentence goes on, *Computers enable **scientists to carry out....*** What do you expect now? Well people always carry out something, so you would expect a noun or noun phrase to tell you what scientists carry out. Let us imagine that the sentence goes as follows: *Computers enable scientists to carry out **complex calculations.*** We now have a sentence which leaves us with no further expectations. Yet, as we have seen, the clause may be extended to include one or more circumstantial elements as in: *Computers enable scientists to carry out complex calculations **at high speed.*** We can show this structure diagrammatically:

N (*Computers*) + V (*have enabled*)

$\downarrow$

Pattern: N (*scientists*) + *to*-infinitive
(*to carry out*)

$\downarrow$

Pattern: N (*complex calculations*)
+ Adv. (*at high speed*)

This simple example suggests how users operate with language. As language producers we string together patterns, filling out the elements as we go along. As receivers we listen and anticipate what is coming.

One of the things that makes language complicated is that we can have one pattern prompting another. In the example above the string

Computers enable ... prompts ... *scientists to carry out* .... The verb *carry out* in turn prompts *complex calculations.* This sequencing of patterns can go on for quite some time. Consider, for example: *He asked me to tell Jean that he wanted to know if she was free on Monday.* Here we have *He asked → me to tell → Jean that he wanted → to know → if she was → free (on Monday).* At each stage the verb creates expectations which are then fulfilled. Once all predictions have been fulfilled we may end the message or we may choose to add supplementary information, in this case: *on Monday.*

The important thing about all this is that it shows how language processing – production or reception – can be described as a linear process. This means it is a process whereby we put things together one after another. We put clauses together piece by piece, and each piece determines to a greater or lesser extent what is likely to follow it. We understand language in the same way, constantly processing what we have in order to predict what is likely to follow. Clause structure emerges as the clause develops.

4.1.1 Teaching and learning clause structure

4.1.1.1 Basic structure

I have argued that the basic structure of the clause is dependent on the verb. If we accept this premise, then the main learning problem with clause structure is to do with verb patterns. Learners need to sort out the patterns which follow verbs, and to assign verbs to those patterns. Usually this is straightforward, depending on the meaning of the verb. Verbs of motion, such as *go* and *come*, are almost always followed by prepositional phrases of place. Verbs describing a mental state and looking to the future are followed by the *to*-infinitive. Examples are *hope, intend, mean* and *want.* The verbs *advise, ask, teach, tell* and *warn* are often followed by N + about + N, as in: *She told me about her problem* or *The organisation informs businesses about environmental issues.*

Learning here involves acquiring frames and patterns based on verbs and beginning to make generalisations based on these patterns. These generalisations may lead learners to categorise the verbs featuring in a pattern and recognising them as, for example, verbs of mental state or verbs of telling and advising. They may lead learners to make generalisations about one of the other words featured in the pattern, recognising, for example, that *about* is frequently used to mean something like *on the subject of.* We can help learners in a number of ways:

- **Recognition:** We can enhance recognition by drawing attention to patterns. We can do this by focusing on instances of the pattern when they occur in text and asking learners to identify, for example, verbs followed by the *to*-infinitive. We can ask them to look back over previous texts to supplement the examples they can find in a particular text. This can work either from the meanings of verbs or from the patterns associated with them. We can ask them to look for verbs followed by a *to*-infinitive and *to* or we can ask them to look for verbs describing a mental state.

- **System building:** We can encourage system building by highlighting the meaning of items such as *about*, meaning *on the subject of*, and asking students to predict which verbs are likely to trigger this pattern. Another way of encouraging system building is by helping learners to organise their lexical knowledge by, for example, encouraging them to recognise and collect verbs of mental state and relate these to the *to*-infinitive. We can encourage them to organise their vocabulary books in ways which will help them to take account of patterns. We can look for students' grammar books which provide lists of patterns.

- **Exploration:** We can provide activities which encourage learners to look critically at text for themselves, asking them to identify patterns and speculate on how these patterns function and what sort of words they involve.

- **Improvisation and consolidation:** We need to give learners opportunities to use the language to provide opportunities for improvisation and consolidation. As they do this they will begin gradually to operationalise the patterns they have learnt. This means that what they have learnt will gradually become a part of their spontaneous language behaviour.

All of these techniques relate to the patterns and frames rather than to clause structure as such. But, as we have shown, clause structure depends crucially on the way words pattern. We shall have much more to say about appropriate teaching techniques when we come to look at patterns in Chapter 7.

4.1.1.2 Circumstantial elements in the clause

A second problem with clause structure concerns the placing of circumstantial elements in the clause. The most frequent circumstantial elements are adverbs and phrases of time and place. These are normally found at the end of the clause, but may come elsewhere, depending on the way we wish to organise information.

Task 4.1:

Look at the sentence:

Police were searching for an eight-year-old boy.

If you want to include the circumstantial element *last night*, where could it go in the clause? How many possible places can you find? Can you remember the text in 3.1.2 above which contained these words? Can you remember where the words *last night* came in the clause? Why do you think the writer chose to put them there?

Commentary on Task 4.1:

This activity encourages exploration. All the following are grammatical sentences:

1. *Police were searching for an eight-year-old boy **last night**.*
2. ***Last night** police were searching for an eight-year-old boy.*
3. *Police were searching **last night** for an eight-year-old boy.*
4. *Police were **last night** searching for an eight-year-old boy.*

Another possibility, though less likely, is: *Police **last night** were searching for an eight-year-old boy.* In the original text the full sentence was *Police were **last night** searching for an eight-year-old boy who attempted to hold up a sweet shop with a pistol.*

The phrase *last night* could have been placed in the usual position, at the end of its clause, *Police were searching for an eight-year-old boy who attempted to hold up a sweet shop with a pistol **last night**.* But this would have created two problems. Firstly, it would have placed the phrase a long way from the verb *searching* which it applies to. Secondly, the sentence would have been ambiguous: was it the searching which took place last night, or the attempted hold-up? Another possibility would have been to put the words *last night* at the beginning of the sentence. But in writing a newspaper article it is important to catch the reader's attention immediately, and the words *last night* would be rather a weak opening. This leaves the writer with the choice between 3 and 4. In the event he chose 4.

As the task above shows, the decision on where to place an adverb of time or place or a prepositional phrase will depend on the way we wish to organise information in the clause. We can begin by establishing the usual position for these elements at the end of the clause. We also need to highlight alternative positions. This can only be done with reference to text. After processing a text for meaning we can ask students to identify phrases and adverbs of time and place, and to note where they occur in the clause. We can ask them to recall sentences from the text. We can also ask students to consider alternative positions for the items, as we did in Task 4.1, and to consider how far these possibilities would be appropriate to the original text.

Adverbs of frequency are also movable, but their normal position is in front of the main verb element in the verb phrase:

*I have **often** met him at work.*
*He is **usually** working in the library.*

But these elements too are variable. Again we need to establish the expected position and then to examine alternative possibilities. In establishing the expected position we can often usefully classify words as, for example:

- **adverbs of frequency**: *often, usually, sometimes, rarely* etc.
- **attitudinal adjuncts**: *apparently, basically, frankly, fortunately, in fact, in general, suddenly* and *surprisingly* – these are usually found at the beginning of the clause.
- **adverbs of manner**: *badly, beautifully, happily* and *well* – these are usually found at the end of the clause.

This kind of classifying activity is an important vocabulary learning activity in its own right, which we will consider in more detail in Chapter 8. We can therefore provide useful guidelines, but we also need to encourage students to observe how these forms are used and to learn from the contexts in which the items are encountered.

4.2 The noun phrase

Some years ago, I read a newspaper article about two reservoirs in Glasgow, which began with this sentence:

Tape-recorded squawks of a seagull in distress have enabled water authorities in Strathclyde to cleanse two reservoirs at Milngavie, near Glasgow, by frightening away an estimated 5,000 seagulls ....

From any reasonable point of view this is a complicated and difficult sentence. The main reason for this complexity is that the sentence contains four complex noun phrases:

- *Tape-recorded squawks of a seagull in distress*
- *water authorities in Strathclyde*

- *two reservoirs at Milngavie, near Glasgow*
- *an estimated 5,000 seagulls ...*

But, if we look at the sentence from the point of view of clause structure and pattern, it is relatively simple. In fact, it is an exact parallel of the sentence we looked at earlier:

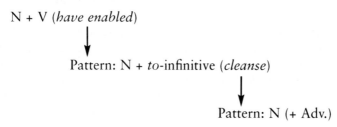

N + V (*have enabled*)

Pattern: N + *to*-infinitive (*cleanse*)

Pattern: N (+ Adv.)

In other words we have a noun which is the subject of the verb *have enabled*. This verb is followed by the pattern N + *to*-infinitive. The *to*-infinitive verb is *to cleanse*. This is followed by its own pattern, N. Finally there is a circumstantial element, the prepositional phrase, *by frightening away an estimated 5,000 seagulls*, which tells us **how** they cleansed the reservoir.

It is only when we fit the noun phrases into the analysis in Fig. 4.1 below that we can see why the sentence is so complicated.

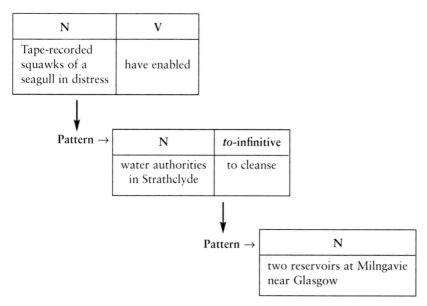

N	V
Tape-recorded squawks of a seagull in distress	have enabled

Pattern →

N	*to*-infinitive
water authorities in Strathclyde	to cleanse

Pattern →

N
two reservoirs at Milngavie near Glasgow

Fig. 4.1

The reason for the complexity of the sentence, therefore, lies in the complex noun phrases. The first N, for example, the subject of *have enabled*, consists of seven words: *Tape-recorded squawks of a seagull in distress*. This illustrates an important feature of language structure: we often have one structure embedded in another. So the noun phrase, *Tape-recorded squawks of a seagull in distress*, has three nouns in it – *squawks*, *seagull* and *distress*. The central noun is *squawks*, because it is the *squawks* that *have enabled ....* . But these *squawks* are defined as *the squawks **of a seagull***. The *seagull* itself is then described as being *in distress*. In theory each of these nouns could be further expanded to produce something like *tape-recorded squawks of a **captive** seagull in **acute** distress*. Theoretically a noun phrase could be extended infinitely, the only limits being those set by our capacity to process the complex meanings.

Another reason for the complexity of the sentence lies in the prepositional phrase: *by frightening away an estimated 5,000 seagulls ....* . This phrase acts in the same way as an adverb of manner, for example: *The water authorities have cleansed the reservoirs **successfully***. It is parallel in structure to the phrase *at high speed* in our *computers* example. As it is, we have this structure in the final part of the sentence:

Preposition +	N +	Pattern
by	*frightening away*	N *an estimated 5,000 seagulls* *which were polluting the water*

The phrase *frightening away* is described here as N. It is true that the word *frightening* is part of the verb *frighten*. But this *-ing*-form of the verb, the gerund, is used as a noun. It may be the subject of a verb as in:

1. a. ***Swimming** is good for you.*
   b. ***Exercise** is good for you.*

or as the object of a verb:

2. a. *I like **swimming**.*
   b. *I like **cornflakes**.*

or as the object of a preposition:

3. a. *I am keen on **swimming**.*
   b. *I am keen on **tennis**.*

In each of these sentences the -*ing*-form acts in the same way as a noun. The gerund, *swimming*, is paralleled by *exercise* in 1.b., *cornflakes* in 2.b. and *tennis* in 3.b. In our seagull text the gerund, *frightening away*, is the object of the preposition *by*.

The -*ing*-form is formed from a verb. Because of this it keeps the same pattern as when it is acting as a verb. Again, in the sentence we are analysing, we have one pattern nesting in another. The use of the verb form in *frightening away* triggers the noun phrase *an estimated 5,000 seagulls*. Again we have embedding. This time, a verbal noun triggers a new noun phrase which could, in theory, contain another verbal noun, which could trigger a new noun phrase ... and so on. Fortunately, noun phrases of this complexity are very unusual even in written English, and almost non-existent in spoken English, as we shall see in Chapter 9. Many native speakers of the language, unless they are journalists, academics or bureaucrats, live happy and fulfilled lives without ever needing to produce such convoluted phrases. Nevertheless, embedding is a common feature of language, and can lead to enormous complexity.

4.2.1 Determiners and quantifiers with nouns

To see how noun phrases are built up, let us begin with two nouns, an uncountable noun, *money*, and a countable noun, *boy/boys*, and see what can be done with them. First of all it is worth noticing that the words *money* or *boys* could be used as they stand to make a general statement:

> **Boys** *should be seen and not heard.*
> *He spends* **money** *as if there were no tomorrow.*

Usually the words are likely to be found with a **determiner**. Determiners are listed in Fig. 4.2. They are listed in two basic categories: **specific** and **general**. We can use any of these forms with countable nouns such as *boy/boys*. With uncountable nouns such as *money* we can use any determiner apart from the indefinite article, *a(n)*.

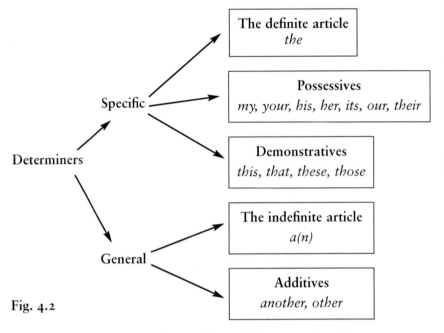

Fig. 4.2

We will look in detail at the teaching of determiners in Chapter 6.

We often find phrases which act as **quantifiers**. Quantifiers may be found in place of determiners or working together with determiners. We talk about *lots of boys, a few of the boys, a lot of bread* and so on. There are three basic patterns:

1. Quantifier + noun: e.g. *all/some money; all/some/both/boys.*
2. Quantifier + specific determiner + noun: e.g. *all the money; all/both the boys.*
3. Quantifier + *of* + specific determiner + noun: e.g. *all/most/some/ any of the money/boys.*

The first step in the acquisition of determiners is lexical and comes, therefore, under the heading of recognition. Learners need to learn the relevant lexical items. In the case of quantifiers there is a closed set of items of around thirty words and phrases: *all, any, both, each, either, enough, (a) few, a little, less, a lot of, lots of, many, more, most, much, neither, no, none of, plenty of, several, some, a bit of, a couple of, a good/great deal of, heaps of, loads of, masses of, piles of, tons of, a great/small number of, hundreds of, thousands of.* One thing to note is that many of these quantifiers are phrases with *of* and should be learnt as phrases. For teaching purposes we can usefully divide quantifiers into three groups:

1. Found with both countable and uncountable nouns:	*all, any, enough, less, a lot of, lots of, more, most, no, none of, some* (Colloquial forms: *plenty of, heaps of, loads of*)
2. Found only with countable nouns:	*both, each, either, (a) few (fewer), neither, several* (Colloquial forms: *a couple of, hundreds of, thousands of*)
3. Found only with uncountable nouns:	*a little, much, a bit of* (Colloquial forms: *heaps of, tons of*) (Found particularly with abstract nouns such as *time, money, trouble* etc.: *a good/great deal of*)

Fig. 4.3

Task 4.2:

As a teacher or materials writer, how would you organise quantifiers for your students? Which ones would you ask them to learn for productive use? Which ones would they need for recognition only? How would you decide which ones to teach first?

Commentary on Task 4.2:

All of these words and phrases are very frequent and very important. Apart from the colloquial forms we can usefully introduce all of them for reception at an early stage. At an appropriate intermediate stage the colloquial forms can be introduced as alternatives to *lots of/a lot of* or, in the case of *a couple of*, as an alternative to *two*.

If there are several frequent words or phrases, which carry more or less the same meaning, it is useful to teach first the words that can be used in a range of grammatical contexts. If there is a choice, as between *many* and *a lot of/lots of*, for example, I would choose *a lot of/lots of* on the grounds that it has a greater grammatical range. You can use *a lot of* or *lots of* with both countable and uncountable nouns, whereas *many* can only be used with countable nouns.

When we want to work on production, we can introduce basic quantifiers with an activity which uses quantifiers with a specific determiner to make statements about specific items.

Teaching Activity 4.1:

Are these statements true or false?

    i. All the boys are playing football.
    ii. All of the boys are playing tennis.
   iii. None of the boys is playing tennis.
   iv. All of the girls are playing football.
    v. One of the girls is playing football.
   vi. Neither of the old men is playing football.
  vii. Both of the old men are sitting on the bench.
 viii. Both the old men are playing tennis.
   ix. Neither of the women is playing tennis.
    x. Both women are talking.

Can you correct the statements that are not true?

This exercise can be done twice, once with books open, and once with books shut, the teacher reading out the sentences. Students, with books closed, can then be asked to work in groups and write down five statements of their own, which may be either true or false. These are read out to the class, corrected by the teacher if necessary, to check if they are true or false. This can be followed by the teacher asking questions with *any*. Finally students can ask their own questions. At a later stage a similar exercise can be done with general statements.

Teaching Activity 4.2:
Do you think these statements are true or false? Correct the ones you think are not true.

1. All animals have four legs.
2. Some animals have two legs.
3. Most birds can fly.
4. Any bird can fly.
5. Most animals live on land.
6. No birds can swim.
7. All birds lay eggs.
8. All fish live in the sea.
9. A lot of animals eat fruit.
10. Some fish can swim.
11. Any fish can swim.
12. All animals can swim.
13. Lots of birds can swim.

All of these are general statements, so the definite article is not used. After doing this exercise, students can be asked to make their own sentences and try them out on other members of the class. And again this can be followed by questions with *any*.

Again it must be emphasised that, even though learners may perform successfully on tasks like these, that does not guarantee that they have control of the quantifier system. The activities aim at recognition and system building; learners still have to consolidate the system by putting it to use. Fortunately these quantifiers are so frequent that students will come across them regularly. Their system will be gradually shaped by exposure, and also by teacher correction, but full control of quantifiers will take some time to develop. In order to use these words and phrases consistently, learners obviously need to distinguish between countable and uncountable nouns and to apply this knowledge to their use of quantifiers. At a later stage in their learning it may be worth reviewing their development. They could be given a list of quantifiers and asked to complete a table like that in Fig. 4.3 above.

Learners also need to master the determiner system before they can have full control of quantifiers. It will be some considerable time before they distinguish consistently between *all animals* and *all (of)* ***the*** *animals*. It is important to recognise that few grammatical systems can be entirely isolated from other systems. We can provide learners with a usable system of quantifiers by treating the words and phrases lexically, but in the long run control of quantifiers depends on control of the countable/uncountable distinction and the system of determiners.

4.2.2 Measurers and nouns

There are a number of ways to describe a part or specific quantity of a noun. The terminology in this section is based on Halliday's description (1994: 194–5). If we take the general term **measurers** to denote these items, we can identify three kinds of measurers:

- **Partitives:** Words such as *beginning, middle, side, back*, which specify a specific part of something.
- **Quantitatives:** Words used to quantify uncountable nouns, such as *an item of furniture* or *a loaf of bread*.
- **Collectives:** Words used to quantify countable nouns, such as *a bunch of flowers; a bag of sweets*.

Partitives are found with nouns of location (*the end of the street, the back of the house* etc.) and time (*the end of the day, the middle of the week, the beginning of the month*). These partitives of location and time are almost always found with the frame *the* + partitive + *of the* + noun. These can be practised from an early stage. Students can be asked: *Who was born at the beginning / end of the month? … in the middle of the month? What lessons do you have at the beginning / end of the day? … in the middle of the day?* Lessons too have beginnings, middles and ends: *What did we do at the beginning / end of our last lesson?* In looking at pictures you can talk about *… the end of the street, the front / back of the house*. The local environment provides opportunities: *What shops are there at the end of the High Street? Where is the butcher's shop?* and so on. Books and stories also have beginnings, middles and ends: *What happened at the beginning / end of the story?* It is not difficult to find ways of introducing and reviewing these partitives in a meaningful context.

Quantitatives are most commonly found in the frame *a* + quantitative + *of* + N. Most of these are found with uncountable nouns. Some of them are very frequent words and have very general application, for example *bit, piece* and *item*. Some less common partitives are found with specific nouns, particularly uncountable nouns – *a loaf of bread, a column of smoke, a sheet of paper, a gust of wind*. Others are found with nouns which are related to one another by meaning. For example the quantitatives *a pool of* and *a drop of* are found with liquids; *a flock of* is used with birds and some animals like sheep. Some quantitatives are measurements – *a pound of, a pint of* etc., others are containers – *cup, bottle, tin, box* etc.

The most generally applicable collective, used with countable nouns, is the word *group*: *a group of boys, trees, houses* etc. Sinclair (1990) offers two productive features which apply to collectives. Nouns which refer to groups, such as *audience, team* and *family*, can be used as collectives. You can also use the area which something occupies as a collective. This would enable learners to produce phrases such as *a forest of trees, a garden of roses* or *a street of shops*.

Since the patterns involved are highly predictable, the main problem with learning measurers is lexical. The problem for the teacher, then, is how best to organise these words. Quantitatives with uncountable nouns are particularly valuable, since they enable us to specify or pluralise these nouns and talk about *two bits of furniture* or *several pieces of luggage*. The words *bit* and *piece* are particularly useful as they can be used with a wide range of uncountable nouns. It is important to introduce these words as soon as learners are introduced to the class of uncountable nouns and to associate them with the appropriate nouns. Learners should learn not only the words *advice* and *furniture*, but also the phrases *some furniture / advice, a piece / bit of advice* and so on. Containers and measures should also be learnt together with appropriate nouns. A lesson which focuses on items of food and drink should include appropriate containers and measures.

At a later stage we can go on to introduce quantitatives and collectives which have a more specific application: *a pinch of salt, a joint of meat, a bunch of flowers, a clump of trees, a gang of kids* and so on. These words could form the basis of a dictionary practice exercise:

Teaching Activity 4.3:

We often talk about *a piece of advice* or *a bag of sweets*. How many phrases like this can you make from the following table? You may use your dictionary to help you.

a

pinch, joint, bunch, block, bottle, pair, drop, slice, packet, grain, bowl, item, spoonful, glass

of

bread, cigarettes, flats, flowers, meat, news, rice, salt, shoes, soup, sugar, trousers, water, wine, grapes

---

Since the aim of this activity is recognition, it could usefully be followed by a memory test. The teacher or a student can call out *a bunch of ...* and challenge another student to complete the phrase from memory with an appropriate word.

4.2.3 Adjectives and noun modifiers with nouns

As we have seen, in English adjectives almost always come immediately in front of the noun: *a little boy, a noisy little boy, some fresh bread, some nice fresh bread* and so on. They may be preceded by a quantifier: *a lot of noisy little boys, a loaf of nice fresh bread.* It is possible, though unusual, to have more than two adjectives with a noun. There are guidelines for the ordering of adjectives: adjectives which express an evaluation normally come before adjectives which are more objectively descriptive, thus we talk about *nice brown bread* rather than *brown nice bread.* Descriptive adjectives generally come in the order size; shape; age; colour. Thus we would talk about *a large brown armchair* rather than *a brown large armchair.* But these are no more than useful guidelines. The positioning of adjectives depends also on the text and the speaker's sense of priorities. Thus it is possible, although unusual, to talk, for example, about *a loaf of fresh nice bread.*

The meanings of adjectives can be made more precise in a number of ways. We can use a comparative or superlative form to talk about *a bigger boy* or *fresher bread, the biggest boy* or *the freshest loaf of bread.* We can use a general **intensifier** such as *very, extremely, exceptionally, really* or *unusually*. With some adjectives we can use an intensifier such as *dangerously, suspiciously, incredibly* or *delightfully* to show how we feel about something. Alternatively we can use a **mitigator** such as *fairly, pretty, slightly* or *rather*. With some adjectives we can use words which indicate a degree of a quality: *almost empty, nearly full* or someone who is *completely exhausted*. In spoken language, particularly, we often use vague terms as mitigators, indicating that we cannot find exactly the right adjective: *I'm feeling **sort of** disappointed. She looked **kind of** surprised.* Or possibly that the right adjective does not exist: *It's **kind of** bluish.*

Some words belong to what grammarians call **closed classes**. A closed class of words is a class which consists of a limited number, so that one can count all the members of the class. Prepositions and determiners are examples of closed classes. Intensifiers also make up a closed class. Sinclair (1990) lists 40 intensifiers, ranging from very frequent words like *very* and *particularly* to relatively infrequent words like *radically* and *wildly*. There are only ten mitigators listed, with *fairly* and *quite* the most frequent, and *mildly* and *moderately* the least frequent. There are 20 items showing the extent of a quality, ranging in frequency from

almost, absolutely and *nearly* through to *exclusively* and *predominantly.*
For all these classes of words the frequent items should be learnt at an
early stage. Other items can be added as they occur.

It is very common in English to put two nouns together as in: *an ice
cube; an ice bucket; the ice age.* When this happens, the first of the two
nouns is a noun modifier. The relationship between the two nouns is not
always clear. The hearer has to work it out. So *an ice cube* is made of
ice, *an ice bucket* is designed to contain ice, and *the ice age* was that
period of time when most of the earth was covered in ice. Sinclair
(1990) cites noun modifiers as a productive feature (see Section 2.5)
since 'almost any noun in English can modify almost any other noun.'
As soon as we put two nouns together listeners or readers begin to
search for an interpretation. Sinclair points out that 'the phrase *trick
finger* for example is grammatically acceptable', and invites us to
imagine a meaning for it. Today's newspaper headlines, for example,
include *York Minster, London residents, health row, fraud team, car
prices, rail misery, tobacco sales, birth defects.*

Nouns ending in *-ing* and *-er*, which are formed from verbs, are very
often found with other nouns: *office worker, pastry maker, potato
peeler, shopping list, swimming lesson, walking holiday, language
learning.* It is also possible to have a series of noun modifiers. I referred
above to *a dictionary practice exercise* – an exercise to enable students
to practise their dictionary skills. Complex noun modifier groups are a
particular feature of newspaper English, since they are another useful
way of compressing information. My newspaper today has a news item
about the *baby injury compensation bill* – the amount of money the
British health service has to pay in order to compensate parents whose
children are seriously injured at birth.

Task 4.3:

As I have shown, noun modifiers are very common in English.
Apart from the phrases in italics there are six phrases with noun
modifiers in the paragraph above, one of them a three-word phrase.
Can you find them?

Commentary on Task 4.3:

The answer is:

*noun modifiers; dictionary skills; noun modifier groups; newspaper
English; news item; health service.*
It is interesting to note that the word *noun* in *noun modifier* is itself
a noun modifier.

The use of noun modifiers is a feature which is very common in English, but is not used in most other languages. As a result it is often underused by learners. Particularly common noun modifiers are those which describe the location of another noun such as *the car door, the kitchen window, the town jail*, which many learners tend to make possessive as in **the car's door* or **the kitchen's window*.

It is useful to point out the use of noun modifiers as they occur in text, and later to ask students to identify these items for themselves. They can be asked, for example, to find or think of a phrase which means *a tray used to make ice in a freezer* or *something which is used to sharpen pencils*. As their course proceeds, students can be asked to explain the meaning of progressively more complex noun modifier groups. They might begin with phrases such as *an English lesson, London restaurants, pet food, a skiing holiday, a football match, a five-hour meeting* or *a food processor*. Later they can go on to look at more complex items such as *a baby sitting service, earth moving equipment* or *a spaghetti eating contest*. At an advanced level, students can be asked to predict the content of newspaper articles headlined *Kabul prison camp riot, City high flier's sex change operation* or *Train strike brings commuter rail misery*.

Task 4.4:

How would you interpret the three phrases above?

Commentary on Task 4.4:

I have the advantage of having seen these phrases in context. This is how I interpreted them in context:

1. Kabul prison camp riot: *a riot which happened in a prison camp in Kabul.*
2. City high flier's sex change operation: *a surgical operation to change the sex of a highly successful businessman.*
3. Train strike brings commuter rail misery: *a strike by railway workers caused inconvenience for people travelling to work.*

4.2.4 Postmodification: Phrases which follow nouns

We now have a fairly complicated noun phrase structure:

(partitive) + (quantifier) + (adjectives) + (noun modifiers) + noun

which will generate fairly complex phrases such as *lots of really crusty brown wholemeal bread* or *a large gang of completely unruly newspaper boys.* But most of the complexity which arose in the seagull text, which we referred to above, was derived from the phrases which followed the nouns, from the way the nouns were postmodified. It is the postmodification of the noun phrase and the possibility of recursion in this **postmodification** which causes the most problems. Elements which are used to postmodify the noun phrase are listed in Fig. 4.4.

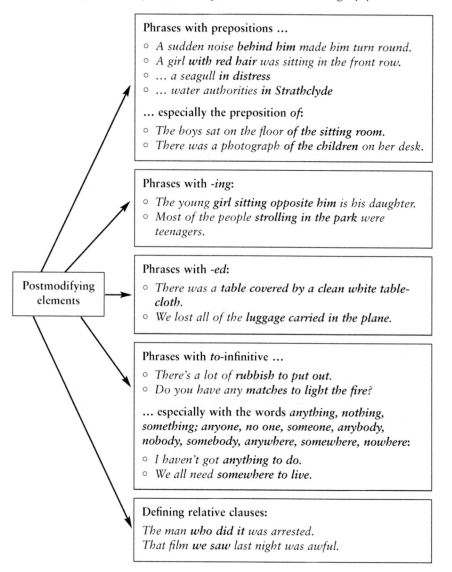

Fig. 4.4 **Postmodifiers**

Teaching Activity 4.4:

Learners can begin to build up fairly complex modification at an early stage. They could begin with a simple memory game: *On my way to school I saw ...* The teacher begins by drawing two boys playing football and saying: *On my way to school I saw two boys playing football.* A student is asked to repeat this. The next picture is added and the teacher says: *On my way to school I saw two boys playing football and a girl in a long dress.* Next is *a dog chasing a cat* and so on.

Again a student repeats. This goes on until learners are trying to remember seven or eight items. The teacher can then begin to rub the pictures off the board and see how many the students can remember. At a later stage students can think of their own phrases and pictures to make up a list. All these activities can be done with students working in groups to help each other to remember and to think of appropriate items.

Teaching Activity 4.5:

A similar activity can be built up using words rather than pictures as prompts. After reading the eight-year-old robber text (see Section 3.1.2) students can be given the simple sentence:

A(n) boy robbed a(n) shop.

The teacher then writes down another element, say, *eight-year-old*, and asks a student to fit this into the sentence and produce: *An eight-year-old boy robbed a shop.* Next the teacher might write down *wearing a balaclava*. The next student produces *An eight-year-old boy wearing a balaclava robbed a shop.* The teacher gradually adds other elements until the blackboard looks like this:

> *A(n) boy robbed a(n) shop.*
>
> 1. *Eight-year-old*
> 2. *Wearing a balaclava*
> 3. *Manchester*
> 4. *And carrying a gun*
> 5. *Sweet*

and learners read out the sentence: *An eight-year-old boy wearing a balaclava and carrying a gun robbed a Manchester sweet shop.*

Teaching Activity 4.6:

At an advanced level, this kind of activity can be carried out with highly complex noun phrases. In Section 4.2 above we looked at the following sentence from a newspaper article about seagulls:

Tape-recorded squawks of a seagull in distress have enabled water authorities in Strathclyde to cleanse two reservoirs in Milngavie near Glasgow, by frightening away an estimated 5,000 seagulls which have been polluting the water.

After they have studied the text, students may be asked to study this sentence carefully. After this they may be given the simple sentence:

Squawks of a seagull have enabled water authorities to cleanse two reservoirs by frightening away seagulls.

They can then be asked gradually to fit in the other elements.

1. tape-recorded, 2. in distress, 3. 5,000, 4. which have been polluting the water, 5. in Milngavie, 6. at Strathclyde, 7. near Glasgow, 8. an estimated.

As they do this, students have to focus at each stage on the structure of the noun group and the elements that make it up. Once students have learnt this technique they can look for complex phrases in the text they read and set up an exercise themselves, challenging others in the class to reconstruct sentences.

4.3 The verb phrase

The structure of the verb phrase is entirely predictable and allows no variation. As a result it is easier to show all the forms than to offer an abstract description of the structure:

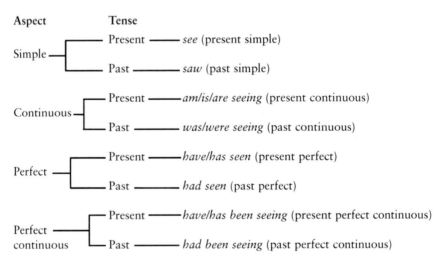

Fig. 4.5

Fig. 4.5 shows all eight tense forms in English. All verbs are either present or past in tense. This combines with what grammarians call **aspect**. All verbs are either **simple** or **continuous** in aspect. In addition to this they may or may not be **perfective**. This gives the combinations shown above. All of these forms are grammatical. Any variation on this combination and ordering, such as *I seeing am* or *I have seeing* is ungrammatical.

In addition to this we have the **modal** and **semi-modal verbs** (*can/could; may/might; must/have to/need to; ought to; shall/should; will/would*) which can also be associated with aspect:

modal + verb (e.g. *I can go* ; *you ought to go*)
modal + *be* + verb (e.g. *I may be going; you ought to be going*)
modal + *have* + verb (e.g. *I could have gone; I might have gone*)
modal + *have* + *been* + verb (e.g. *I might have been going*)

We will look in detail at the meanings carried by tense, aspect and the modals, and at the teaching of the verb phrase in the next chapter.

Finally we have the passive voice. As we saw in Task 2.3 in Section 2.2, the passive is used to provide an alternative way of organising information in the clause. Instead of saying: *The castle is on a hill above the town. Sir Robert Fitzwilliam built it in the twelfth century*, we can say: *The castle is on a hill above the town. It **was built** in the twelfth century by Sir Robert Fitzwilliam*. This keeps *the castle* as the focus of the new clause. The passive voice is formed by using the appropriate tense of the verb *be*, followed by the past participle: *built, discovered, broken, seen* etc.:

*These toys **are made** in Taiwan.*
*She **should be congratulated** on her performance.*

In theory this can produce a highly complex verb phrase:

*He **might have been being questioned** by the police.*

Fortunately phrases of this complexity are extremely rare.

4.4 Specific structures

The structural patternings we have looked at so far operate at a very general abstract level. They provide a template for **all** clauses and for **all** phrases. There are additionally a number of specific structures. In Sections 1.2 and 1.6 in Chapter 1 we looked at the problems involved in learning *do*-questions. Question forms are an example of the way structure is used to signal the function of an utterance. Negative clauses with *do* also involve structural manipulation, as we can see if we compare: *I enjoy teaching English* and *I do not enjoy teaching English*.

Relative clauses too have a specific structure which causes problems for learners who tend to produce:

*I met a man who he was going to St. Ives.
*That's the man who I met him.

Learners reproduce the antecedent (*a man*) as a pronoun in the relative clause (*he, him*). In Section 1.6 we suggested difficulties like these should be handled by a progression from improvisation to consolidation, through recognition and system building.

I have used *do*-questions as an example of something which is strangely resistant to teaching. The same applies to negative clauses and relative clauses. Teachers can help with these forms by drawing attention to them (recognition) and explaining how they are formed (system building), but they will only become a part of the learner's spontaneous language use if learners are given plenty of opportunities to engage in these meanings in improvisation and consolidation activities.

4.5 Summary

In Section 3.2 we looked at three different kinds of teaching activity – recognition, system-building and exploration which can be seen as providing a scale of teachability. The grammar of structure can be explained or demonstrated for learners without too much trouble. Shortall (1996) reports that Japanese learners have few problems with basic clause structure even though Japanese has the order *subject → object → verb* as opposed to the English *subject → verb → object* order of elements. Similarly, Japanese learners rapidly come to terms with the fact that English has prepositions which come in front of the noun, whereas equivalent words in Japanese come after the noun. The same seems to be true of other learners.

There is an element of exploration in acquiring structure. For example, learners need to identify classes of adverbs and recognise the usual position for each class. So the learning of structure will be linked to the learning of vocabulary, with teachers helping learners to organise their lexis into appropriate classes. Learners also need to recognise that almost all adverbs are movable. Again this can be taught explicitly, and students can also be encouraged to take note of these features in text.

Learners need to be encouraged to take full advantage of the resources of the language. This applies particularly to the use of intensifiers and mitigators with adjectives. It also applies to the use of complex noun groups, particularly in written English. The role of the teacher is not to help students to avoid error, but to help them to build up a usable meaning system.

There can never be any guarantees that what is taught will become a part of the learner's meaning system, but there are a number of things teachers can do to help students acquire the grammar of structure:

- **Explanation:** For example, adverbs of frequency normally come in front of the main verb in the verb phrase. This is a fact about English which is worth pointing out. As learners become familiar with the use of quantifiers it is worth identifying explicitly those quantifiers which are found only with countable or with uncountable nouns. This can be done by the teacher, or it may be done by students working in groups with teacher guidance.

- **Selection:** Often this is the role of the syllabus designer or materials writer rather than the teacher, but it is important for someone to select what items are to be highlighted for learners, and in what order. Since it is important to select those items which learners are likely to meet when they come to use the language outside the classroom, frequency is a valuable guide to selection. Another guide is what we might call grammatical range. As quantifiers, for example, the phrases *lots of* and *a lot of* have greater range than *many* or *much*. *Lots of* and *a lot of* can be used with both countable and uncountable nouns, whereas *many* is restricted to countable, and *much* to uncountable nouns.

- **Organisation:** Teachers can help students organise their vocabulary in useful ways. We have seen, for example, how adverbs can be organised into classes according to meaning and therefore according to their position in the clause. Partitives can be systematically related to the nouns or types of nouns with which they are normally found.

- **Memorisation:** There are two kinds of memorisation that are worthwhile for learners. Firstly there is the accumulation of useful words and phrases for their own sake. Secondly there is the learning of phrases, clauses and sentences which provide a useful exemplification of a valuable language item or feature. Several of the activities we have looked at are designed to help students memorise things. The picture-based activity focusing on quantifiers (see Teaching Activity. 4.1, 4.2.1) is, for example, a useful first step towards memorising quantifiers. The exercise on postmodification exemplified in Teaching Activity 4.4 in Section 4.2.4 is an example of a memorisation exercise which encourages students to focus on the structure of the noun phrase, and helps them to recognise the potential of this unit of language.

5 The grammar of orientation: The verb phrase

5.1 What is orientation?

In Chapter 2 we referred to grammatical devices of orientation which 'act as "pointers", showing how items relate to one another and to the outside world in terms of time, place and identity'. The elements in a clause, *wife – work – garden – weekend*, may show us what the clause is about, but they do not supply any 'orientation' so that we cannot identify exactly who the message is about: whether it refers to past, present or future time; whether it refers to a particular wife and garden or to wives and gardens in general. But given the clause, *My wife works in the garden most weekends*, we can identify the wife as the wife of the speaker, and the garden as their garden. The tense of the verb reinforced by the adverbial *most weekends* shows that the statement is a general statement relevant to present time.

We have to make choices relating to orientation in every clause. For every verb we have to choose tense, aspect and modality. For every noun phrase we have to choose from the determiner system. This means that orientation is central to language and may explain why traditional pedagogic grammars devote so much time to this feature of the grammar.

Unfortunately the systems of orientation are highly complex and resistant to teaching. In this chapter we will look at two different ways of describing verbs and their tense forms and then go on to propose pedagogic strategies to help learners cope with this aspect of orientation.

5.2 The 'traditional' pedagogic description of the verb

In building up the grammar of the English verb most English courses begin, entirely sensibly, with the present tense of the verb *BE*. Very often the next form to be introduced is the present continuous of a range of verbs. This is followed by the present simple tense. Usually the next stage is to contrast the present simple and the present continuous. The course proceeds in this way, introducing the tense forms one after another. As the learner progresses, the use of established forms is extended and new meanings are introduced. Learners are shown, for example, how the present continuous is used with reference to future time.

At regular stages learnt forms are contrasted with new forms or with one another. The past simple, for example, is contrasted successively with the present perfect, the past continuous and the past perfect. These processes of extension and contrast build a valuable measure of recycling into the learning process. The picture that emerges is one of a large number of verb forms – present simple, present continuous, present perfect, present perfect continuous, past simple, past continuous etc. – some of which, such as the present simple and the present continuous or the present perfect and the past simple, are related to one another contrastively. But there is no unifying system, at least none that is explicit in the description.

Learners discover at an early stage that the present simple is used to refer to states or to regular or habitual actions:

*Both our children **live** in London.*
*We usually **phone** them several times a week.*

This use of the present tense is strongly associated with adverbs of frequency such as *often, sometimes, every day, usually* and so on. This is contrasted with the present continuous, which is used for actions which are going on at the present time, and which, according to the usual contrastive description, is not found with adverbs of frequency:

George *is playing* tennis.
I'*m cooking* the dinner.

A clear distinction is made between the two forms. This provides a sharp learning focus so that the system, as described, is, in principle, readily learnable. Unfortunately these generalisations are also misleading:

Task 5.1:
1. a. *Our daughter **lives** in London.*
   b. *Our daughter **is living** in London.*

2. a. *I **work** in London, but Jane **works** in Birmingham.*
   b. *I **work** in London, but Jane **is working** in Birmingham.*

Clearly sentences 1.a. and 2.a. refer to a present state. What about 1.b. and 2.b.? Do they contradict the rule that the present simple must be used for present states? What is the difference in meaning between the highlighted forms in 1.a. and 1.b., and between those in 2.a. and 2.b.?

Key to Task 5.1:

Both 1.b. and 2.b. refer to present states and therefore break the rule as it is stated above. Both sentences are, however, entirely grammatical. The present continuous tense is probably used to indicate that the states are temporary rather than permanent. This is sometimes made explicit:

> *Our daughter **is living** in London **at present**.*

A second possibility is that the use of the present continuous marks a change of some kind:

> *Our daughter has left Birmingham. She's **living** in London now.*

In the same way it is also possible to use the present continuous to refer not only to present states, but also to regular or habitual actions:

> a. *I'm **taking** tablets **every day** for my sore throat.*
> b. *We're **usually having** breakfast when the post comes.*

In sentence a. the continuous form seems to signal **temporariness** – I believe that I will soon be able to give up taking the tablets. In the second case the continuous form signals **interruptedness** – the taking of breakfast continues before and after the arrival of the post. In this sort of sentence, it is quite possible for the present continuous to be used with adverbs of frequency such as *every day* and *usually*.

We can also find examples which show how the traditional description is incomplete and not sufficiently detailed. As a result, it fails to recognise important generalisations. In many coursebooks and grammars learners are introduced to a man who is involved in some mundane activity such as reading the newspaper or watching television. While he is engaged in this activity, a number of things happen, which enable the learner to generate sentences such as these:

> *While he **was watching** television the telephone **rang**.*
> *While he **was watching** television the postman **called**.*
> *While he **was watching** television the house **caught** fire.*

These sentences illustrate the rule that, when an action or state in the past is interrupted by another action, the interrupted action will be in the past continuous tense and the other action in the past simple. Again there is a precise focus and the distinction is readily learnable. This pedagogic model has the virtues of simplicity and learnability, but this limited focus on the interrupted *past* also provides a good example of the way in which the traditional description is unsystematic and incomplete:

Task 5.2:

Do the following sentences refer to the **past**, the **present** or the **future**?

   a. The kids **are** usually **watching** television when I **get** home.
   b. The kids **will be watching** television when I **get** home.
   c. The kids **may be watching** television when I **get** home.

Key to Task 5.2:

Sentence a. makes a general statement about the *present.*
Sentence b. refers to the *future.*
In sentence c. the modal *may* with the continuous form of the infinitive is used to refer to the future.

Although the interrupted past is taught in most coursebooks and student grammars the interrupted present and future are hardly ever taught. The important generalisation here is that all continuous forms can be used to signal interruptedness – the meaning is carried in the -*ing*-form. But continuousness, or continuous aspect, is not usually one of the categories of the traditional pedagogic description, which confines itself to treating each tense form separately and fails to deal with abstractions like aspect. Since the description fails to recognise abstractions such as 'continuousness' it fails to recognise the meaning of the *-ing*-form. Because of this it is unable to generalise from the interrupted past to the interrupted present and future, and to enable learners to make this valuable generalisation.

Another example of a failure to generalise is the treatment of the **second conditional:** *I would come* round *if I had time.* This incorporates an important generalisation about the verb forms it contains. Both the modal *would* and the past tense forms are regularly used to express hypotheses. They both talk about something which is imagined rather than real.

Task 5.3:

Are the following sentences about something **real** or **imaginary**? Do they describe something which **did** happen or are they about something which **could possibly** happen?

    a. Suppose you *got* lost. What *would* you do then?
    b. Someone who *didn't know* the background *wouldn't* understand the story.
    c. I wish you *would* listen.
    d. What advice *would* you give to a young person leaving school?

Key to Task 5.3:

All these sentences are about something imaginary, about something which could possibly happen. In a. listeners are asked to imagine what would happen if they got lost. In b. listeners are asked to imagine the situation of someone who did not know the background to the story. In c. the speaker is talking to someone who is not willing to listen. In d. listeners are asked to imagine what advice they would give if they were asked.

We know that the modal *would* is very frequently used to express something imaginary in an explicitly conditional sentence with an *if*-clause. The sentences in Task 5.3 show that it is also frequently used to talk about something imaginary even in sentences which have no *if*, no explicit conditional. In fact, corpus studies suggest that the hypothetical *would* is found about six times as often without an accompanying *if*-clause as in an explicitly conditional sentence with *if*. This means that the important generalisation that learners need to make is that the past tense and *would* both carry this hypothetical meaning. Given this we could adopt one of two teaching strategies:

- Highlight the hypothetical meaning first, then go on to point out the second conditional as a specific example of this use.
- Begin with the second conditional as an effective way of highlighting the hypothetical meaning, then go on to show that the same meaning occurs in a range of other environments.

Unfortunately most pedagogic grammars adopt neither of these strategies. A lot of time is spent teaching the second conditional, but this is not usually extended to show that hypothesis is part of the meaning of *would* and of the past tense. Indeed the second conditional is often highlighted because it is regarded as unusual, as an exception to the normal use of the past tense. But we shall see below (Task 5.4) that this is a normal function of past tense forms.

It takes a very long time for learners to develop a consistently accurate model of the verb phrase. The use of the continuous and perfect tenses seem to be particularly problematic. This is certainly in part due to the complexity and subtlety of the meaning and concepts involved. But it may also be due to the fact that traditional pedagogic models are unsystematic and uneconomical. They fail, for example, to make the generalisation that all continuous forms can signal interruptedness. In determining a pedagogic strategy for the verb phrase we want to retain the advantages of the traditional pedagogic model, its simplicity and the fact that it is relatively easy to demonstrate.

At the same time we must seek to supplement this with a more powerful and systematic description. In doing this we must be prepared to allow for the fact that the learner's ability to use the system will develop slowly. Learners may learn relatively quickly to use verbs to distinguish between past, present and future time. But the meanings of the continuous and perfect forms of the verb and the use of the verb phrase to signal hypothesis are subtle and complex. If learners are to use verbs to realise these more complex meanings they must be allowed time and they must be given guidance based on a systematic description of the meanings involved.

5.3 A systematic description

5.3.1 Past and present tenses

We talk about things which are in the past:

1. *I **met** her last week.*

We use present tense forms to talk about things which are true in present time:

> 2. *I **meet** her every day.*

But these present tense forms are often seen with an adverbial which shows that they refer to the future:

> 3. *I **meet** her **at ten o'clock tomorrow.***

As we shall see, all the present tenses (present simple, present continuous and present perfect) are frequently used to refer to the future.

Verb phrases can be very complex:

> 4. *I **had been going to meet** her at ten o'clock ...*

and all the parts of the phrase make their own contribution to the overall meaning. It is the first part of a verb phrase that always tells us if we are talking about the past:

> 5. a. *I **was** talking to her last week.*
> b. *I **had** been talking to her last week.*

In 5.a. it is the past tense form of the auxiliary, *was*, which marks the past continuous tense. In 5.b. it is the past tense form *had*. Similarly, it is the first part of the phrase that tells us if the verb is in one of the present tenses:

> 6. a. *I **am** talking to her.*
> b. *I **have** met her.*

In 6.a. the form *am* signals a present tense, the present continuous, and in 6.b. the form *have* signals present perfect. Again these present tenses may be marked by context as occurring in the future:

> 6. a. *I **am** meeting her at ten o'clock tomorrow.*
> b. *I will tell you as soon as I **have** met her.*

In 6.a. the adverbial phrase *ten o'clock tomorrow* marks the meeting as taking place in the future. In 6.b. the verb *will tell* in the main clause marks the meeting as occurring in the future. We can make a powerful generalisation about all present tense forms: all present tenses can be used to refer to the future.

We can also make powerful generalisations about past tense forms. They do not always refer to past time.

Task 5.4:

How many of the verbs highlighted below refer to past time? Why are they in the past tense?

 a. You wouldn't be insured if you **had** an accident.
 b. If Jack **was playing** we'd probably win.
 c. Excuse me, I **was wondering** if this **was** the emergency ward.

Key to Task 5.4:

None of the verbs refers to past time. In sentence a. the verb *had* refers to the possibility of an accident in the future. In b. *was playing* could refer to the present. It could be said by someone watching a game and regretting the absence of a star player. It could also refer to the future since it could be said by someone looking at the team sheet before a game. In both a. and b. a past tense is used to mark a clause as imaginary rather than real. As we saw in Task 5.1, above, this use of the past tense to express a hypothesis is very common. In c. the past tense is used to encode politeness. This use is infrequent and is found only with a few fixed expressions like *I wondered ...; I was wondering ...; I didn't know ...; I wasn't sure ...; I was hoping ...; I had hoped ... .*

Because they have these different uses the past tenses are sometimes referred to as **remote** rather than past. The term **remote** suggests that the speaker is distanced from a proposition either in time or in seeing it as unreal or unlikely. The term also carries the notion of the social 'distance' implied in the use of an extremely polite form.

The simple examples above illustrate two important features of present and past tenses. The first is that they do not relate simply to present and past time. Present tense forms are very frequently used to refer to the future. Past tense forms are used to encode not only past time, but also hypothesis and politeness. The second important feature is that these generalisations refer to all present tenses and to all past tenses. In other words, when we say that present tense forms frequently refer to the future this applies not only to the present continuous form, but also to the present simple, present perfect and present perfect continuous – the generalisation is true of all present tenses.

5.3.2 Talking about the future

When we talk about the past or present we can speak with confidence – we know what happened or what is happening. The same is not true when we are talking about the future – we can never be sure what is going to happen in the future. When we talk about the future, what we are interested in is very often not the timing of an event, but the likelihood of its occurrence.

We have seen that the present tenses can be used to refer to the future. We use a present tense form when we have confidence in the occurrence of a future event. So the present continuous form is used for something which is already arranged:

> *I'm going to the cinema on Monday.*
> *England are playing Australia next week.*

When we are talking about something which is regularly scheduled we may use the present simple tense:

> *The next train leaves at two-thirty.*
> *I have my golf lesson on Monday.*

We also use the present tense form, *going to*, when we are talking about an intention: *I'm going to see the children next week*, or for a prediction for which we have some observable evidence: *It looks like it's going to rain.*

It may be the case, however, that we are not interested in the timing of an event, but rather in the likelihood of its occurrence. The orientation is one of possibility rather than time. We use modal verbs (*can/could; will/would; may/might; must; shall/should*) to make statements about degrees of possibility:

> 7. a. *It will take a long time.*
>
> 7. b. *It may take a long time.*
>
> 7. c. *It could take a long time.*

Such statements vary from near certainty 7.a. through possibility 7.b. to something which appears unlikely 7.c. We will look at modal verbs in more detail below (Section 5.3.6).

The modal *will* is so frequently used for the future that it is often referred to as 'the future tense'. Because it is so frequent it is useful to introduce learners to the *will*-future at an early stage, and to think of *will* as expressing the future tense. But although this generalisation provides a useful starting point, it can also be misleading and will need to be refined at a later stage. It is more accurate to think of *will* as having two meanings. The first of these is prediction:

Task 5.5:

Look at these sentences. Do they all refer to the future? Are any of them grammatically incorrect? Why?

1. The children are tired. They**'ll** probably **fall** asleep quite soon.
2. Jack's playing well. I think he**'ll win** tomorrow.
3. It's Saturday morning. The traffic **will be** very heavy.
4. Mary starts school tomorrow. I'm sure she**'ll enjoy** it.
5. Most of you **will know** Professor Bryant from his many books and articles.
6. If it **will rain** you**'ll need** your umbrella.

Key to Task 5.5:

Sentences 1, 2 and 4 refer to the future, 3 and 5 refer to the present. The modal *will* is used because they are predictions, predictions about the present. Sentence 6 is ungrammatical. Students are often given the rule that *will* is not found in an *if*-clause. This is generally true, because *will* is mostly used to make a prediction. The word *if*, on the other hand, is used when we are unsure of something. It is used in order to **avoid** making a prediction. So there is a contradiction in meaning if we include a predictive *will* in an *if*-clause. The same is true of clauses introduced by *when, as soon as, until* and other conjunctions expressing time.

The second meaning of *will* is volition. We use *will* to express willingness to do something. Because of this, *will* is used to make a promise or undertake an agreement:

I'll write to you when I get home.

By declaring a willingness to write the speaker is seen as making an agreement to write. In the same way *will* is used for requests:

***Will** you help?*

Asking someone if they are willing to help is the same as requesting help. When *will* has the meaning of volition it can be use in an *if*-clause:

*If you **will help** me I **will help** you.*

This means, *If you are willing to help me, then I am willing to help you.* So *will* can be used in *if*-clauses, but only when it has its less frequent meaning, that of willingness or volition.

It seems therefore to be an acceptable strategy to introduce *will* as the future tense. But there are two disadvantages to this strategy. First learners will not recognise that *will* can be used with the meaning of prediction to refer to present time:

*Most of you **will know** Professor Bryant from his many books and articles.*

Secondly, if learners see *will* simply as expressing the future, they will naturally be drawn into over-generalising and using it in *if*-clauses and in temporal clauses. If they are to have a full understanding of *will* and its meanings, they need at some stage to work through an exercise like that in Task 5.5. This will make them aware of the meanings of *will*, and will prepare them to take advantage of exploration activities to help them choose between *will* and other ways of expressing the future, such as the present tenses, *going to* and other modal verbs.

5.3.3 Lexical verbs

It is the last word in the verb phrase that provides the lexical element. It labels the action, process or state we are talking or writing about. If it is the only word in the verb phrase, it will be marked, as we have seen, for tense (see examples 1 and 2 above: *I **met** her last week, I **meet** her every day*).

If there is more than one word in the verb phrase then the lexical verb may be marked as an *-ing*-form:

*I am **going**.*
*I will be **going**.*
*I might have been **going**.*

Or it may be marked as a past participle (pp) form:

*I have **gone**.*
*I will have **gone**.*
*I might have **gone**.*

What do these forms mean? We will look at these two forms in the next two sections.

5.3.4 The -ing-form

Let us look first at the *-ing*-form. The *-ing*-form is used in the continuous tenses:

8. a. *I am working.*
    b. *I was working.*
    c. *I will be working.*

The *-ing*-form takes its timing from the first part of the verb. In 8.a. the *working* is in the present, signalled by *am*. In 8.b. the *working* is in the past, signalled by *was*, and in 8.c. it is in the future, signalled by *will be*. The *-ing*-form is used to express what most grammarians refer to as continuous aspect. We saw in Section 5.2 above how continuous aspect, the *-ing*-form, is used to signal interruptedness. It is also used to express a number of other meanings:

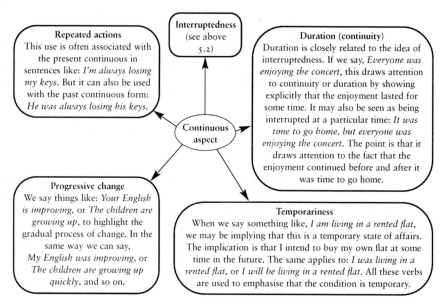

Repeated actions
This use is often associated with the present continuous in sentences like: *I'm always losing my keys*. But it can also be used with the past continuous form: *He was always losing his keys*.

Interruptedness
(see above 5.2)

Continuous aspect

Duration (continuity)
Duration is closely related to the idea of interruptedness. If we say, *Everyone was enjoying the concert*, this draws attention to continuity or duration by showing explicitly that the enjoyment lasted for some time. It may also be seen as being interrupted at a particular time: *It was time to go home, but everyone was enjoying the concert*. The point is that it draws attention to the fact that the enjoyment continued before and after it was time to go home.

Progressive change
We say things like: *Your English is improving*, or *The children are growing up*, to highlight the gradual process of change. In the same way we can say, *My English was improving*, or *The children are growing up quickly*, and so on.

Temporariness
When we say something like, *I am living in a rented flat*, we may be implying that this is a temporary state of affairs. The implication is that I intend to buy my own flat at some time in the future. The same applies to: *I was living in a rented flat*, or *I will be living in a rented flat*. All these verbs are used to emphasise that the condition is temporary.

Fig. 5.1 Continuous aspect

The *-ing*-form as part of the verb phrase takes its timing from the first word in the verb phrase. Sometimes the *-ing*-form stands on its own and takes its timing from another verb in the clause.

Task 5.6:
Do the *-ing*-forms below refer to past, present or future time?

1. *I saw her **standing** there.*
2. *You will find him **working** in the library.*
3. *Look, there's George **talking** to the chairman.*
4. *After **shopping** we can go for a cup of coffee.*
5. ***Realising** his mistake he apologised profusely.*

Key to Task 5.6:

1. past; 2. future; 3. present; 4. future; 5. past

In each case we take the timing of the *-ing*-form from the associated verb. So in 1 we take the timing *past* from the verb *saw*. In 2 we take the timing *future* from the verb *will find* and so on.

All the examples of *-ing*-forms we have looked at so far have been participles or adjectival forms. But the rule that the *-ing*-form takes its timing from the associated time marker also applies to the gerund, the form of the verb which functions as a noun. So in: *I enjoy playing golf*, the *playing* takes its timing from the present tense *enjoy*. In the sentence, *I enjoyed playing golf*, the *playing* would be seen as in the past, and in *I will enjoy playing golf*, the *-ing*-form would be seen as occurring in the future.

We have, then, powerful generalisations about the timing of the *-ing*-form and its associated meanings. It has a range of possible meanings, as shown in Fig. 5.1., and it takes its timing from an associated verb. Once we are aware of this we can apply these principles to any occurrence of an *-ing*-form.

5.3.5 *The past participle form*

The past participle form denotes an action or a situation which is prior to the tense marker:

9. a. *I have **seen** 'The Third Man'*.
   b. *It was 1999. I had **lived** in Birmingham for ten years.*

In 9.a. the seeing took place at a time prior to the present, but the present tense marker *have* shows that it is relevant to present time. In 9.b. the *living* had taken place for ten years prior to 1999. The past tense form *had* marks the verb phrase as relevant to the past, in this case to 1999, and the past participle form *lived* marks a situation established prior to the tense marker *had*, but still relevant to the past time, 1999.

The past participle form is used for the perfect tense forms. These tenses are used:

- for an event or situation which was prior to an established time, but continues to be relevant up to that established time. The present perfect is used for actions and situations which began in the past and continue up to the present: *I have lived in Birmingham for ten years*. Because this is a present tense with the present tense marker *have* the established time is the present and the proposition is seen as being relevant up to the present.

Task 5.7:

What verb forms are highlighted in the following sentences? Why is perfective aspect used?

    a. I'm tired. **I've been walking** all day.
    b. I was exhausted. We **had been walking** all day.
    c. It's our wedding anniversary next month. We'll **have been married** for thirty years.

Key to Task 5.7:

Sentence a. uses the present perfect continuous, b. uses the past perfect continuous and c. uses perfective aspect with the modal *will* referring to the future.

The **present** perfect in a. refers to an action which began in the past and continues up to the present. Because it began in the past but continues up to the present the present perfect is used. The continuous form is used because the speaker wants to emphasise the duration of the action. In b. the **past** perfect refers to an action which began in the past and continued up to a given time in the past – the time at which the words were spoken. Again the speaker or writer uses continuous aspect, probably to emphasise duration. Sentence c. refers to an event which started in the past and is seen as continuing up to a time in the future, up to next month.

- to talk about experience up to an established time. We might say, *I have read that book three times*. This makes it explicit that I am referring to the situation up to the present and leaves open the possibility that I will read the book again at some time in the future. In the same way we might say, *I had read it twice by the time I left school*. This describes the situation up to a given time in the past – the time when I left school.

Task 5.8:

What verb forms are highlighted in the following sentences? Why is perfective aspect used?

a. I was looking forward to seeing George. **I had** only **met** him once before.
b. If I go to that film again tomorrow, **I'll have seen** it three times in one week.
c. She's not at home. She **may have gone** to work.

Key to Task 5.8:

Sentence a. uses the past perfect, b. uses perfective aspect with the modal *will* referring to the future and c. uses perfective aspect with the modal *may* referring to present time.

In a. the past tense verb *was* sets the utterance in the past so the past perfect refers to experience up to that time in the past. In b. the adverbial *tomorrow* sets the sentence in the future, so the perfective with *will* refers to experience up to a time in the future, up to tomorrow. In c. we have a possibility referring to the present, expressed by *may*. The past participle, *gone*, refers to an event accomplished before the present.

- for a situation which is in the past, but which is relevant at the established time. We might say: *I have finished that book you lent me. I'll bring it back tomorrow.* The form *have finished* refers to an action which was accomplished in the past, but which is relevant at the time of speaking, in this case the present: *Because I have (now) finished the book ...*

Task 5.9:

What verb forms are highlighted in the following sentences? Why is perfective aspect used?

a. **I had finished** the book so I promised to return it the next day.
b. **I will have finished** the book tomorrow, so I'll return it then.
c. **I might have finished** the book tomorrow. I'll return it if I have.

Key to Task 5.9:

Again a. uses the past perfect and b. uses perfective aspect with the modal *will* referring to the future.

In a. the relevant time is set in the past by the past tense verb *promised*, so the past perfect form is used. In b. the relevant time is set in the future, *tomorrow*, so the modal *will* is used to refer to the future with perfective aspect used to show that the action of finishing will be complete at the relevant time. Sentence c. is the same as b. in that it is set in the future. But the modal *might* expresses possibility, rather than the certainty of *will*.

So the past participle form is used for an event which took place or a situation which began prior to a tense marker, but which is still relevant at the time of that tense marker. This general rule applies not only to the perfect tenses but also to other uses of the past participle form:

10. a. *The windows are **broken**.*
    b. *Peter was **rescued** by one of his companions.*
    c. *I lay down **exhausted**.*
    d. *A van **equipped** with a loudspeaker toured the reservoir.*
    e. *Be careful. You'll get those papers **mixed up**.*

Sentence 10.a. is talking about the present. This is shown by the tense marker *are*. The past participle form *broken* is used for an action which was prior to the tense marker and therefore describes the current state of the windows. The tense marker *was* shows that 10.b. is talking about the past. The past participle form *rescued* is used for an action which was prior to the tense marker and so describes Peter's state at the time of the tense marker. In 10.c. and 10.d. the same logic operates. We are concerned with the past as shown by the past markers, *lay* and *toured*. The past participle *exhausted* describes a state brought about by previous exertions. The past participle, *equipped,* describes the state of the van established by an action prior to the touring. In 10.e. the speaker looks to the future. By an unspecified time in the future an event will have occurred to account for the state of the papers: someone will have done something to mix them up.

When it combines with the auxiliary *have*, the past participle is active in meaning. In all other uses it is passive in meaning. The timing is consistent – it always denotes an event or situation established prior to the established time.

5.3.6 Modality

The modal auxiliaries orient us to the certainty or possibility of something occurring. They show how far a speaker is committed to the truth of a statement. So people who say, *It will rain tomorrow*, are committing themselves to the truth of what they say. They are making a prediction. But if someone says, *It might rain tomorrow*, there is no commitment to the truth of the statement. The modals also carry meanings like obligation (*You should be more careful*) and ability (*I can speak French*). Because they carry these meanings they are often associated with specific functions. When you say to someone, *You should be more careful*, you are pointing out an obligation, and this is likely to be seen as giving advice.

The teaching and learning of the modals are initially lexical. It is a matter of getting to know what these forms mean. Once learners are aware of the meanings of the modals they can begin to combine them with the meanings of continuous and perfective aspect. They can also begin to see how the meanings are exploited with subtle differences in discourse. Here is a very brief summary of the meanings and uses of the modal verbs:

- Meanings
  a. Certainty and possibility:
  Prediction: *will* (Past: *would*)
  Deduction: *ought to; should; must* (negative = *cannot*) (e.g. *They left at six. They ought to/should/must be there by now.*)
  Possibility: *can; could; may; might* (e.g. *It can be very cold in winter.*)

  b. Other meanings:
  Obligation/duty: *should; ought to*
  Obligation/necessity: *must/have to*
  Volition: *will* (Past: *would*)
  Ability: *can; be able to* (Past: *could*)
  Past habit: *used to; would*

- Functions
  Permission: *can; could; may*
  Instructions and requests: *can; could; will; would*
  Suggestions: *could; may; might; shall*
  Offers and invitations: *can; could; shall; will; would*
  Intentions: *going to*

Task 5.10:

Expressing hypotheses or conditions
Look again at Task 5.5. Now think which of the modal verbs listed above you could use to complete the conditional sentence below.

If she had our address she _____ send us an email.

Why do you think this is? Why can't you use the other forms?

Commentary on Task 5.10:

Could, might and *would* are the past tense forms of *can, may* and *will.* As we saw in Task 5.5, the past tense carries the meaning of hypothesis. This is why the forms *could, might* and *would* are used to express hypothesis, but not *can, may* and *will.*

Task 5.11:

Look back to Task 5.4. Which of the following pairs do you think is more polite, a. or b.? Why?

  1. a. Can you help me please?
     b. Could you help me please?

  2. a. Will you call round some time please?
     b. Would you call round some time please?

  3. a. Shall I lead the way?
     b. Should I lead the way?

Commentary on Task 5.11:

As we saw in Task 5.4, the past or **remote** tense is used as a marker of politeness. So 1.b., 2.b., and 3.b. would normally be considered the more polite forms, since they use the past tense forms of the modals.

As we saw in Section 4.3, the modals can combine with *-ing* and past participle forms. The meanings of these forms relate to the meanings of aspect which we looked at above (see Fig. 5.1). For example, *Don't phone them now, they might be having supper*, carries the meaning of interruptedness. *They might be staying with friends*, carries the meaning of temporariness.

Tasks 5.7, 5.8 and 5.9 above show how the meaning of perfective aspect combines with the modals *will, may* and *might.* It combines equally effectively with the other modals.

5.4 Using the grammatical description

The traditional description has the advantage of simplicity. It is straightforward and relatively easy for teachers and students to use. It has a long tradition behind it and, as a result of this, it has developed a number of useful teaching routines and techniques. It has, however, three serious weaknesses:

- It rests on making distinctions which are not valid. Task 5.1 shows that the contrast between continuous and simple forms is based on a misunderstanding. We saw in Section 5.3.1 that the traditional formulation of the contrast between the past simple and the past perfect does not work.
- It fails to make powerful generalisations which apply to the verb system as a whole. We saw in Task 5.2 how it fails to generalise about the continuous tenses realised by the *-ing*-form. Tasks 5.7, 5.8 and 5.9 show generalisations about perfective aspect which are not revealed by the traditional description. We have also seen how generalisations apply to all present tense forms (they can all refer to the future) and to all past tense forms (they can all be used to encode hypothesis and politeness). These generalisations are not made within the traditional description.
- Finally, the traditional approach links tense too closely to time. The use of present tense forms to refer to the future is treated by the traditional approach almost as though it were exceptional. Learners need to recognise early on that present tense forms are frequently used with reference to the future. They also need to recognise that past tense forms are associated with hypothesis and with politeness.

The systematic description can compensate for the weaknesses we have identified in the traditional approach. It provides an antidote to the false contrasts made under the traditional approach. It also makes available powerful generalisations that are missing in the traditional approach.

The problem with the systematic model is that it is highly abstract. There is no way it can be made directly accessible to learners through grammatical explanation. If we are to harness the power of systematic description we must find appropriate pedagogic techniques to achieve this. We will now go on to look at an approach to teaching the verb phrase based on the five-stage model of language development outlined in Chapter 1.

5.4.1 Improvisation

From a very early stage learners will improvise with verb forms to get their message across. They will, for example, use a base form of the verb with a past adverbial to encode past time:

*I see her yesterday.

There is no way to avoid this without restricting their language production to teacher-controlled utterances. They will certainly make a great many errors. But there are a number of reasons why we should be prepared to accept this. The first is that learners will make errors anyway. We saw in Chapter 1 how errors are a part of the developmental process which is the basis of language learning. The second is that it is the learners' attempts to mean that pave the way for learning. By trying to realise a range of meanings in English they become aware of the shortcomings of their existing system. Thirdly we need to recognise that learners will not and should not be content to wait until their language is error-free before they begin to put their language to work. For an elementary or intermediate learner, one of the most valuable skills they can acquire is the ability to make the most of the little language they have, the ability to exploit their limited language to realise a wide range of meanings.

We need to put in place as quickly as possible the resources to make reference to present, past and future. For obvious reasons of frequency and utility the first verb form normally introduced in the classroom is the present tense of the verb *BE*. Learners begin to talk about themselves using the present simple of the verbs *be, have* and a range of other verbs to do with their everyday lives such as *live, like* and *go*. Apart from this, the first tense form to be introduced is usually the present continuous referring to an action taking place here and now. This is not a particularly frequent use of the tense but it has the advantage that it is easily demonstrable through pictures and actions.

We saw above (Section 5.2) how the traditional contrast between present simple and present continuous is false and misleading. We have shown elsewhere how the contrast between past simple and past perfect is a misleading oversimplification. It is reasonable to show the present simple tense as showing a habitual action or state, and to show the present continuous as showing an action in progress. But it is not reasonable to contrast these and so to imply that the present continuous is not used for something habitual and the present simple is not used for something in progress.

It may be argued that these contrasts help to define forms. This is true only if the contrasts are valid. False contrasts are likely to make learning inefficient as there must be a stage at which what has been learnt has to be unlearnt. What happens is that, if we offer learners only examples where the supposed contrast holds true, we may give an appearance that they have mastered the forms. They then go on to hear and read language which contradicts the conclusions they have reached.

Under the traditional approach there is an attempt to grade forms and to allow time for mastery of one form before moving on to another. The gradual presentation rests on the belief that we can define tenses independently of one another. But this is not the case. As part of the system of orientation tense aspect and mood are a matter of choice. This means that learners must learn to make choices from a range of possibilities. To enable them to do this we need to introduce the forms rapidly and encourage learners to look carefully at verb forms in context. We should therefore move on rapidly to the uses of the present tenses for future and the introduction of past tense forms.

We use adverbials as well as verb tense to signal time. We rarely find references to the past or future that are not contextualised by a time adverbial. This does not mean that we have adverbials in every clause, but that there is always an adverbial available in the discourse. Given this, we should introduce a range of time adverbials early in the learning process: *always; often; today; tomorrow; this/next/last week/month/ year; ... days/weeks/months ago* etc. This gives elementary learners the capacity to operate in lexical mode signalling time by adverbials:

> *Yesterday I go cinema.
> *Tomorrow I go cinema.

Almost certainly, when they are under pressure, this is the improvisational strategy they will adopt. It also creates the possibility of relating adverbial references more and more to the appropriate verb forms, moving to:

> Yesterday I *went to the cinema.*
> I *am going to the cinema tomorrow.*

We should move on rapidly to the introduction of the present perfect and modals *will* and *might*. The present perfect can usefully be contrasted with the past simple, using well established traditional techniques. Unlike the simple/continuous contrast, the contrast between past simple and present perfect is a valid one, but it is subtle and takes a long time to assimilate. Again it needs to be associated with adverbs and adverbial phrases which highlight its uses: *for a long time; since ...; often* etc.

The purpose in this rapid introduction of a series of tense forms and associated adverbials is to provide learners with the capacity to improvise and to begin to improve on their improvisations, gradually moving from a reliance on a lexical, adverbial mode to the development of a grammatical mode. This is in line with natural acquisition processes.

5.4.2 Recognition

The improvisational process outlined above also involves recognition and can be assisted by exercises which support recognition. After learners have worked with verb forms and adverbials in context we can begin to highlight their meanings explicitly. This process may be reinforced by grammar-focused exercises:

Teaching Activity 5.1:

Are these sentences present activities, or are they future plans?

1. Be quiet. *I'm listening* to the radio.
2. *We're having* a party for Joe's birthday. Can you come?
3. Look, *Jenny's wearing* her new dress.
4. When do *you leave* for Paris?
5. What *are you doing* tonight? Do you want to come round for dinner?
6. *We live* next door to Joan and Peter.

Commentary on Teaching Activity 5.1:

This activity draws attention to the fact that the present continuous and the present simple can be used for both present and future – that they are, in fact, non-past rather than present tenses.

The activity is not intended to test students, and there is certainly no guarantee that successful completion of activities like this will mean that students will be able to use these forms accurately when they are using language spontaneously. The activities will, however, make students aware of the use of these tense forms and will make them more sensitive to the forms when they meet them in future input.

Recognition is a necessary first stage in learning, but it must be supplemented by system building, exploration and consolidation. Some of the Tasks above, such as Tasks 5.1, 5.2, 5.3 and 5.5 could easily be adapted to produce similar teaching activities.

Teaching Activity 5.2:

Each student will be asked to do one of the following. They can be given written instructions in both English and their first language.

- Find three people who have been to the US. Find out when they went there.

- Find three people who have read a *Harry Potter* book. Find out when they read it.
- Find three people who live near you. Find out how long they have lived there.

Commentary on Teaching Activity 5.2:

These activities can be carried out as a classroom task. One way to do this would be simply to give learners the task instructions before asking them to do the task. When they do the task very few of them will use the tense forms appropriately with any consistency, but they will find ways of getting their meanings across.

After the task the teacher can go through, checking the results of the student surveys. At this stage the teacher will be saying things like:

Okay Maria, tell me three people who have been to the US. Okay, let me write those up:

> *José, Pablo and Juanita have been to the US.*
> *José went there in 1998.*
> *Pablo went there last year.*
> *Juanita went there in September.*

After the teacher has elicited a few responses she can move to a memory test, removing information from the board and asking students how much they can remember.

When students first begin to work with the past simple and present perfect they will be moving from improvisation to the stage of recognition. There will be mistakes and inconsistencies. Again recognition is only the first stage in the learning process. It serves to prepare the way for other learning processes.

It is tempting to use activities of this kind as part of a presentation process. Learners are introduced to new forms and expected to use them after explanation, demonstration and controlled practice. All we know about language acquisition processes suggests that this is unlikely to happen. These activities will promote recognition. They will make learners more aware of the input they experience. Learners will begin to have an awareness of the use of these forms. As they build these forms into their language systems, they will begin to use them productively. As they are exposed to more language, they will begin to discover how the forms are used in discourse and will use this information to refine their system. Recognition cannot be more than an introductory stage which facilitates the subsequent stages.

5.4.3 System building

Tense forms do not exist in isolation; the use of each tense is determined by its relationship with all the other possible forms. System building, therefore, requires activities which relate the forms to one another. The traditional approach seeks to achieve this through a series of one-to-one contrasts between the present simple and the present continuous, the past simple and the present perfect, and so on. An approach based on a systematic description will look to demonstrate truths about all present tenses, all continuous tenses, and so on.

Teaching Activity 5.3:

Put the verbs in brackets into the past simple or the past continuous:

1. The baby *(wake)* us up when we *(try)* to go to sleep.
2. When we were in England it always *(start)* raining when we *(play)* tennis.
3. Sally *(look)* as if she *(enjoy)* herself.

Now rewrite the sentences using present tenses.

Teaching Activity 5.4:

Complete the following sentences using the present perfect continuous tense of any of the verbs below:

live – play – study – wait – walk – watch – work

1. We _____ in London since 1995.
2. You're a bit late. I _____ here for ages.
3. It's time to go to bed. You _____ television for four hours.

etc.

Complete these sentences using either *have*, *had* or *will have* with the continuous form:

1. a. It was 1998. We _____ been living in London for three years.
   b. By the end of this month we ____ been living in London for five years.
   c. We're still in London. We ____ been living here since 1998.

---

2. a. John was late. I _____ been waiting for two hours.
   b. Ten minutes from now I _____ been waiting for two hours.
   c. John's late. I _____ been waiting for two hours.

etc.

Commentary on Teaching Activities 5.3 and 5.4:

These activities may be seen as mechanical, but they demonstrate the important generalisation that all continuous tenses and all perfect tenses have the same meaning. As a result of exercises like these learners will begin to see that verb phrases are systematic.

5.4.4 Exploration

The grammar of orientation is highly complex and resistant to explanation. We often cannot give satisfactory explanations for the choice of the present continuous rather than the present simple, or the past simple rather than the present perfect. We can help learners to recognise and systematise verb forms in ways like those shown above, but they still have to make complex choices when they come to use the tenses. We cannot solve these problems or make these choices for them, but we can offer a number of activities to help them with this.

Teaching Activity 5.5:

I received this letter from a business contact:

Dear Dr Willis,

I am writing to say that I have made the travel arrangements for my visit to Singapore. I will be travelling by Jordanian Airways and should arrive in Singapore at 1350 on 18th April.

I have not yet got confirmation for my return flight, but I hope to catch a flight which leaves at 0530 on 4th May. I shall write to confirm this as soon as I receive further information.

Yours sincerely,

Bruce Kay

(B.J. Kay)

Enclosed with it was this airline booking slip:

CL	DATE	APT	TO	DEP	ST	ARR	COST
Y	18APR	LHR	AMM	0855	OK	1740	£875
Y	18APR	AMM	SIN	2100	WL	1350+1	
Y	04MAY	SIN	AMM	0530	WL	1045	
Y	04MAY	AMM	LHR	1200	WL	1710	

1. What do you think all the entries on the booking slip mean?
2. Mr Kay has got something wrong in his letter. He has given some false information. Can you find what it is?

At the same time I received this letter from another contact who was hoping to meet Mr Kay in Singapore.

Dear Dave,

Thanks for your letter. I am planning to arrive on Sunday May 4th and to leave either p.m. May 7th or a.m. May 8th.

I have spoken to your London office about payment for my ticket and I am hoping to finalise the details this week.

I do not know yet whether I shall be staying with Y.K. Tan, but I'll let you know as soon as I have heard from him.

I would certainly be grateful if you could arrange a meeting with Bruce Kay during my visit.

Regards,

John

(J.B. Green)

3. Will it be possible for Green and Kay to meet if they keep to their arranged flights?
4. Look carefully at both letters. How many ways can you find of referring to the future?
5. Write a letter to either Bruce Kay or John Green suggesting that they change flights so that they can meet in Singapore.

Commentary on Teaching Activity 5.5:

These letters highlight a misunderstanding which actually happened. Bruce Kay failed to realise that the notation +1 on his booking slip referred to the fact that his arrival in Singapore would be on the day after his departure from Amsterdam. He would arrive in Singapore on the 19th of April, not the 18th. Nevertheless he would be able to meet with John Green provided they could meet in the morning of May 4th.

The letters allow students to look at a number of ways of referring to the future. Question 4 asks students to look consciously at possible ways of doing this:

> Modals: *will be travelling, should arrive, shall write, would be grateful, could arrange.*
> Verbs of wish/intent: *hope to catch, am planning to arrive, am hoping to catch.*
> Present simple: *which leaves, as soon as I receive.*
> Present perfect: *as soon as I have heard.*
> Yet: *I have not **yet** got confirmation* (implies that I expect to get confirmation).

It will be useful to discuss the possible reasons for these choices: the difference between **should** *arrive* and **shall** *write*, for example, and the similarity between *as soon as I **receive*** and *as soon as I **have heard**.*

Again it must be stressed that, even if students do this exercise successfully, this is no guarantee that they will be able to use all these forms appropriately when they come to produce language for themselves. But it is beginning to open up for them the range of choices available for future reference, and to suggest criteria for making appropriate choices.

Question 5 will provide them with an opportunity to compose their own letter incorporating similar forms. This is an activity which moves from exploration to consolidation. It gives students a chance to build what they have learnt into their language production. To supplement this consolidation they could be offered a grammaticisation exercise (see Chapter 3, Teaching Activity 3.8):

Look at the following words. Can you remember exactly what was in Green's letter?

> Thanks letter. Plan arrive Sunday May 4th leave p.m.
> May 7th/a.m. May 8th.

Speak London office payment ticket. Finalise details this week. Not know stay Y.K. Tan. Let you know as soon as hear. Grateful arrange meeting Kay during visit.

Here students try to recall the original letter. It is, of course, unlikely that they will be able to do this in detail. As they try to do so, however, they will face the same choices as the writer of the original. They may not always make the same decisions. Where they make different decisions, some will be different but acceptable and others may be unacceptable. The important thing is that they are obliged to make choices.

Unfortunately few texts have such a rich variation of verb forms, so it is unusual to find a text that can be exploited in exactly this way. If you look at most narratives, for example, you will find almost all the verbs in past simple, with a few occurrences of the past perfect or past continuous. An alternative strategy is to gather together a number of occurrences from a series of texts which the learners have already used as listening or reading texts.

Teaching Activity 5.6:

Review of *would*

(This activity is taken from Willis, D. and J. Willis 1996)
Here are some sentences with *would* which you have seen before in earlier reading and listening work. Find sentences in which:

a) *would* is used as a conditional
b) *would* is used as the past tense of *will*
c) *would* means *used to*.

How many sentences are left over?

1. If you were designing a poster which two *would* you choose?
2. Yes, I *would* think so.
3. My brother *would* say, 'Oh your mother spoils you.'
4. *Would* you like us to do anything about it?
5. That's not the sort of letter I *would* like to receive.
6. *Would* people in your country talk freely about these things?
7. Then we said we *would* play hide and seek.
8. Often there *would* be a village band made up of self-taught players.

9. Some *would* write their own songs or set new words to tunes.
10. What advice *would* you give to someone about to leave school?
11. I never had the lights on. My parents *wouldn't* allow it.
12. Yes, I *would* agree with that.

Commentary on Teaching Activity 5.6:

Would used:

- as conditional: 1, 5, 6, 10.
- as past tense of *will*: 7.
- as *used to*: 3, 8, 9, 11.
- left over: 2, 4, 12 (polite expressions).

This is an exploration activity because it encourages students to analyse samples of language which they have already processed for meaning but may not have processed grammatically. The problem with a methodology, which rests simply on processing for meaning, is that learners can often process a text for meaning without paying detailed attention to the grammar.

An important feature of this activity is the use of sentences that the students have already come across in their reading and listening. The activity not only encourages them to look at these specific examples and to think carefully about *would*; it also encourages them to look carefully at other texts they come across and to develop good learning habits.

Not all the answers are straightforward. In sentence 3, for example, *would* could be used either in a hypothetical sense or as *used to*. In this case, a look at the original context confirms that *used to* was the meaning intended. When students identify a hypothetical use, they need to make the hypothesis explicit:

5. That's not the sort of letter I would like to receive *if someone sent it to me*.
6. Would people in your country talk freely about these things *if you asked them?*

Students may see 4 as a hypothesis: Would you like us to do anything about it *if we offered to?* Or they may see it simply as a fixed phrase. It is certainly a fixed phrase, but probably one which originated as a hypothesis.

Teaching Activity 5.7:

Review of *-ing*

(This activity, with slight adaptation, is taken from Willis, J. and D. Willis 1988)

The *ing*-form of the verb is used for:

1. Describing someone or something:

    There were *two girls eating fish and chips*.
    Write down one or two *interesting things* about each person.

2. After *am, is, was, be* etc.

    One girl *was carrying* a white bag.
    Your partner *will be asking* you questions about what you have done.

3. After *see, look at, hear, listen to* etc.

    Listen to them *talking*.

4. Before *am, is, was, be* etc.

    Dialling 999 is free.

5. After *stop, start, like* etc.

    She likes *watching* television.
    Everyone stopped *talking*.

6. After *when, before, instead of* etc.

    Remember that *when dialling* a number from within you do not need a prefix.
    Before attempting to break the door down the man tried ...

What categories do these sentences belong to?

1. Put in the money before making your call.
2. Listen to David and Bridget discussing the same problem.
3. The conversation stopped and she heard gasping sounds.
4. Using a cardphone is not difficult.
5. You can telephone your family back home without using money.
6. The cards are available from shops displaying the green 'Cardphone' sign.
7. I really like running. Swimming is good too.
8. You have quite a long working day, don't you?

Commentary on Teaching Activity 5.7:

This exercise is taken from an elementary coursebook at the end of a unit about using telephones. Almost all the examples are taken from texts which are familiar to the learners.

The activity is exploratory because it encourages learners to look carefully at text and to begin to recognise the range of uses of the *-ing*-form. As with all exploration activities, there is no guarantee that the forms will be immediately assimilated. It is most unlikely that learners will immediately begin to use all these forms. The activity forms a part of a learning process. It does not of itself guarantee learning.

5.5 Summary

Learning the verb system in English, and almost certainly in any other language, is a long and complex business. The traditional approach often depends on false contrasts and it fails to generalise in a way that is maximally helpful to learners. On the other hand, it has developed a lot of valuable teaching techniques and procedures which we should draw on.

If learners are to move towards a verb system of complexity approaching that of a fully competent speaker of the language they need to go through a series of stages:

- **Improvisation:** Learners will begin by making the most they can of a very limited system. They should be encouraged to do this. The early introduction of a range of adverbial forms will enable learners to realise a range of meanings and will encourage them to link the meanings of verb forms to the meanings of adverbials.
- **Recognition:** It is useful to give rules of thumb to help learners to recognise the value of different forms. These rules do not teach the system, they simply provide a starting point for the process of development.
- **System building:** The meanings of the verb phrase are highly systematic. We need to devise teaching activities which highlight this systematicity.
- **Exploration:** We also need to design activities which will encourage learners to look carefully at text and to reach conclusions for themselves about the way different forms are used.

- **Consolidation:** Finally we need to provide learners with plenty of opportunities to use the language for themselves to enable them to implement their developing system.

Another feature of traditional approaches to teaching the verb forms is that they have all recognised the need for recycling. This acknowledges implicitly that the learner's system develops slowly, and that learners continue to make errors for a very long time. But recycling should be principled. There is little point in simply going through the same procedures again and again. The progression outlined above offers the possibility of principled recycling. At each stage the same material is covered, but at each stage further demands are made on the learner. This does not mean that each element in the system progresses neatly from one stage to the next. It should mean, however, that students have a growing awareness of the system, and that they continue to learn from future input.

6 Orientation: Organising information

In Section 2.2 we looked at the need to organise information in text in a way which moves in a reader-friendly way, from given to new. In this chapter we will look at the devices in the grammar which enable us to organise text in this way. We will look first at the definite and indefinite articles, *the* and *a(n)*. We will then place the articles within their grammatical context as part of the determiner system (see Fig. 4.2, Section 4.2.1). We will then go on to look at the determiner system as part of the referential system of language. Finally we will look at other devices used to organise elements of the message.

In Task 2.3 we looked at two possible versions of the same text:

Text A

1. There is *a new castle* situated on a hill high above the town.
2. Sir Robert Fitzwilliam built *it* in the twelfth century. 3. Raiders from Scotland attacked *it* regularly over the next two hundred years without success. 4. Cromwell finally captured *it* in 1645 and destroyed *it*. 5. Once Cromwell had taken *the castle* he set about subduing the surrounding countryside ...

Text B

1. There is *a new castle* situated on a hill high above the town.
2. *It* was built in the twelfth century by Sir Robert Fitzwilliam.
3. Over the next two hundred years *it* was regularly attacked without success by raiders from Scotland. 4. It was Cromwell who finally captured and destroyed *the castle* in 1645. 5. Once he had taken *the castle* he set about subduing the surrounding countryside ...

In the five sentences in each text the castle is introduced in sentence 1 as *a new castle*. Once the castle is established as shared knowledge between the writer and the reader, the writer is able to deploy the referential systems of the language in order to refer to the castle in successive sentences as something which is given. In Text A this produces the chain of reference: *a new castle* → *it* → *it* → *it* → *it* → *the castle*. The corresponding chain in Text B is: *a new castle, it, it, the castle* and *the castle.*

I suggested that both texts are grammatical, in the sense that they are made up of grammatical sentences, but that in Text B information is organised in a more reader-friendly manner. The focus in the first three sentences in both texts is *a new castle.* In the preferred version, Text B, the passive voice is used to ensure that the pronoun *it*, referring to the castle, is the first noun in sentences 2 and 3. In sentence 4 the focus shifts to Cromwell, and in Text B this shift is marked by the use of the cleft form, *It was Cromwell who ...*, together with the opening of a new paragraph.

This is a simple example and certainly oversimplifies the processes involved in creating coherent and readable text. But it illustrates the basic principle that in composing sentences, and therefore in composing text, we move from what is given or established to what is new.

6.1 Definite and indefinite articles

The basic contrast between the definite and indefinite articles involves notions of *given* and *new.* The basic distinction between the definite and indefinite articles is to do with whether or not the noun we are talking about is given – something that can be identified by the reader/listener:

The definite article:

We use the definite article, *the*, to mark a noun phrase as something known or identifiable. It may be identifiable because:

- it has been mentioned and identified earlier in the text or conversation;
- there is only one in existence:
  The sky was bright blue.
  We have landed men on **the moon.**
- there is only one in the shared environment or context:
  The prime minister is speaking on TV this evening.
  Do you need **the car** this evening?
  I'm going to **the letter box.**
- you are going on to specify the thing you are talking about, using a postmodifier such as a prepositional phrase or a relative clause:
  I'm interested in **the history of Cumbria.**
  This is **the book I was telling you about.**

Fig. 6.1 The definite article

The indefinite article:

If we are talking about a singular noun, which our listener cannot or does not need to identify, we use the indefinite article *a(n)*:

There was **a** little boy sitting in the corner.
I read **a** great book last week.

If we are talking about an uncountable noun or a plural noun, which the listener cannot or does not need to identify, we omit the article altogether. Grammarians refer to this as the **zero article**:

Beauty is only skin deep.
Cats hunt mice.

Fig. 6.2 The indefinite article

The distinction between the definite article and the indefinite article, then, is to do with whether or not the noun can be identified. There are, however, a few complications. For example, the definite article can be used instead of a plural form to make general statements about countable nouns:

The computer *enables us to carry out complex calculations.*
(Computers enable us to carry out complex calculations.)
My favourite flower is **the rose**. *(My favourite flowers are roses.)*

But the distinction is, in principle, clear enough. In the early stages of learning there is a strong tendency for learners to omit articles altogether, although some students rapidly acquire the basic distinction.

Task 6.1:

Do your students have problems with the basic distinction between definite and indefinite articles? Or is this basic distinction fairly clear, leaving them with only a few specific problems?

Commentary on Task 6.1:

The answer to this question probably depends on your students' first language. Speakers of Japanese, Chinese or Arabic, for example, have considerable problems with this distinction, because their first language operates a very different system. For speakers of Greek, on the other hand, the basic distinction is clear, but there are

---

difficulties with proper names. In Greek these always take a definite article, but the way proper names are handled is inconsistent in English. In general, we do not use the definite article with names but it is used with the names of seas and oceans, for example, although not with lakes. There is no logical reason why English should talk of *Lake Geneva* and *Lake Superior,* but insist on *the Atlantic Ocean* and *the North Sea.* French is like English in that it operates an inconsistent system, but the inconsistencies in French are different from those in English. For example, French uses the definite article for the names of countries (*la France; la Grande Bretagne*), but not for towns or cities. It uses the definite article for days of the week, but not for the months of the year. There is, therefore, a certain amount of 'tidying up' to do for all learners, but for many, including speakers of most European languages, the basic distinction between definite and indefinite articles is straightforward.

Some learners of English, however, continue to have problems with the use of articles even after they have evolved a grammar which is almost indistinguishable from that of a native speaker. I once supervised an Arabic-speaking PhD student, whose written English was eloquent and persuasive at a level way beyond all but a tiny minority of native speakers. But her article system was still, on occasions, noticeably non-native.

6.2 Building grammatical systems

When we discussed system building in Section 1.4 in Chapter 1 we looked at the game *What's in the bag?*, which was aimed, among other things, at developing routines to provide initial insights into the use of the articles and other referential devices in English. Routines of this kind play an important part in promoting recognition of the referential system, and in building an understanding of the parameters which govern the system.

At a later stage we can build on this initial introduction by offering rules-of-thumb for the use of the definite article, such as those set out in Figs 6.1 and 6.2 above. Learners move from accumulating routines to solving problems, often with the help of a basic rule system. We can reinforce this by contrasting specific statements using the definite article, with general statements using the indefinite article or the zero article.

There is an example of this in Teaching Activities 4.1 and 4.2 in Section 4.2.1.

But we cannot give definitive rules for the use of the articles in the same way as we can give rules for the structure of the noun phrase. This is because, unlike the structure of the phrase, which is entirely rule-governed, the use of the articles is often a matter of user's choice – as the task below shows:

Task 6.2:

Without looking back, can you say which of the following, **A** or **B**, are the paragraphs used to introduce the text about the eight-year-old robber we looked at in Section 3.1.2? How do these two texts differ? Are they both grammatically acceptable?

> **A:** POLICE were last night searching for the eight-year-old boy who attempted to hold up a sweet shop with a pistol, *writes David Ward.*
>
> A boy, wearing a balaclava, threw a carrier bag at a shopkeeper at a corner store in Ashton-under-Lyme, Greater Manchester, and ordered her to fill it up.

> **B:** POLICE were last night searching for an eight-year-old boy who attempted to hold up a sweet shop with a pistol, *writes David Ward.*
>
> The boy, wearing a balaclava, threw a carrier bag at the shopkeeper at the corner store in Ashton-under-Lyme, Greater Manchester, and ordered her to fill it up.

Commentary on Task 6.2:

The journalist's original version was B, but version A is also grammatically acceptable.

As we have seen, it is usual to use *the* with a noun that is specified by a relative clause. The journalist decided to use *a*, probably to emphasise the fact that the boy has not yet been identified by the police.

He has chosen to follow on by taking the boy and the corner shop as given. This means he refers to *The boy, the corner shop* and *the shopkeeper.* As shown in Text A, however, he could have treated the introduction as something separate and, taking the second paragraph as the beginning of a story, gone on to refer to *a boy, a corner shop* and *a shopkeeper.*

> If you look at any text, you are likely to find occurrences where the use of the definite or indefinite article is clearly a matter of choice rather than simply a matter of following a rule.

This means that, if learners are to acquire full use of the article system, they must continue to look critically at text. Command of the system will eventually come not from decontextualised system building activities but from exploration, from looking critically at text.

We can help to build up this critical faculty by working with texts the students have become familiar with. When we reach this stage, however, we need to see the articles not as a self-contained system, but as part of the wider determiner system and referential system of English. After working with the eight-year-old robber text, for example, we might, as we did in Teaching Activity 3.6, ask students to recall the text by offering them part of it as a gapped exercise:

— boy went into — shop and bought — Smarties for 25p. "— gave me — 50p piece and as I gave — — change — man came in. — waited until — man went. Then — threw — plastic carrier bag at me, pointed — gun at me and said: 'Put everything in'." — fled when — woman, who had — two children with —, pressed — alarm.

Students can usefully work in groups to recall the text. They may offer acceptable alternatives to the original text. They could, for example suggest *the woman, ..., pressed **the** alarm,* on the acceptable grounds that there was only one alarm in the shop which is seen as part of the shared context. Students will be looking at the article system as a part of the determiner system, which includes elements like ***her** two children* and ***his** change.* They will also be placing the articles in their context as part of the referential apparatus used to build up a coherent text. There is, for example, a choice between, ***He** threw a plastic carrier bag at me* and ***The boy** threw a plastic carrier bag at me.*

This learning process involves both recognition and system building. A text can be seen as a complex routine which exemplifies the use of language in the same way as the simple routine involved in a game such as *What's in the bag?* In order to fill the gaps, learners will use their recall of the text, together with their subconscious feel for how the language works, and they will be using their explicit rule system to monitor what is produced in this way.

The process also involves exploration. The only way learners can acquire the referential system is by working with it in a context. In their group discussions, learners are likely to produce alternative versions of the text. Some of these will be grammatically acceptable, some will not. Some of these possible versions will be discussed in the class discussion which follows the group work. One function of such an exercise is to raise student awareness and to make them more receptive to these systems in future exposure and exploration. Learners will also go on to produce their own texts. As they produce their own stories or retellings as part of their future learning, they will be experimenting with the system they have built up.

A useful alternative to asking students to fill gaps is to ask them to identify **reference chains** in a text. They might, for example, be asked to work through the eight-year-old robber text and underline all the references to the robber or to the shopkeeper.

The development of the article system and its integration with other systems, then, will involve the following stages:

- **Improvisation:** In the early stages of learning students will be inconsistent in their use of articles, often omitting them altogether.
- **Recognition:** Through the use of games and other classroom activities, learners acquire routines, which they are later able to draw on when they are producing their own texts (see, for example, the game *What's in the bag?* in Section 1.4). This process is reinforced by their encounters with the articles in the texts they work with. Teachers can help by highlighting appropriate elements in texts.
- **System building:** With teacher help, learners begin to develop a rule system to account for the occurrence of articles in text.
- **Exploration:** Learners are encouraged to work with text in a way which encourages them to refine their article system and integrate it with the general system of determiners and with other referential devices.
- **Consolidation:** As learners produce their own written or spoken text, or take part in spoken interaction, they begin to work with a coherent and consistent system which has been refined by exposure.

6.3 Devices for organising text

In Chapter 4 we looked at excerpts from a text about seagulls to illustrate features of the grammar of structure. Here is the full text:

How a reservoir is gulling[2] the gulls

from ROGER KERR in Glasgow

1. TAPE-RECORDED squawks of a seagull in distress **have enabled** water authorities in Strathclyde to cleanse two reservoirs at Milngavie, near Glasgow, by frightening away an estimated 5,000 seagulls which were polluting the water.
2. Although the technique **has been used** successfully at airports, Strathclyde officials believe this is the first time it has been operated at a reservoir.
3. Throughout the country, water authorities **are plagued**, mainly in winter, by roosting seagulls mucking up the reservoirs. 4. Three years ago Strathclyde Regional Council's water department found that seagulls were causing a potential health risk on two reservoirs serving Glasgow.
5. The cost **prohibited** covering the two reservoirs at Milngavie or building an improved treatment plant. 6. **Instead**, Dr. Patricia Monagham, a lecturer at Glasgow University's zoology department, and research student Colin Shedden found the answer: scare them off with a seagull's distress call.
7. So, during the winter months, **a van equipped with a loudspeaker and tape bearing the agonised squawks of a captured seagull held upside down** slowly toured the reservoirs for two hours before dusk, a period when gulls fly in to roost.
8. 'When the birds come in looking for a safe place to roost, a fellow bird's distress call will scare them off', said Dr. Monagham.

The agonised squawks of a seagull held upside down.

(From: *The Observer*)
Let us look more closely at the text to see how it is organised. It begins with a headline, *How a reservoir is gulling the gulls*. This contains an

[2]To *gull* is an old-fashioned word meaning to deceive.

implied question: *How is the reservoir gulling the gulls?* Sentence 1 opens with an answer to the question. Briefly the answer is: *tape-recorded squawks of a seagull in distress.* Since we normally expect to have a human or other animate subject for a verb, a more neutral ordering of the elements in this sentence would be: *Water authorities have frightened away an estimated 5,000 seagulls by using the tape-recorded squawks of a seagull in distress.* In order to bring the required words, *recorded squawks of a seagull in distress,* to the front of the sentence, the writer uses the verb *enabled.*

Sentence 1 describes the technique used to cleanse the reservoirs. In sentence 2 the use of the passive *has been used* enables the writer to use the words *the technique* as the subject of the sentence, neatly picking up the element established in the first sentence. *Strathclyde officials* in sentence 2, is picked up by *water authorities* in sentence 3, but in order to bring this element to the front of the sentence the writer uses the passive form *are plagued.* In sentence 4, the *water authorities* theme continues with a reference to *Strathclyde Regional Council's water department.*

Sentence 4 also implies a question. If the authorities have identified a problem, the question is: *What did they do about it?* This is taken up in sentences 5 and 6. The obvious solutions – covering the reservoirs or improving the facilities – were too expensive, so the authorities found an alternative. By opening with the phrase, *The cost prohibited ...,* the author is able to list two unsatisfactory solutions and to contrast them immediately with the successful alternative by opening sentence 6 with the word *Instead.* Sentence 7 uses the word *So* to announce that a summary is coming and then uses a complex noun group to summarise the whole article. Sentence 8 provides an explanation to round off the text.

Obviously this is not the only way the text could have been put together, but the writer has produced a coherent text by exploiting a number of the resources of the language:

- **The passive voice:** As we have seen, this enables the writer to bring the object of an active verb to the front of the sentence by making it the subject of a passive verb.
- **Metaphorical use of words:** The act of *prohibiting* would normally be thought of as requiring a human subject, it is normally people who prohibit things. But the language allows us to use words metaphorically, so the word *cost* is used as the subject of the verb *prohibited.* Some verbs are regularly used metaphorically with an abstract subject. Others are rarely used in this way except perhaps

to make a joke. I might say, for example, *This computer doesn't seem to **like** me very much. It won't do what I ask it to*, speaking of the computer as though it were animate rather than inanimate.

- **Lexical choice:** It was the choice of the verb *enabled* that allowed the writer to open the article with an answer to the question implied in the headline. Lexical choice also enables a writer to summarise and refer back to items in the text. In sentence 2 above, the word *technique* refers back to the use of *tape-recorded squawks*; and similarly the word *officials* refers back to *water authorities in Strathclyde*.
- **Fronting:** The text highlights a successful solution to a problem by contrasting it with the unsuccessful solutions; it marks this by bringing the marker of contrast, *instead*, to the front of the sentence. Other words and phrases used to mark contrast are: *actually, certainly, undoubtedly.*
- **Logical connector:** The word *so* is a logical connector used here to introduce a summary. We use a range of words and phrases, such as *therefore, however* and *as a result*, to show how a sentence relates logically to the preceding text.

In addition to the devices exemplified here we also have:

- **Clefting:** There is an example of clefting in Text B, at the beginning of this chapter: *It was Cromwell who* ... There is another example in my definition of Lexical Choice above: *It was the choice of the verb* enabled *that* ..., but in general clefting is more frequent in spoken than in written language.
- **Pseudo-clefting:** Some years ago there was an advertisement for a brand of beer which used the slogan: *What we want is Watney's*. This is a way of highlighting the final element in the clause, in this case the name of the advertised brand.
- **Focusing words and phrases:** A number of words and phrases are used, in the same way as the word *instead* is used above, to show the function of a sentence, for example:
  - we use *in fact, as a matter of fact, in reality* or *in practice* to mark a contrast;
  - we use phrases such as *in my opinion, in my view* or *to my mind* to highlight an opinion;
  - we use phrases such as *then, suddenly, all of a sudden, fortunately, unfortunately* to mark critical stages in a narrative.
  - we often use phrases with *it* and *that's* to highlight the coming sentence in a number of different ways: *it is true that* ..., *it is possible that* ..., *it is likely that* ..., *that's why* ..., *that's what* ...;

- the frame, *the* + Adj. + *thing is ...*, is often used to show the relevance of the sentence which follows: *the main thing is ...; the annoying thing is ...; the worrying thing is ...* etc. The same applies to a range of other general words: *the best way is to ...; the only way is to ...; the problem is that ...;*
- the demonstrative pronoun *this* is often used in text to link back to something that has been said. It is used with verbs to explain the significance of a previous stretch of text: *this means that ...; this suggests that ...; this shows ...* . It is also used with abstract nouns which refer back to elements in text as in: *this problem ...; this attitude ...; this proposal ...* . In the seagull text we have the phrase *the technique*. It could equally well be ***this*** *technique ...* .
- The determiner *one* or the phrase *one of the* is used in the same way as *this*, to indicate one of a number of possibilities: *One reason is that ...; One possibility is that ...; One solution would be to ...; One of the problems is that ...; One of the proposals was to ...* .

6.3.1 Recognition of text-organising devices

Some of these organising devices fit readily into the existing syllabus. When we are teaching relative clauses, it would be easy to add on cleft devices which, structurally, are simply *it* + *BE* + relative clause. Similarly, pseudo-cleft phrases can be linked to reported questions. Particularly common phrases such as *what I said was ..., what I meant was ..., what I did was ...* can be singled out for special attention. Phrases with *that's* + *WH-* can also be linked to reported questions, again highlighting particularly common forms such as *that's what I said/thought/did* and *that's where I live*.

Words and phrases which are commonly used as text organisers can be taught lexically. Teachers can help with this by grouping them functionally in ways exemplified above, with words and phrases marking opinion or stages in a narrative. Logical connectors can usefully be grouped under headings such as cause and effect (e.g. *therefore, as a result*), addition (e.g. *besides, moreover, what's more, also*), adversatives (*but, however, in spite of this, nevertheless*). But the use of many of these items is complex and recognition needs to be supplemented with exercises which focus on system building and exploration.

6.3.2 System building and exploration.

To provide examples of text-building devices in use it is useful to draw attention to some of the devices, which learners have already encountered in their reading and listening.

Teaching Activity 6.1:
We might, for example, collect a number of sentences, Set A, which exemplify clefting:

Set A
1. EL: Right. Yeah. It's quite a long way in from Forest Hill, mm?
   CB: It's quite a journey into erm, Central London. *It's Hatton Garden I work in.*
2. RS: Yes. It's very clear, in the foreground. The background's sort of nice and shimmery.
   BB: *Yes. It was a German friend of my wife's who* took it, so maybe that had something to do with it because er, normally we – our photos are absolutely terrible.
3. I do a few concerts and competitions, but I'm still at the beginning of my career. *It's very hard work getting established as a musician.*
4. *One of the things I really hate is* spiders and insects.
5. This time *it was a woman who* answered the door. Grimble preferred men.
6. James Bond fans have seen quite a bit of John without knowing it. *It was John's legs that* did the spectacular dash to safety over the backs of alligators in *Live and Let Die.*

We might then rewrite these sentences, removing the cleft elements, to produce Set B:

Set B
1. EL: Right. Yeah. It's quite a long way in from Forest Hill, mm?
   CB: It's quite a journey into erm, Central London. I work in Hatton Garden.
2. RS: Yes. It's very clear, in the foreground. The background's sort of nice and shimmery.
   BB: Yes. A German friend of my wife's took it, so maybe that had something to do with it because er, normally we – our photos are absolutely terrible.
3. I do a few concerts and competitions, but I'm still at the beginning of my career. Getting established as a musician is very hard work.

---

4. I really hate spiders and insects.
5. This time a woman answered the door. Grimble preferred men.
6. James Bond fans have seen quite a bit of John without knowing it. John's legs did the spectacular dash to safety over the backs of alligators in *Live and Let Die*.

The students look at Set B as we play a recording of Set A, or read out Set A. Students are asked to listen for any differences. After one playing we ask the students, working in groups, if they can rewrite Set B to produce Set A. Then we play or read Set A again before asking students to read out their rewritten version. The teacher might then go on to ask students if they can recall the sentences from minimal prompts: *1. Hatton Garden – work; 2. Photo – German friend; 3. Hard work – musician* etc. Finally the teacher might list a number of phrases used to achieve this effect: *What I did was …; What we are going to do is …; What I said was …; What I think is …; That's why …; That's what …* etc.

It is possible to collect similar sets of sentences to illustrate the use of the passive, logical connectors and fronted elements. We can use a range of devices to prompt recall of these elements. The exercise described above uses a simple rewriting technique. We could use gap-filling, giving students a list of items to complete sentences. We can use 'jumbled' sentences:

I / one of the things / really / spiders and insects / hate / is.

Students can begin by working in groups to reconstitute these sentences. They may then be asked to listen to a reading of the sentences to help them before they are asked to produce their own versions. The important thing about these activities is that it encourages learners to pay careful attention to the wordings as well as the meanings.

6.3.3 Text-based exercises

The real difficulty with text-organising devices is not one of form or structure but one of use. The best way to help with these items is by highlighting them when they occur in text. Again there are a number of ways of doing this. In 6.2 above we gave an example of a gap-filling exercise to be done after processing a text for meaning. Gap-filling does not have to be done in the written form. It can be done as a dictation. The teacher can read out the text, pausing at appropriate points.

Students may be asked to write down the words that complete the text, or they may be asked to select from a multiple-choice format the items that complete the text, or they may be asked to choose items from a list.

Teaching Activity 6.2:

We might, for example, use the first three sentences of the seagulls text as the basis for a gap-filling exercise:

1. TAPE-RECORDED squawks of a seagull in distress have enabled water authorities in Strathclyde to cleanse two reservoirs at Milngavie, near Glasgow, by frightening away an estimated 5,000 seagulls which were polluting the water.
2. Although the technique has been used successfully at airports, Strathclyde officials believe this is the first time it has been operated at a reservoir.
3. Throughout the country, water authorities are plagued, mainly in winter, by roosting seagulls mucking up the reservoirs.

First students are given a gapped version of the text:

1. (1) of a seagull in distress have (2) water authorities in Strathclyde to cleanse two reservoirs at Milngavie, near Glasgow, by frightening away an (3) 5,000 seagulls which were polluting the water.
2. Although the (4) has been used successfully at airports, Strathclyde (5) believe this is the first time it (6) at a reservoir.
3. Throughout the country, (7) are plagued, mainly in winter, by roosting seagulls mucking up the reservoirs.

They are asked to complete the text from memory. Then the teacher writes up or hands out a list of words:

a. technique b. officials c. estimated d. tape-recorded squawks e. has been operated f. enabled g. water authorities.

Students check their solutions. Finally the teacher reads the full version of the text again to allow students to check their answers.

There are ways of adjusting the difficulty of a gapped exercise such as this one. An exercise is always easier to do if students work in groups and help each other. Another advantage of group work is that it encourages students to explain the thinking behind their choices. The disadvantage, of course, is that it may allow some students to sit back and leave the others to do the work. You can minimise this disadvantage by asking them to work first individually and then to pool their ideas in their groups, and by asking one or two of them for some ideas before the group stage.

Gapped exercises can be used to draw attention to any number of lexical or grammatical features which a teacher feels are worth highlighting. But they are particularly useful for the grammar of orientation where the real learning problems are to do with the organisation of information.

6.4 Summary

Let me summarise by relating the teaching of orientation to the five processes described in Chapter 1.

- **Improvisation:** Learners will begin by improvising in a number of ways. They will, for example, simply bring to the front of the sentence elements they wish to emphasise. Instead of saying, *It was a German friend of my wife's **who** took it* they will say things like: *German friend of my wife, she took it*, or: *My wife, German friend, she took it*. It will probably be some time before they use explicit cleft phrases such as *It was ... who ...*. Instead of using a passive, as in *Although the technique has been used successfully at airports* ..., learners may write things like *Although the technique have used successfully at airports ...*. This may just be a simplification designed to bring to the front of the clause the element they want to emphasise. Teachers should realise that learners feel the need to improvise because they recognise the need to organise text in a reader- or listener-friendly manner. They are not simply making mistakes, they are deliberately extending their grammars to meet new demands. In doing this they run the risk of producing unacceptable forms, but it is a risk that is worth taking.
- **Recognition:** We should make available to learners the structural devices, such as the passive and cleft forms, which are used to organise information. We should highlight and bring together logical connectors and focusing phrases. We should, on appropriate occasions, highlight metaphorical uses of particular words, and should point out that this is a regular feature of English. Which words, for example, can be used as subject of the verb *say*? We regularly refer to what books, newspapers, reports, letters, TV and radio *say*. And the word may have a large number of other metaphorical subjects:

The rules say that we need a two-thirds majority to win.
My watch says quarter to twelve.
This incident says something about the way the company is run.
Your home says a lot about you.
This music says nothing to me.

Very frequently the subject of *says* is *it*, as in: *it says on his T-shirt ...; it says here ...; it says somewhere ...* . Many other frequent verbs are used with a similar range of subjects. Look, for example, at the dictionary entries for *come* and *go*. Such verbs are frequent enough to justify detailed treatment, and one aspect of the treatment is to do with their range of metaphorical uses.

- **System building:** Discourse-organising devices do not exist as a definable system in the same way as verb tenses or determiners. There is no closed set of exponents which can be readily identified. But we need to recognise that the organisation of information is an important part of language.
- **Exploration:** The grammar of structure is relatively simple, and consequently it is well described in grammars. Text organisation on the other hand is extremely complex and not nearly so well described. This means that learning must depend very much on exploration. We need to devise exercises like those outlined above in 6.3.3, which focus on the use of a range of organisational devices in text. With adult learners it may be well worthwhile looking at organisational devices in their own language. The purpose of these exercises is not only to provide direct teaching input, but also to encourage learners to look critically at future input.
- **Consolidation:** Learners must have plenty of opportunities to create text for themselves.

7 Lexical phrases and patterns

7.1 What is a lexical phrase?

It is not easy to define a lexical phrase. Skehan (1992) sees them as 'ready-made elements and chunks', items we can deploy 'without the need to construct each chunk independently'. Sinclair (1988) talks of 'semi-preconstructed phrases that constitute single choices, even though they might appear to be analysable into segments'. It is clear that *as a matter of fact, at least* and *from a _____ point of view* are lexical phrases. They are strings of words which we can call to mind and produce as fixed units in the way Skehan and Sinclair describe. The phrase *as old as the hills* is one which will be called to mind as a single unit by most British speakers of English. Within this we can identify the frame *as ... as*, which will be familiar to almost all competent speakers of English, and which should therefore qualify as providing the framework for a number of lexical phrases. Sometimes a lexical phrase may be no more than two words which are often found together, such as *familiar to* or *qualify as,* but which do not constitute units on their own. Let us see if we can reach a workable agreement on what constitutes a lexical phrase, even if we cannot provide a watertight definition.

Task 7.1:

We looked at the following paragraph from Widdowson (1989) in Section 3.1.:

> ... communicative competence is not a matter of knowing rules for the composition of sentences ... It is much more a matter of knowing a stock of partially pre-assembled patterns, formulaic frameworks, and a kit of rules, so to speak, and being able to apply the rules to make whatever adjustments are necessary according to contextual demands. Communicative competence in this view is essentially a matter of adaptation, and rules are not generative but regulative and subservient.
>
> (Widdowson, 1989: 135)

How many lexical phrases of two or more words can you find in Widdowson's paragraph? The term *communicative competence* is one example. As an applied linguist I carry this term around in my head and produce it as a phrase on appropriate occasions. Another example is *a stock of*. The word *stock* is almost always found with the indefinite article rather than the definite article, and it is usually followed by the word *of*.

Key to Task 7.1:

I would identify the following lexical phrases:

1. *is not a matter of ...___ing*: This phrase predicts a frame extending over several sentences. As soon as we read the negative *is not a matter of*, we anticipate that an affirmative form will follow, probably an affirmative with a comparative in it such as *rather* or *more*. And this is exactly what happens with *it is much more a matter of ...___ing* and later *is essentially a matter of*.

2. *rules for ...*: The word *rules* is frequently followed by the word *for*.

3. *the composition of*: *composition* is usually preceded by the definite article, and almost always followed by *of*.

4. *a stock of*: The word *stock* is usually found with the indefinite article, and normally followed by *of*.

5. *a kit of*: Again this is a frequent combination.

6. *so to speak*: This is very much a fixed phrase. Widdowson could not have said *so to write*, even though this would make very good sense in this context.

7. *being able to*: The word *able* is often followed by *to*.

8. *apply the rules*: What do we do with rules? We *make* and *break* rules. We *follow* rules and we *apply* them. So we can predict a small set of verbs which are likely to be found in the vicinity of *rules*.

9. *make ... adjustments*: Adjustments are like rules in that there are not many things we can do with them. If we have *adjustments* as object of a verb then the verb is very likely to be *make*.

10. *whatever ... are necessary*: Another frequent frame.

11. *According to*: The word *according* is almost always followed by *to*.

12. *In this view*: There are a number of frequent phrases with the word *view*. Again the possibilities are restricted: *In my view* and *in this view* are both frequent occurrences but, interestingly, *in that view* is not.

13. Finally Widdowson uses the phenomenon of phrases as a stylistic device. He ends with *rules are not generative but regulative and subservient.* As a grammarian I am very used to the idea of rules being *generative* and *regulative.* But *subservient* is not a word that is normally associated with rules. This makes the word *subservient* stand out and gives it a powerful impact, strongly reinforcing the point that Widdowson is making.

Widdowson illustrates his own point very neatly. Around two-thirds of his paragraph is made up of lexical phrases. Most discourse, whether spoken or written, is made up of frequently occurring phrases. There is a large element of predictability in language. This has obvious implications for pedagogy. As far as possible we should identify the frequently occurring words and phrases, and try to organise these in a way which makes them accessible to learners and helps to make them memorable.

It will, I think, be clear from the outcome of Task 7.1 that there are identifiable elements which can reasonably be identified as lexical phrases, ready-made elements or semi-preconstructed phrases, and that these elements make up a large proportion of language.

Before looking at ways of organising lexical phrases for teaching I will first identify different types of lexical phrase:

- **Polywords:** Some of the items in Task 7.1, like *according to, so to speak* and *in my view,* can be regarded as polywords. These phrases are made up of a number of words, but they can reasonably be learnt as if they were single words because the same string of words occurs again and again without variation.

- **Frames:** Examples of frames in Task 7.1 are *whatever ... are necessary* and *are not ... but ... .* Here we have a lexical phrase, which is not a continuous string of words, but which consists of a frame that can be completed in any number of ways, depending on the context.

- **Sentences and sentence stems:** Some lexical phrases constitute full sentences. Many of these are social acts such as *How do you do?* or *How are you?* Others are simply sentences which occur with great regularity in given contexts: *What time is it? How do you know? I'm not sure about that.* There are also sentence stems which provide an introduction to a sentence: *Would you like ...? Do you mind if I ...? What I mean is ...* and so on. Very often these stems signal strongly the way in which a sentence is to be interpreted. *Do you mind if I ...?*, for example, introduces a request. *What I mean is ...* introduces some sort of clarification or justification.

- **Patterns:** In Section 2.3 we identified patterns as part of the grammar. As an example we cited the fact that the word *relationship* often features in the pattern noun + *between*. We listed a few other words which figure in the same pattern: *agreement, quarrel, fight*. When we have a pattern it is possible to characterise the kinds of words that will complete the pattern. In the case of noun + *between* the items that fill the *noun* slot will be nouns denoting conflict (*war, argument*) resolution (*agreement, compromise, treaty*) and relationships (*love, rivalry, partnership*). A pattern is thus like a frame with an additional feature: the words which complete the frame are to some extent predictable according to their meaning.

7.2 Polywords

Nattinger and DeCarrico (1990) cite a number of items which they describe as *polywords*. These are phrases which recur again and again without variation, for example: *so far so good, what a pity, in fact.* Basically, these polywords need to be learnt as lexical items. There is very little difference between the meaning and use of the word *actually* and the meaning and use of the phrase *in fact*. There is no reason why they should not be learnt in the same way. Polywords are central to language, functioning as all parts of speech.

If we see a polyword as a string of elements we can identify a large number of polywords based on verbs:

1. Two-part verbs:
   a. Verb + preposition: *look at, work for, listen to, look after.*
   b. Verb + adverb: *break out, carry on, go away.* Here the words *out, on* and *away* are adverbs rather than prepositions because they are not followed by a noun. Very often, as with *carry on*, these combinations have a meaning which is quite different from the sum of the parts – in other words, learners cannot guess their meanings by looking at each word in turn, they need to recognise and learn these items as polywords.

2. Three-part verbs:

   catch up with, get on with, talk down to etc. Again many of these items have a meaning which is different from the sum of their parts.

The important thing about these units is that, although the form of the verb may vary (e.g. *looks at, looking at, looked at*), the units always occur as a string. This means they can be learnt as though they were single word items.

A large number of polywords act as nouns. Very often these feature a noun modifier: *potato peeler, washing machine, wine glass, ice cube, income tax*. Sometimes an adjective is closely attached to its noun: *plastic carrier bag, brown bread, fresh eggs, instant coffee*. Many technical terms are polywords: *communicative competence, transitive verb, noun modifier, visual reaction time, autonomic nervous system*. All of these items are best regarded as single units and will be learnt as such, although the learning is made easier if the learner is already aware of the value of the individual parts.

Many adverbials are polywords:

- Time adverbials: *last week/month/year; the other day/week; the day before yesterday; the day after tomorrow; next week* etc.
- Place adverbials: *over there; on the left/right; in the middle* etc.
- Sentence adverbials: *in fact; as a matter of fact; by and large* etc.

There are polywords which function as adjectives: *spick and span; black and blue; as old as the hills; tried and tested* and so on. We use polywords to express logical relations: *in spite of, as a result of, owing to*; and as prepositions: *in front of, next to, to the left/right of* etc.

There are, therefore, a large number of items which need to be recognised and learnt as single items even though they are made up of more than one word. It is important that learners recognise this from an early stage and begin to look out for polywords.

7.3 Frames

In Task 7.1 we identified phrases like *whatever ... are necessary* and *are not ... but ...* . These are clearly useful items, but they are not polywords because they are not a continuous string. They are frames with gaps which could be filled by a whole range of words depending on the context. In fact, they are somewhat abstract frames since, in each one, the place of the word *are* could be filled by any form of the verb *BE*, depending on the context. They could also be manipulated in other ways. Widdowson could, for example, have written *whatever adjustments **seem to be** necessary*. We have, therefore, frames which can be manipulated in a number of ways according to the context, which, in Widdowson's words, can be adjusted according to contextual demands.

In Section 2.5 we drew attention to frames and productive features, citing as an example the frame *from a(n)* adj. *point of view*, used to limit or focus a statement:

*Everything looks good **from a** financial **point of view**.*
*That would be a risky decision **from a** political **point of view**.*

Like polywords, frames can fulfil a range of functions. Some function as what Nattinger and DeCarrico (1990) call sentence builders: *not only X but (also) Y; the ____er X, the ___er Y*, providing a framework for a whole sentence. In Task 7.1 we have frames which are used to structure a whole paragraph: ... *communicative competence **is not a matter of** knowing ...; It **is much more a matter of** knowing a stock of partially pre-assembled patterns .... Communicative competence in this view **is essentially a matter of** ...* . We have, therefore, frames operating at a number of levels to structure phrases, sentences and whole paragraphs.

Under the heading of polywords we looked two- and three-part verbs. Most grammars would define such verbs as phrasal verbs. It seems to me that they are much better regarded simply as polywords. I would limit the term **phrasal verb** to apply to verbs with the following characteristics:

1. If the object is a noun or noun phrase, it may come directly after the verb (*fill the bag up*) or after the particle (*fill up the bag, hold up a sweet shop*). If the object is a long noun phrase, it will almost certainly come after the particle. The sentence, *She filled the green plastic bag she was carrying up*, is possible, but most unlikely.
2. If the object is a pronoun it must come after the verb: *fill it up*, not **fill up it*.

There are then a number of verb/particle combinations which are polywords, in which there is an unbroken sequence. There are also combinations in which the verb/particle combination functions as a frame: it leaves a space for other information, in this case for a grammatical object.

7.4 Sentences and sentence stems

Sometimes a phrase constitutes a whole sentence. Much social interaction is made up of predictable utterances: *Hi, how are you?, See you later, Thanks a lot, Lovely weather*. We also have sentence stems, elements which introduce a sentence, *Would you like ...?*, introducing an offer or invitation, or *Do you think I could ...?* or *Do you mind if*

I ...?, introducing a request. Such items are sometimes referred to as form/function composites since the form strongly signals the function it fulfils. We will look in detail at these predictable forms in conversational English in Chapter 9.

In Section 6.3 we looked at devices used to organise discourse. Among these devices were a number of introductory sentence stems: cleft and pseudo-cleft sentences introduced by phrases such as *It was ... who; X was the one who ...; What I want/think/do is ...;* other phrases which highlight the use of the sentence, or the way it is to be interpreted: *It is true that ...; It is likely that ...; That's why ...* etc. In academic discourse many sentence stems are used for hedging: *it seems/appears that ...; it may well be that ...; our findings/results suggest that ...*. There are also predictable ways of introducing a research topic, for example: *The aim/purpose/goal/object of this study is to analyse/investigate/establish ....*.

7.5 Patterns

Patterns are a sub-class of lexical phrases. They are like frames in that they are discontinuous and need to be completed, but, unlike frames, patterns are systematically related to identifiable sets of words as we saw when we looked at the pattern noun + *between* above.

Consider the word *about*. It has three basic meanings:

1. Concerning a particular subject: *Think **about** it. I read a book **about** that recently.*
2. Approximately: *It takes **about** two hours to drive to London. It'll cost **about** a hundred quid.*
3. To indicate general spatial orientation: *It's late. There's nobody **about**. We spent the morning just walking **about** town.*

Each of these meanings is likely to be found in association with predictable sets of words. With 1 we are likely to find verbs, such as *think, forget, talk* and *read*. We are also likely to find nouns denoting items which communicate, such as *book, programme, story* and *article*, as well as nouns denoting acts of communication, such as *advice, agreement* and *opinion*. We would also expect to find adjectives which describe attitudes towards information, states or events, such as *happy, pleased* and *sorry*. With 2 we will find numbers, such as *a hundred, a thousand* or *a dozen*; measurements, such as *a kilometre, an hour and a half* and *a ton*. With 3 we tend to find phrases like *hanging about, lying about* and *waiting about*. If we have access to a computerised corpus of language we can check to find which words occur with *about*.

Most patterns involve the use of highly frequent words in the language, like *about*, and their relationship with identifiable sets of words. Francis *et al.* (1996) list around thirty prepositions (*about, as, at, between, by, for, from, in, off, on, over, through, to, with* etc.) which feature in patterns with verbs. They list around 25 similar words as featuring in patterns with nouns, and fifteen with adjectives. They also list a number of patterns with verbs, nouns or adjectives followed by clauses introduced by *that* and by WH-words:

> *The same learner may have been made **aware that** the pattern is used to **indicate that** someone is thought of in a particular way.*

> *There are a number of **reasons why** patterns like this one are pedagogically important.*

> *Can you **say which** of the following are the paragraphs used to introduce the eight-year-old robber text?*

There are also words followed by non-finite verb forms, such as the *to*-infinitive or the *-ing*-form:

> *Each of these meanings is **likely to** be found in association with predictable sets of words.*

As we have seen (2.3 and 2.5), the way words feature in patterns is not random. The verbs associated with the first meaning of *about* are all to do with communication. Francis *et al.* (1996) list over 120 verbs associated with this meaning. These range from words like *ask, know, talk, think* and *write*, which would be found in an elementary course, through to words like *mutter, quibble* and *whinge*, which might not be found even in an advanced level course. In the same way, Francis *et al.* (1998) identify around thirty nouns denoting items used to communicate, which are associated with *about*. These include very frequent words, such as *book, story* and *letter*, and also relatively infrequent words like *anecdote, fable* and *yarn*, which would probably be found only at a very advanced level, if at all. Their list of adjectives runs to over 400, varying from *happy, sad, worried* and *angry* to infrequent words like *bullish, phlegmatic, leery* and *effusive*.

There are a number of reasons why such patterns are pedagogically important. First, as we saw in Chapter 2, in order to use language fluently and quickly, learners need to assimilate not just words, but patterns and phrases. We do not have time to apply complex grammatical rules to create utterances in real time, so we are dependent on lexical phrases or 'chunks'. If we are to help learners to develop this capacity we need to find ways of identifying and highlighting relevant patterns.

The second reason concerns the function and power of words like *about*. Imagine learners who hear the sentence: *He'll probably spin you a yarn about all his problems.* The phrase *spin you a yarn*, meaning *tell you a story*, is unlikely to be known. But the word *about* provides a powerful clue. Given *He'll probably___ you a ____ about all his problems*, they would probably infer that the blanks involved an act of communication, something like telling a story. The more learners are aware of the patterns and meanings associated with *about*, the more likely they are to make this inference. Patterns and the pivotal words they contain, like *about*, provide powerful clues to meaning. Francis *et al.* (1996) give an example featuring the word *as* from a newspaper report:

Elisabeth and Thomas were hailed as heroes.

They argue that, although a learner at, say, the intermediate level, may not know the meaning of the word *hail*, the same learner may be aware of verb patterns with *as*, and 'may have been made aware that the pattern is used to indicate that someone is thought of in a particular way, usually as something good or bad'. The general meaning of *hail* can therefore be guessed, and the specific meaning can be checked if necessary.

Task 7.2:

The sentences below are taken, with minimal adaptation, from Francis *et al.* (1996 and 1998). Can you guess the meanings of the words that go in the blanks below? Can you guess the words themselves?

 1. He went to hospital by ****.
 2. Revealed as a fraud who had **** her way to the top of her profession, she resigned after a month.
 3. They can **** you a room.
 4. The Prime Minister's speech **** me of the need to improve the education system.
 5. The main **** to reform is the employees' lack of interest.

What clues helped you to find the answers?

Commentary on Task 7.2:

The actual words are: 1. *helicopter;* 2. *lied;* 3. *book;* 4. *convinced;* 5. *obstacle.*

---

1. You probably guessed that the missing word denotes some form of transport. The words *went* and *by* together strongly predict this. Given the word *hospital* you may well have guessed *ambulance* as the missing word. In fact, the word is *helicopter.*
2. The missing word is *lied*, although you may well have guessed *cheated, bribed, schemed* or some other word which denotes dishonesty. The pattern **** *her way to* suggests some sort of deliberate action and the word *fraud* suggests dishonesty.
3. The double object structure in **** *you a room* suggests that the missing word refers to a service of some kind. It must be a service which could apply to a room. The answer is *book.*
4. There are relatively few words which might fit into the frame **** *me of the need to.* The missing word is *convinced.* Other possibilities are *persuaded* and *reminded.*
5. *The main* **** *to reform* could be either something positive like *incentive* or it could be something negative like *obstacle* or *threat.* The word *lack* subsequently identifies it as negative.

Finally a focus on patterns is likely to encourage a productive approach to the organisation of vocabulary. Words will be organised into groups according to meanings. Teaching materials will be likely to start by grouping basic words like *talk* and *ask*, later adding to these items like *enquire* and *complain*, and possibly going on at a later stage to add items like *boast* and *mutter*. To sum up, there are three good reasons for organising words into patterns:

- This organisation will make it more likely that learners will begin to process language as patterns and phrases rather than as individual words. Without this capacity they will be unable to use language fluently.
- Patterns, and the words which are pivotal to patterns – words like *about, as, by* and *her way to* – provide valuable clues to the interpretation of meaning.
- The recognition of patterns will encourage teachers and materials writers to organise words in ways which assist learning and recall.

In terms of pedagogic organisation, however, the difficult question is how we handle information on patterns. There are two questions here; the first question is: what constitutes a pattern? The second question is: given that there will obviously be a very large number of patterns, and an impossibly large number of words associated with those patterns, how will we select and organise patterns for teaching?

7.5.1 Patterns with prepositions

We saw in Section 7.1 that the preposition *about* has three basic uses. All the patterns associated with *about* relate closely to these uses. Let us look briefly at the basic meanings of the preposition *for* as given in an elementary coursebook, Willis and Willis (1988).

Basic meanings of 'for':

1. **How long?**

1.1. Time:
He paused *for a moment.*
Bridget lived in Sussex *for a few years* before coming to London.
They are out *for the afternoon.*

1.2. Distance:
We walked *for three miles.*

2. **Why?**

What are they for?

She was waiting *for a friend.*
Look at these forms. *What are they for?*
For example ...

2.1. Ask/look for
Look *for* more examples.
Ask four students *for* their names and addresses.

3. **Who wants or needs ...?**
Can you spell your name *for me?*
This next record is *for Pat Malone.*
Wait a minute. I'll do that *for you.*

3.1 After *good/bad, easy/difficult, right/wrong*
It's *good for you* to take a lot of exercise.
I hope this isn't too *difficult for you.*

Obviously this is a very simplified presentation of a very complex word, but it does provide a useful foundation for a general understanding of *for*. Francis *et al.* (1996) identify 20 categories of meaning for verbs with the pattern V *for* N, as in *I'm looking for my friend*. These incorporate over 200 verbs. But it is possible to allocate most of these words to categories in the description set out above:

Verb patterns with 'V *for* N':

1. How long?

1.1 Time:
Under this heading we would accommodate the verbs which Francis *et al.* list under THE 'LAST' GROUP: *endure, keep, live, last.*

1.2. Distance:
This would accommodate other members of THE 'LAST' GROUP: *extend, stretch.*

2. Why?
The preposition *for* introduces a reason or explanation. One of the semantic groups that Francis *et al.* list is called THE 'WAIT' GROUP. When we say someone is waiting, we are also likely to explain why they are waiting – *for* a friend or *for* a bus. The same applies to THE 'PLAN' GROUP, which includes words like: *plan, arrange, provide*; as well as THE 'PREPARE' GROUP, which includes *study* and *train*; and THE 'COMPENSATE' group: *pay, answer, apologise.* Closely allied to these is THE 'VOLUNTEER' GROUP: *report, sign on, show up, enrol.*

2.1 *Ask/look for*
Francis *et al.*'s largest groups are THE 'SEARCH' GROUP and THE 'ASK' GROUP. The first of these includes the words *hunt, look, shop* and *listen.* The second includes *ask, beg, send, shout* and *call.*

3. Who wants or needs …?
Francis *et al.*'s third largest group is THE 'WORK' GROUP which includes: *act, fight, play* and *speak.* When the word *for* occurs with words from this group, it can be paraphrased as *on behalf of.* The same applies to words which Francis *et al.* list under THE DEPUTISE (e.g. *substitute, stand in*), ARGUE (e.g. *argue, pray, speak up, vote*) and CARE (e.g. *feel, grieve*) GROUPS.

There are also 12 groups of verbs with the pattern V N *for* N, as in: *He asked his father for a loan.* The first of these is THE 'ASK' GROUP and corresponds closely to the same group with the V *for* N pattern. In all the other groups but one the preposition *for* introduces a reason for the action in the verb:

I admired her for her determination.
He was criticised for his behaviour.
They are wanted for armed robbery.

The final group is THE 'SCHEDULE' GROUP. This contains only three words: *schedule, reschedule* and *time*. With verbs in this group the preposition *for* introduces a time, as in:

The meeting is scheduled for ten-thirty.

There are two further uses of *for* which need to be covered. The first, which answers the question *How much?*, includes the verbs *buy, sell, go* and *pay*. The second, which Francis *et al.* characterise under THE 'HEAD' GROUP, includes *depart, leave* and *set off*. Both of these sets can usefully be covered under the notional headings of *buying and selling* and *travelling* respectively.

It is, therefore, possible to offer a reasonably economical characterisation of the preposition *for* and to relate this to verb patterns. Learners will begin by assigning a value to words like *about* and *for*. They will achieve this in a number of ways. They will relate the word *for* to phrases like *for a moment* or *for a long time*. They will then abstract from this to recognise the pattern *for* + adverbial of duration. They may paraphrase one of the meanings of the word *for* in their minds as meaning *on behalf of*. This will enable them to account for or to generate sentences like: *Can you do something for me?*

In some cases they may usefully relate particular uses of *for* to items in their first language. But these relationships can be complex. The French *pour* and the Spanish *para*, for example, relate to the basic meaning shown above under *Who wants or needs?* But they do not relate in the same way to the verb patterns with *for*, and in the categories *ask for* and *look for* there is certainly no consistent relationship between the English *for* and the French *pour*.

Task 7.3:

Think of a language other then English which you know well, possibly your own first language. How do the categories of meaning set out for the word *for* relate to words in that language?

Commentary on Task 7.3:

It is almost certain that no other language has a word which corresponds to the English *for* in all its meanings. In most cases, as with French and Spanish, there will be a highly complex relationship. We can draw two conclusions from this:

- The organisation of English is economical and logical in that *for* has a restricted and related number of uses. This is, however, not the only possible form of organisation – other languages will have ways of organising words which are different, but just as economical and logical.
- Since other languages have fairly different forms of organisation, learners need to acquire the patterns which are specific to English. To a large extent this will be a piecemeal job. It will involve a growing realisation and refinement of the meanings of the prepositions and the gradual build-up of an inventory of patterns. Teachers can help with this by characterising and grouping the meanings and uses of *for* in English, and also by listing the most frequent verbs found with a particular pattern, but a good deal of learning must be exploratory.

7.5.1.1 Helping learners with patterns with prepositions

We can help learners to acquire patterns with prepositions by characterising the meanings and uses of prepositions in the way shown for *about* in Section 7.5 and *for* in 7.5.1. We might then ask learners to categorise further instances of the words according to the categories given.

Teaching Activity 7.1

Look at the basic meanings of *for* in Section 7.5.1. Which group does each of these sentences belong to?

1. Will you do something **for** me?
2. I'm going to be away **for** a few days.
3. It's nice **for** children to have plenty of free time.
4. We were all listening **for** the telephone.
5. He swam **for** a hundred yards before he reached the shore.
6. Remember the words that are useful **for** you.
7. This knife is **for** cutting cheese.
8. That house is **for** sale.

Commentary on Teaching Activity 7.1:

This is a recognition exercise which aims to establish the meanings and uses of *for*. When other examples crop up in future texts it might be useful to refer learners back to this exercise to classify the uses. This is the sort of thing that can be set as supplementary homework.

As far as possible in such exercises we should use examples which are familiar to the learners, examples taken from texts that they have already studied. If there are not enough examples, it is worth looking ahead in their coursebook to find examples that will occur in future texts. This provides them with a context for the example, and serves to make the examples more memorable.

Key to Teaching Activity 7.1:
1: 3 Who wants or needs?; 2: 1.1 How long?: time; 3: 3.1 After *good/bad* etc.; 4: 2 Why? or 2.1 *Ask/look for*; 5: 1.2 How long?: distance; 6: 3 or 3.1 Who wants or needs?; 7: 2 Why?; 8: 2 Why?

We might move on to system building by designing exercises which will encourage learners to think for themselves about the kind of words which are likely to be found with a particular pattern.

Teaching Activity 7.2:
1. Use these phrases to complete the sentences below:

applied for – fight for – hoping for – leaving for – listen for – looking for – play for – sent away for – stick up for – trying for – working for.

a. Every professional footballer would love to _____ his country.
b. My father is _____ Mercedes, but he's just _____ a job with BMW.
c. I've just _____ the latest CD.
d. You should _____ your friends when they are in trouble.
e. My sister is _____ a scholarship to University.
f. I'm _____ my keys. I can't remember where I left them.
g. We are _____ London tomorrow.
h. Everyone should _____ the things they believe in.
i. I can _____ the baby and phone you if she wakes up.
j. We are _____ a good attendance.

2. We can put these words into groups:

A: Doing something for someone: *play for, work for, write for.*
B: Supporting or helping someone or something: *stick up for, fight for.*

C: Trying to find something or get something: *apply for, look for, listen for, send (away) for, try for.*

Which groups do you think these phrases belong to?

   a. We are **collecting for** the National Society for the Blind.
   b. I've **hunted** everywhere **for** it.
   c. She's **aiming for** a job in television.
   d. I'm going to **vote for** Peter Jackson.
   e. **Look out for** Michelle when you're at school.
   f. The church should **speak for** the poor.

3. Can you translate the sentences in 1 and 2 into your own language? How many ways are there of translating the word *for*?

Commentary on Teaching Activity 7.2:

1: a play for; b working for – applied for; c sent away for; d stick up for; e trying for; f looking for; g leaving for; h fight for; i listen for; j hoping for.

2: a A; b C; c C; d B; e C; f A.

The purpose behind all these activities, 1, 2 and 3, is system building. It is an attempt to encourage learners to recognise groups of verbs which are followed by *for*, and therefore to be able to predict what other verbs will be used in the same way.

The translation exercise, 3, will encourage learners to look closely at the relationship between the organisation of English and the organisation of their own language. Obviously that relationship will depend on their first language.

In selecting words for such an exercise it is important to choose the most frequently occurring words. All the words here are among those marked as frequent by Francis *et al.* (1996). It is worth noting that the word *for* is repeated in all the gap filler items in 1. This is to help learners to associate the verb and its preposition. Again, if it is possible, it is a good idea to choose sentences that learners have already seen.

7.5.2 *Patterns with gerunds, infinitives and clauses*

A good deal of time is spent in the classroom looking at verbs followed by an infinitive or gerund. Similarly, indirect speech takes up a good deal of classroom time, highlighting reported statements with words like *say, suggest,* etc. followed by a (*that*)-clause, reported questions with words like *ask* and *wonder* followed by *if* or a WH-clause. But all these forms, gerunds, infinitives and clauses with (*that*) or WH-words have a wide range of uses.

In Task 2.2 in Chapter 2 we looked at the use of *it* as a dummy subject. We saw an example of this, *it + BE + Adj. + to + verb*, in Section 2.3.:

it	*BE*	*Adj.*	*to*-infinitive
it	*is*	*nice*	*to meet you.*

In a sense the real subject here is *to meet you*. It is just possible to say, *To meet you is nice*, but we would be very much more likely to say, *It's nice to meet you*. The same applies to a sentence like: *It's not surprising that he is so successful*. It would be possible to say, *That he is so successful is not surprising*, but the formulation *It's not surprising that he is so successful*, or *It's not surprising he is so successful*, omitting the word *that*, is very much more likely – there is a reluctance in English to have a *to*-infinitive or a *that*-clause as the subject of a sentence. To a lesser extent the same applies to phrases with *-ing*. We are more likely to see or hear, *It was a real pleasure working with George*, than *Working with George was a real pleasure*. It is very common, therefore, to see the patterns:

$$It + BE \left. \begin{array}{c} \\ + \\ \\ \end{array} \right\} \begin{array}{c} \text{Adj.} \\ \\ \text{Noun} \end{array} \left. \begin{array}{c} \\ \\ \\ \end{array} \right\} \begin{array}{l} + (that)\text{-clause} \\ + to\text{-infinitive} \\ + \text{-}ing\text{-phrase} \end{array}$$

Let us look at a few examples:

> *It's a pity (that) you can't come tomorrow.* (*It + BE + Noun + (that)-clause*)
> *It's good (that) Jack has passed his exams.* (*It + BE + Adj. + (that)-clause*)
> *It's my turn to wash the dishes.* (*It + BE + Noun + to-infinitive*)
> *It's nice sitting out in the sun.* (*It + BE + Adj. + ing-form*)
> *It's hard work carrying all this stuff.* (*It + BE + Noun + -ing-form*)

In each case we use an *It + BE + Noun/Adjective* to comment on a statement expressed as a (*that*)-clause, or an action expressed as a *to*-infinitive or an *-ing*-form. Most of these are evaluative in some way and this is a very common function of this 'dummy *it*' pattern.

It is very common in English to draw attention to a proposition or an action by labelling it as *an idea, a problem, a solution* and so on, and then go on to comment on it. Such phrases are, therefore, frequently used as discourse organisers:

The problem is that ...
The idea is that ...
The best way is to ...
The solution is to ...

Frequently occurring nouns found with a *that*-clause are *claim, danger, difficulty, news, story, theory*. Perhaps the noun most commonly found in this frame is *thing*. It usually occurs with an adjective: *the funny thing, the annoying thing, the silly thing, the best thing, the other thing* etc. Nouns found with the infinitive include: *answer, decision, idea, plan, solution*. Again the word *thing* is found, often with a superlative as in *the best thing, the easiest thing, the wisest thing*.

Many nouns are frequently postmodified by a *that*-clause, which serves the function of expanding on the noun and defining it.

There are fears that the use of GM crops will upset the natural balance.
I have a feeling that she's going to do well.

Nouns followed by a *that*-clause include words like *belief, chance, danger, fact, hope, idea* and *opinion*. Particularly common is the use of the noun *fact* built into phrases like *in spite of the fact that; due to the fact that*, and *apart from the fact that*. The infinitive is used in the same way where a noun is defined as an action of some sort:

The secret of his success is his burning desire to win.
I had a sudden urge to break out laughing.
There is a conspiracy to keep things secret.

Nouns followed by an infinitive include *ability, agreement, chance, order, responsibility* and *way*.

In Section 7.5 we looked at patterns with *about*. When looking at patterns which involve a preposition like *about* followed by N it is important to recognise that N may be the *-ing*-form of a verb:

*He wrote books **about walking in the Lake District**.*

or a noun clause introduced by a WH-word.

*Think **about what you need to do**.*

In some cases, as in the case of adjectives followed by *about*, an *-ing*-form or a noun clause is more likely than a simple noun phrase:

*I'm not sure **about coming** round tomorrow.*
*He wasn't sure **about what he needed to do**.*

A number of nouns are frequently followed by *of* + *-ing*:

> We had no **way of knowing** how to proceed.
> He made the fatal **mistake of underestimating** the opposition.

Again the function of the *-ing*-form is usually to expand on the noun which precedes it.

Gerunds, infinitives, *(that)*-clauses and WH-clauses enable us to define and label propositions and actions and so build them into the discourse. They are common in all forms of English, but they are absolutely central to genres which seek to convey complex information with conciseness and precision. Academic English, business English and newspaper English all have a high incidence of these forms. It is important to draw learners' attention to them, and to the variety of ways in which they are used.

7.6 Making learners aware of lexical phrases

As we saw in Section 2.5, Skehan suggests that we need to have access to lexical phrases to enable us to communicate in real time. If this is the case, then phrases of this kind must be a feature of all languages. In spite of this, there is often a tendency among learners to think of language as being made up of words and to believe that language is processed word by word. From the very earliest days, therefore, teachers should begin to point out phrases and the importance of phrases. Pronunciation practice, for example, should aim to identify phrases like *there is a …* as a consolidated unit, pronounced almost as if it were a single word. The same applies to phrases like *a cup of tea, a piece of cake, a glass of water, I've got a …, Have you got any …?* and so on. Learners can be encouraged to pronounce such phrases as quickly as possible, running the elements together. It is good for them to hear some recordings of speakers of English speaking at normal speed, running words together. All too often the careful enunciation of the language, which learners hear in the early stages, reinforces the notion that English is made up of a series of isolated words.

One way to make learners aware of the importance of lexical phrases in English is to make them aware of the phenomenon in their own language. A teacher who has a good knowledge of the learners' L1 can explain and demonstrate to them this feature of language. This can be underlined at various stages of their study. In looking at clause and sentence connectors, for example, it is useful to ask learners to identify items in their own language which serve the same function. Almost certainly these will include a number of phrases.

We also need to encourage learners to look for themselves for phrases in English text. Whenever they have worked with a text, there are a number of ways of asking them to identify phrases. They can be asked to pick out all the phrases with a particular form or word, as students were asked to pick out *to*-infinitives in the eight-year-old robber text in Teaching Activity 3.3. They may be asked, for example, to pick out all the phrases to do with time or place. In a text which is specifically to do with travel they might be asked to pick out all the phrases to do with movement. Their search may cover more than one text. They may be asked to look at a number of the texts they have processed during their course and pick out phrases with the word *in* or *as*, or any other word which is worth studying.

7.7 Teaching phrases and patterns

One way of helping learners with phrases – polywords, frames and patterns – is to organise them into meaningful groups. The functional syllabuses of the 1970s offer useful ways of organising phrases under functional headings. In Section 9.1.6 we will look at examples of formulaic phrases used in spoken discourse and in Sections 9.2.4 and 9.2.5 we will look at ways of teaching these phrases. We can also group together phrases which relate to particular notions or topics. In Section 7.2 above we listed adverbials of time and place and sentence adverbials. These would be useful notional categories to help learners organise their language.

In Section 4.2.2 we suggested an exercise to focus on partitive expressions like *a bunch of flowers, a glass of water, a bottle of wine, a slice of bread* and so on. This is a structural classification bringing together phrases with the structure *a* (Partitive) *of* N. Many of the phrases can be recycled under the topic food and drink, providing a notional heading. There are, then, a number of ways of organising and recycling phrases.

Teaching Activities 3.3, 3.4, and 3.5 provide an example of how we can call on students to identify and categorise patterns for themselves. In this particular case, there were enough examples of the pattern in one specific text to provide a reasonable picture of the target pattern. Often, this will not be so. It may, however, be possible to ask learners to trawl through two or three texts to enable them to find instances of, for example, patterns with *as*. Another possibility is to share the work by dividing learners into groups and ask each group to look at one or two texts and then pool the results. Each group can then list the phrases they have found and show them to the class on OHTs or pin a list on the classroom wall. Another possibility is for a member of the group to read out the phrases they have found and ask other groups to see how many they can recall.

In Section 7.5.1 above we suggested a way of characterising the preposition *for* in order to pave the way for recognition of patterns with *for*. Teaching Activities 7.1 and 7.2 provide examples of exercises focusing on patterns with *for*. This kind of work might be supplemented by asking learners to keep pages of their vocabulary notebooks dedicated to specific words and forms, and the phrases and patterns associated with them. Again the work can be shared. Students can be divided into groups, and each group may be given responsibility for a set of five or six prepositions so that the class between them can cover the 30 prepositions which account for so many of the patterns of English. Similarly, groups might be given responsibility for collecting phrases based on the *to*-infinitive, or *-ing*-forms, or the word *it*.

The problem with phrases and, to a lesser extent, with patterns is that there are so many of them. There is, therefore, a responsibility on the teacher to keep track of the language that learners have experienced and what they can be expected to learn from that language. Here is an exercise focusing on the pattern N + of + *-ing*:

Teaching Activity 7.3a:

Underline the nouns in these sentences which are followed by *of* + *-ing*.

1. Another way of doing it is to work abroad.
2. I think it's more a question of specialising in the country in which you work.
3. Their first memory of singing together was during their days in the boy scouts.
4. His prayer had been answered and he gave up the idea of committing suicide.
5. I always had this fear of falling down stairs.
6. This would have the twofold effect of getting the job done cheaply and making it safe for local people to cross the river.
7. He took every opportunity of visiting the zoo.
8. So the thought of competing with a three-year-old is quite difficult.
9. It shows how to reduce the risk of falling victim to violent crime.

Commentary on Teaching Activity 7.3a:

The nouns are: *way, question, memory, idea, fear, effect, opportunity, thought, risk.*

All these examples are taken from a coursebook, Willis, J. and D. Willis (1990). They are a part of the language that learners have processed for meaning. This body of language could be described as a **pedagogic corpus**. Grammarians and lexicographers work with a corpus of language, a set of texts, to enable them to describe the grammar and vocabulary of the language. In the same way, learners process a set of texts to enable them to develop their own vocabulary and work out their own grammar of the language. We can describe this set of texts as a pedagogic corpus. Once we see things in this way we can suggest that one of the roles of the teacher and the course designer is to highlight important features of the pedagogic corpus and to help learners familiarise themselves with it.

This exercise could also be done as a listening exercise. Students could be given the instructions and the first sentence as an example. The rest of the sentences could then be read out to them.

Teaching Activity 7.3b:

Listen to the following sentences. What words are followed by *of + -ing?*

1. I think it's more a matter of specialising in the country in which you work.
2. Their first recollection of singing together was during their days in the boy scouts.
3. His prayer had been answered and he gave up the thought of committing suicide.
4. I always had this terror of falling down stairs.
5. So the idea of competing with a three-year-old is quite difficult.
6. It shows how to reduce the possibility of falling victim to violent crime.

Commentary on Teaching Activity 7.3b:

This is a way of extending the range of words used with the target pattern.

The exercises above focus on a pattern. As we have seen, there is some predictability with patterns. Other phrases are less predictable, but it is still possible to draw learners' attention to them as they occur in text, and also to provide exercises summarising what learners have experienced.

Teaching Activity 7.4:

Look at the following sentences. Two words can be used to complete all of these sentences. Which word goes in which sentences?

1. BB: That actually looks like you, doesn't it. Don't you think?
   RS: Yes it does actually. Yeah, it's not _____.
2. EL: Do you get headaches in thunder? Some people get really _____ headaches.
3. If there is a well at the top of the hill there is a _____ chance that there is water at the bottom too.
4. Work together and try to come up with one _____ reason why a normal leopard should turn into a man-eating leopard.
5. .... a medal from South America, given him by his wife for _____ luck.
6. ... being cautious and taking more time is not always such a _____ thing.
7. A _____ deal of mystery surrounds this disappearance.
8. It's perhaps not a very good er basis for friendship between parents and er son-in-law, but I think I would try and make the best of a _____ job there.
9. BB: Offer to provide any more information if they so wish.
   EL: That's a _____ point, yeah.
10. In the real world, a lot of news is _____ news: disasters, wars, crashes and crises.
11. I think a country where flowers grow beautifully is _____ to live in.
12. It's no _____ writing a very detailed economic assessment for a newspaper which is more interested in purely personal stories.
13. EL: But we all thought we were going to crash – I mean, it was really _____.
    BB: It was as _____ as that, was it?
14. I was no _____ at games.
15. Helms himself found that Christmas was not such a _____ time to be alive, after all.

Commentary on Teaching Activity 7.4:

The words are, of course, *good* and *bad*. The word *bad* is used to complete sentences 1, 2, 6, 8, 10, 13, and 15, *good* completes the others.

Again this activity is most effective if it exploits the pedagogic corpus, using examples from texts learners have already encountered or will encounter later in their course.

Many phrases are built round frequent words such as *good* and *bad*. A quick look at dictionary entries for the words *fact* and *point*, for example, will confirm this. It is worth pointing out some of these uses and encouraging learners to use their dictionaries to help them build up a picture of the uses of such words.

Teaching Activity 7.5:

How would you translate the word *strong* into your own language in the following expressions?

strong tea; a strong drink; a strong argument; a strong marriage; a strong team; someone's strong points; a strong wind; a strong leader; a strong stomach; a strong accent; a strong possibility.

Commentary on Teaching Activity 7.5:

This exercise focuses on collocations involving the English word *strong*. It is an attempt to build links between metaphorical patternings in the first language and patternings in English. Obviously, such an exercise will work best with a monolingual class. But you could also try it with a mixed language class, asking them at the end to compare how many different words were used in French, for example, as opposed to Japanese, in order to realise the meanings of *strong* in English.

The same kind of exercise can be usefully done with any frequent word. We saw an example earlier in this chapter in Teaching Activity 7.1 which focused on the word *for*. You could use the technique with any preposition, or with words like *big, little, point, fact, thing* and so on.

7.8 Summary

Pedagogically the main problem with phrases is that there are so many of them. This means that many phrases must be treated as though they were lexical items – they simply have to be learnt. Teachers can help with this task in the same way as they help with the learning of lexis, by organising words under useful headings to assist recall. Phrases can be organised structurally, functionally and notionally to help learners. At an early stage learners should be encouraged to recognise the importance of phrases in English, both by looking at English text and by looking at phrases in their own language.

Many phrases are generated from patterns featuring the most frequent words in the language. Learners should be given the opportunity early on to recognise the general uses of words such as *about* and *for*, paving the way for the recognition and assimilation of patterns at a later stage. It is also important for learners to recognise how patterns follow one another and nest within one another. Particularly important in this regard are patterns which use *to*-infinitives, *-ing*-forms, (*that*)-clauses and WH-clauses to define and expand propositions and actions.

It is useful for learners to identify phrases, including patterns, for themselves. Teachers can help with this by exploiting the pedagogic corpus to devise exercises which help learners familiarise themselves with valuable phrases. There are a number of advantages to using a pedagogic corpus as the basis for exercises. Firstly, by using language which learners have already processed for meaning, you are providing an instant context. A teacher can, if necessary, provide a reference for the examples used. Secondly, because the examples cited are taken from real texts, they tend to come in association with other important features of language. Take, for example, the sentence: *Work together and try to come up with one good reason why a normal leopard should turn into a man-eating leopard*, which was used in Teaching Activity 7.4 above. As well as highlighting the phrase, *one good reason*, this citation reviews other useful phrases: *work together, come up with, reason why, turn into*. It also illustrates an important use of the modal *should*. When we concoct examples for our students we tend to focus simply on the feature of language we want to exemplify. So for *one good reason* a teacher would be likely to offer something like: *Give me one good reason why you are late*. Teachers use such examples because they are simple and do not detract from a focus on the main point. But examples taken from the pedagogic corpus do not need to be simple. They will be readily recognised and understood. It is possible that they may detract from the main point, but, on the other hand, learners are much more likely to recall a citation which has real meaning for them than a decontextualised example which is made up simply to illustrate a language point.

Perhaps the most important reason for using the pedagogic corpus, however, is that it sends learners the right kind of message. Teacher-controlled and teacher-concocted examples increase the learner's dependence on the teacher. They tell learners: *Your teacher is the guide and mentor, who will show you what to learn and how to learn it. Listen to your teacher and do as you are told. Then you will learn.* By recycling language, which is familiar to them, we tell learners: *Look at this. You have valuable experience of the English language. If you look at that experience and use it, then you will learn from it.* This is a way of encouraging learners' curiosity and self-reliance.

8 Class: The interlevel

8.1 Grammar and lexis

We argued in Chapter 2 that there are classes of word which relate to all aspects of grammar. The whole basis of pattern grammar is that patterns relate to groups or classes of words which share meanings. Class also relates to structure and orientation. As they acquire the language, learners observe regularities in the language, and which words in the language are associated with those regularities. They go on to allocate those words to classes according to their meaning and use, and go on from this to form hypotheses about the behaviour of other words. In putting together phrases, clauses and sentences we draw not only on the basic rules governing clause and phrase structure, but also on the behaviour of individual words.

Once we see language from this perspective then lexis and the behaviour and patterning of individual words assume an enormous importance. And if we accept this, then the concept of class becomes central both to language description and to language learning. It is this concept of class which provides a link between grammar and lexis. When we learn words we also need to learn about their behaviour, their place in structure and the way they pattern with other words.

In Chapters 4 to 7 we have looked at different aspects of grammar – structure, orientation and pattern. As we have done this, we have looked at words and phrases which fulfil particular functions and, very often, at ways of classifying those words. Much of this chapter will review what has been said in earlier chapters, looking explicitly at the notion of class as the interlevel between grammar and lexis.

8.2 Class and structure

In Section 4.1 in Chapter 4 we looked at the sentence, *He asked me to tell Jean that he wanted to know if she was free on Monday*, to demonstrate how a sentence is made up of a series of patterns: *He asked → me to tell → Jean that he wanted → to know → if she was → free (on Monday)*. In this case, the verbs are central to the way the sentence develops. The verb *asked*, meaning request, predicts the pattern N + *to*-infinitive. In turn, the verb *wanted* predicts either a noun phrase, or *to*-infinitive, or N + *to*-infinitive. The verb *was* could be followed by a range of patterns such as an adverbial (*at home*), a noun (*the winner*) or an adjective (*free*). This suggests that clause structure is a product of the choices that are made in terms of words. At each stage the verb selected constrains the possibilities that follow. It also suggests that we compose messages in chunks. In producing, *He asked*, with the meaning of requesting an action, a speaker must have the intention of following this with N + *to*-infinitive. In selecting the verb *tell*, the speaker has the intention of reporting a statement of some kind. So the message unfolds piece by piece rather than word by word.

The same kind of predictability often applies to the structure of phrases. The 'sentence', *He expressed the view*, has the appearance of being grammatically complete, made up of a subject, a verb and an object. It is, however, fairly obviously, incomplete as an utterance. The word *view* demands some kind of expansion. Once we get this expansion: *He expressed the view **that the government must take responsibility***, there is a sense of completeness. So phrases, in this case a noun phrase, also have a measure of predictability.

8.2.1 Clause structure

We have suggested more than once that clause and phrase structure are best seen as sequences of patterns rather than sequences of words. The verbs *give, bring* and *send*, for example, all figure in the pattern V + N + N – they are all commonly followed by a double object structure. The basic structure of a clause featuring one of these verbs is likely to be N (subject) + V + N + N. The important insight of pattern grammar is that the words associated with a particular pattern can be allocated to groups, or classes, according to their meaning. So it is not only the verbs *give, bring* and *send* that are followed by two nouns. They are representatives of classes of verbs to do with transferring (*give, hand, lend, pass, promise* etc.) or to do with providing a service of some kind (*bring, buy, cook, fetch, find, get, make* etc.) or with communicating messages (*ask, post, send, teach, tell, write* etc.).

The verb *look*, meaning *appear* or *seem*, is a **link verb**. This means it can be followed by an adjectival phrase: *You look very tired*. Most link verbs can be followed by a noun phrase acting as a complement. The verb states some sort of equivalence between the subject of the verb and the complement:

> *Tokyo is a vast city.*
> *Britain remains a democracy.*

But *look* is also a member of a small subset of link verbs (*feel, look, smell, sound, taste*), which are followed not simply by a noun but by the preposition *like* followed by a noun:

> *He looks just like his father.*
> *It smells like rotten eggs.*

We can classify *look*, then, as a link verb and also as a member of a subclass of link verbs, those to do with the senses, found with the pattern V *like* N.

Thus, the structure of the clause relates to the verb it features, and we can predict that structure by allocating verbs to classes according to their meaning. We recognise the meaning of a verb, the class to which it belongs, and the patterns associated with that class. This is how basic clauses are built, and, as we saw in Teaching Activities 3.3, 3.4 and 3.5 in Chapter 3, it is important to help learners by identifying the frequent members of each class of verb and drawing them together. Learning develops according to the processes we outlined in the Commentary on Teaching Activity 3.5.

Basic clause structure is determined by verbs and their associated patterns. But many clauses also feature adjuncts or adverbials. In Section 4.1.1.2 we looked briefly at the positioning of adverbials in the clause. This can be varied in order to achieve a particular emphasis, but the usual position for most classes of adverb is at the end of the clause. This applies to adverbials of manner:

> *Everyone sat down **quietly**.*

and to adverbial phrases of time and place:

> *We hope to meet **at six thirty**.*
> *There is a huge oak tree **at the bottom of the garden**.*

But some adverbials behave differently. Adverbs of frequency, for example, are normally found immediately in front of the main verb:

> *Adverbs of frequency are **normally** found in front of the main verb.*
> *I have **never** been here before.*

There is another class of adverbials which are normally found at the front of the clause. These are known as **sentence adverbials** and express some attitude to the clause which follows (*fortunately, luckily, naturally, of course, sadly, surprisingly, suddenly* etc.).

Fortunately *we were ready for anything.*
Suddenly *there was a loud bang.*

Similar to sentence adverbials are adverbials used to change topic or emphasis in conversation (*actually, anyway, well* etc.). These too tend to come first in their clause. Some learners have particular difficulties with adverbs of degree, tending to place them between the verb and its object:

I enjoyed **very much the party.*
I admire **greatly your father's work.*

Adverbs belonging to this class (*completely, enormously, nearly, perfectly, well* etc.) are, like most adverbials, normally found at the end of the clause:

*I enjoyed the party **very much**.*

although most of them can also come in front of the main verb:

*I **greatly** admire your father's work.*

Students will go through the usual stages in building up their knowledge of how adverbials fit in the structure of the clause:

- **Improvisation:** Most learners will probably develop a usable system with little prompting from the teacher. They may begin to recognise that most adverbials come at the end of the clause and they may adopt a strategy like putting adverbials at the front of the clause for emphasis.
- **Recognition:** It is worth pointing out the general rule that most adverbials come at the end of the sentence. It is also worthwhile highlighting classes of adverbials which are exceptions to this rule, such as adverbs of frequency and sentence adverbials, and grouping the most frequent members of these classes together systematically. This can be done by asking students to suggest as many ways as possible of filling a gap in a sentence. At the same time, it will be necessary to point out particular mistakes, such as **I enjoyed very much the party.* Since the positioning of adverbials can vary so much there is no way that learners can identify such errors without teacher correction.
- **System building:** Learners begin to organise words into classes according to their meaning, and to recognise how adverbs of different classes typically fit into clause structure.
- **Exploration:** The positioning of adverbials for emphasis can only be learnt from seeing the system at work in context. Students can

usefully do reconstruction exercises like the one below (Teaching Activity 8.2). They can also look at sentences taken from previously studied texts and replace the adverbials (see Teaching Activity 8.3).

Teaching Activity 8.1:

How many words can you think of to replace the word *always* in the following sentence?

> *I always get up early in the morning.*

Use these words to make sentences that are true for you:

    1. I _____ do my homework on time.
    2. I _____ speak English at the weekend.
    3. I _____ go to the cinema during the week.
    4. I _____ use a computer.
    5. I _____ do the cooking at home.

Can you remember what your classmates said?

Commentary on Teaching Activity 8.1:

Students at the elementary level will probably come up with a range of adverbs of frequency, such as *sometimes, never* and *always*. After the first part of the activity you may want to supplement their list by adding useful items they have omitted, such as *seldom* and *hardly ever*. You may also want to introduce phrases like *nearly always* and *quite often*.

    You can introduce an element of memory work by asking a group of five or six students to come to the front of the class. They then make true statements based on sentence 1, for example, and other members of the class try to remember what each of them said.

    After completing the activity, you may ask students to work in groups to see who can produce the longest list of adverbials of frequency.

It is possible to devise exercises of this kind for other classes of adverbial.

Teaching Activity 8.2:

1. Go through the text and underline all the phrases to do with time.

I got up at 7.30 and had my usual cup of coffee and a couple of slices of toast. Since my sister died I've had various people staying in her room. At the moment I have an old friend from University staying, so I usually take him a cup of coffee in the morning. Then I went straight into the office in time for a meeting on marketing policy.

At 12.30 I took some time off to go to an exhibition at the National Gallery. I had a quick sandwich for lunch and then I went to Head Office for another meeting.

In the evening I went to see a film at my local cinema. I got home at about ten o'clock and realised my flat badly needed cleaning. I had friends coming round for breakfast the next morning, so I stayed up until about 2 a.m., scrubbing floors and dusting furniture.

2. Now the time phrases have been removed from the passage. Here they are listed in the same order as they occur in the passage. Can you put them back in the right places?

at 7.30 – at the moment – usually – in the morning – then – in time – at 12.30 – then – in the evening – at about ten o'clock – the next morning – until about 2 a.m.

I got up and had my usual cup of coffee and a couple of slices of toast. Since my sister died I've had various people staying in her room. I have an old friend from University staying, so I take him a cup of coffee. I went straight into the office for a meeting on marketing policy.

I took some time off to go to an exhibition at the National Gallery. I had a quick sandwich for lunch and I went to Head Office for another meeting.

I went to see a film at my local cinema. I got home and realised my flat badly needed cleaning. I had friends coming round for breakfast, so I stayed up scrubbing floors and dusting furniture.

Commentary on Teaching Activity 8.2:

Students will already have processed the text for meaning before being asked to identify the time phrases. The first part of the activity highlights the form of time phrases, particularly the use (or the omission) of prepositions. It will also prepare them for the second part of the activity, which looks at the place of the adverbials in their clauses.

During their discussion and in their solution to the second part of the activity students will probably suggest a number of other positions for the time adverbials. This will provide opportunities for class discussion and, where necessary, for correction.

Teaching Activity 8.3: (For this activity it is necessary to go back through texts the students have studied previously and pick out examples of the grammatical feature you want to highlight.)

You have seen all these sentences before. Can you remember where the words in brackets go in each sentence?

1. EL: I was just, erm, going up north in a bus to Durham and er, it was absolutely pitch black outside and really pelting down. *(last week)*
2. But the Government denied this. *(only yesterday)*
3. Eight children died, and many were injured, as fire swept through a hospital in Paris. *(early yesterday)*
4. Italian concert violinist Luigi Alberto Bianci paid a world record price of four hundred and forty thousand at Christie's in London for the Stradivarius Colossus violin. *(yesterday)*
5. Patchy rain will move north turning to sleet in parts of North Wales, the Midlands and East Anglia and turning to snow over much of Northern Ireland. *(tomorrow morning)*
6. We hope we have made up for our earlier error, a board spokesman said. *(yesterday)*
7. Jaguar's American subsidiary reported that US sales had collapsed in April. *(yesterday)*
8. A strike by Madrid underground workers demanding a pay rise cut the number of morning rush hour trains by half, affecting an estimated one million people. *(yesterday)*
9. A car bomb exploded in a central bazaar of the Afghan capital, Kabul, and another loud blast was heard across the city. *(on Tuesday)(yesterday)*

Commentary on Teaching Activity 8.3:

This activity illustrates another advantage of exploiting the pedagogic corpus (see Section 7.8). Learners are asked to recall

---

where an adverbial actually occurred in a particular text. This means that there is an 'answer' to the problem. Of course it is unlikely, though not impossible, that they will be able to recall texts with this amount of detail. They may, however, pick up clues from the citations themselves. In sentence 2, for example, the use of the modifier *only* suggests that the speaker wishes to emphasise the timing of the denial. If it is to be emphatic, it is more likely to be at the beginning of the sentence than in the standard position at the end. The discussion generated by acceptable but 'wrong' answers will be valuable.

1. EL: I was just, erm, going up north in a bus to Durham **last week** and er, it was absolutely pitch black outside and really pelting down.
2. But **only yesterday** the Government denied this.
3. Eight children died, and many were injured, as fire swept through a hospital in Paris **early yesterday.**
4. Italian concert violinist Luigi Alberto Bianci paid a world record price of four hundred and forty thousand at Christie's in London **yesterday** for the Stradivarius Colossus violin.
5. **Tomorrow morning** patchy rain will move north turning to sleet in parts of North Wales, the Midlands and East Anglia and turning to snow over much of Northern Ireland.
6. We hope we have made up for our earlier error, a board spokesman said **yesterday.**
7. Jaguar's American subsidiary reported **yesterday** that US sales had collapsed in April.
8. A strike by Madrid underground workers demanding a pay rise **yesterday** cut the number of morning rush hour trains by half, affecting an estimated one million people.
9. A car bomb exploded in a central bazaar of the Afghan capital, Kabul, **on Tuesday,** and **yesterday** another loud blast was heard across the city.

Adverbs can, then, be classified according to the function they fulfil and their usual position in structure. As we have seen, there is a small, but interesting class of adverbs which are sometimes called **broad negative** adverbs (*barely; hardly; never; rarely; scarcely* and *seldom*). They are normally found in front of the verb:

I could hardly believe my eyes.
You seldom see him nowadays.

If, however, the verb is the simple present or simple past tense of the verb *BE*, the adverb comes after the verb:

> *She is barely six months old.*
> *The office was hardly ever empty.*

At an advanced level learners may need to know that these adverbs can come at the beginning of a clause, but that, when they do, they have drastic effects: the verb and the auxiliary are inverted.

Seldom have I seen such incompetence.

> *Seldom have I seen such incompetence.*
> *Hardly had we reached safety when the avalanche struck.*

Alternatively, an auxiliary *DO* must be supplied.

> *Rarely do you find such an abundance of animals in this area.*

We will have to make teaching decisions at each stage about how much learners need to know about a class of words. At an intermediate stage they need to be aware that broad negative adverbs come before the verb or after the verb *BE*. These words occur very frequently in these positions; only rarely are they found at the beginning of the clause. We may therefore postpone giving or highlighting this information until students have reached an advanced level.

The structure of the clause, therefore, depends firstly on the verb and its associated patterns, and secondly on the position of the adverbials in the clause. The position of the adverbial depends on the class of that adverbial, though it may vary according to whether or not the writer wants to place some emphasis on it.

8.2.2 Class and the structure of the noun phrase

In Section 4.2 in Chapter 4 we looked at the structure of the noun phrase. In doing so we identified a number of elements. We can regard each element as containing a class of words. When looking at quantifiers we were able to identify a closed set of items consisting of around 30 words which provides a fairly comprehensive system of quantifiers. We also identified measurers, which we subdivided into a number of categories. We identified partitives of location (*beginning, end, middle, back, front* etc.) and time (*beginning, end, middle* etc.), which feature in the frame *the* + partitive + *of* + *the*. We also identified quantitatives found with uncountable nouns: *bit, piece, item*, and specific partitives, such as *a loaf of bread, a column of smoke, a sheet of paper, a gust of wind*. Other classes of partitive are containers (*a bottle of, a box of* etc.) and measurements (*a kilo of, a pint of, a quarter of* and so on). We also looked at adjectives and at intensifiers, words like *absolutely, almost, fairly, quite* and *thoroughly*, which are used to modify adjectives.

It is possible to classify nouns in the same way, according to how they behave. They can, for example, be classified as countable and uncountable. It is then possible gradually to build up a list of the most frequent uncountable nouns, those that learners are most likely to need. There is a smaller class of **plural nouns**, which have only a plural form. For example, you can buy and sell *goods*, but you cannot buy *a good*. One group of plural nouns refers to clothes or implements which are made up of two matching parts. Again, we can identify and list those most likely to be needed by learners, for example *glasses, trousers, tights, pyjamas, jeans, trainers* and *scissors*.

What is happening here is that we are identifying the elements of structure in the noun phrase. Each element constitutes a class of words. For each class we can go on to classify the members. In some cases, for quantifiers or general partitives for example, we can list all of the members. In other cases, as with specific partitives, it is possible to list the most frequently used members of the class and link them to their associated nouns, as was done in Teaching Activity 4.3. Nouns themselves can be classified according to their behaviour. We begin with the potential for the noun phrases, in terms of structure, then go on to show what class of words may be used to complete each element of structure.

One of the most complex features of the noun phrase is the way in which nouns can be postmodified. We looked at postmodification in Section 4.2.4. There are, as we have seen, nouns which are frequently followed by a clause introduced by *that*. We looked at one of these noun phrases above in Section 8.2: *He expressed **the view that the government must take responsibility**.* For such nouns the *that*-clause provides some sort of definition or description of an otherwise empty noun (*appearance, case, effect, fact, grounds, problem*). Many of these nouns can be characterised as having to do with saying (*argument, claim,* *complaint, demand, explanation, promise, rule, suggestion* etc.) or thinking and feeling (*belief, fear, feeling, idea, impression, knowledge, suspicion, theory, view* etc.) or possibility (*chance, danger, hope, possibility, probability, risk*). When one of these nouns occurs, it needs to be defined, and the most frequent way of defining is a *that*-clause. So a noun phrase featuring one of these nouns is likely to be a complex phrase involving a postmodifying *that*-clause:

> There is always *a risk that you will lose everything.*

In the same way we can identify nouns which are frequently followed by a *to*-infinitive or by *of* + *-ing* (see Teaching Activity 7.3). And a large number of patterns involve the postmodification of nouns by a phrase with a particular preposition. We looked, for example, at nouns which are typically followed by *about*: nouns denoting items which communicate like *book, programme, story* and *article*, and nouns denoting acts of communication like *advice, agreement, information* and *opinion*. The rules governing the structure of the noun phrase (see Section 4.2) set out what is possible in the language, the grammar of class helps us to identify what is probable or typical in the language. Any noun can be postmodified. Particular nouns are likely to be postmodified in particular ways.

It is, therefore, possible to build up the noun phrase in terms of classes. We have classes of quantifier and partitive which come in front of the noun. We can classify adjectives of *size, shape, age* and *colour* (see Section 4.2.3). This helps to determine where they appear relative to one another. Adjectives are modified by words which we classified as **intensifiers** and **mitigators** (see Section 4.2.3). After the noun we have nouns which are likely to be postmodified in particular ways identified by pattern grammar. As the interlevel the grammar of class spells out the potential of individual words and the way they build up larger units.

8.3 Class and orientation

The grammar of orientation relates information to the real world. The verb phrase works together with adverbials to locate an action in the past, present or future. It tells us if an action or state is to be seen as temporary, or if it is relevant to the present or to a specific time in the past or future. The determiner system in the noun phrase is one of the devices which enables us to organise information and to relate entities in the discourse to the outside world. The definite determiners tell us that an entity can be identified by the listener or reader. An indefinite determiner signals that an entity cannot be identified or does not need to be identified. In Section 6.3 we listed a number of devices which are used for organising text so that it moves in a way easily accessible to the reader, usually from known to unknown, from given to new.

In looking at the relationship between class and orientation we need to look at classes of verb, which use the tense system in particular ways, and at adverbials which help to signal the orientation of the verb phrase. We will then go on to look at the classification of text organising devices.

8.3.1 Class and the verb phrase

There are some verbs, often referred to as stative verbs, which are rarely found in the continuous tenses. These can be classified as follows:

Being: *be, exist, consist of* etc.
Mental state: *believe, forget, imagine, know, realise, recognise, suppose, think, understand, want, wish* etc.
Liking/disliking: *dislike, hate, like, love, prefer* etc.
Possession: *belong to, contain, have, include, own* etc.
Appearance: *appear, look, seem, smell, sound, taste* etc.

This is a relatively small class of verbs, but these verbs feature very prominently in text because the list includes some of the most frequently occurring verbs in English, notably *be* and *have*. There is a further sub-class of stative verbs consisting of verbs of perception: *hear, see, smell* and *taste*. When these verbs are used to refer to the here and now they are usually found with the modal *can*.

In Section 5.3.4 I drew attention to the use of the present continuous to express an action or event which is happening here and now. This is the first use that learners generally encounter. It may be a useful generalisation as a starting point, but it can lead learners into error and confusion. They are led into error because they make sensible but false generalisations, so that they produce sentences like: **I am having two sisters*, or **I am liking the picture*. They may be confused by the fact that they are constantly given input which challenges the generalisation. They may hear someone say, *This pencil belongs to me*, when they expect **This pencil is belonging to me*, or *I prefer that book* when they expect **I am preferring that book*.

The problem is compounded by the fact that most of these stative verbs are sometimes seen or heard in the continuous tenses. This is because they are used with a different meaning:

We are having a party. (*have* here means *celebrate* or *organise*)
You're being silly. (*be* here means *behaving in a particular way*)
Be quiet, I'm thinking. (*think* here denotes a deliberate, active process rather than a mental state)

The problem is how do we deal with this conflicting input. We can consider this problem by looking at language use and language learning processes summarised in Section 1.5:

- **Improvisation:** Learners are unlikely to have problems in understanding the standard forms even if their own grammar varies from this. They will, for example, understand someone who says, *That pencil belongs to me*, even if their own preferred form would be, *That pencil is belonging to me*. Similarly, they will be readily understood if they say, *I am not seeing the blackboard*, rather than, *I can't see the blackboard*.

- **Recognition:** It is worth correcting utterances, such as *This ... is belonging to me*, by simply saying, 'We don't normally use *belong* in the present continuous'. It is certainly worth providing a model for *I can see* as opposed to *I am seeing*. If learners continue to have problems with these forms it may well be worth bringing these verbs together in the way I have done above.

- **System building:** It is worth at some stage bringing these words together and commenting on their behaviour. But we should bear in mind that these verbs are not actually exceptions at all. It is not surprising that they are not normally found in the continuous tenses – it is because they refer to states rather than actions or events. This is a point which should be made when listing the verbs as apparent exceptions.

- **Exploration:** It is worth highlighting specific examples of these verbs as they occur in text. They can provide the focus for grammaticisation exercises, or they may simply be pointed out in passing. What we need to recognise is that the apparently unusual behaviour of these verbs is not highly significant in itself. It is significant because it may distort the learner's growing picture of the tense system as a whole. Teacher intervention, therefore, should be aimed at illuminating the system as a whole rather than simply at these specific verbs.

Some verbs, on the other hand, are very frequently found in the continuous forms. Although the simple tenses are ten times as frequent as the continuous forms, Biber *et al.* (2002: 163) list verbs which occur over 80 per cent of the time in continuous aspect:

activity/physical verbs: *bleed, chase, shop, starve*
communication verbs: *chat, joke, kid, moan*

And others which occur over 50 per cent of the time as continuous forms:

> activity verbs: *dance, drip, head (for), march, pound, rain, stream, sweat.*
> communication verbs: *scream, talk.*
> mental/attitude verbs: *look forward, study.*

Corpus studies of the language are uncovering more and more tendencies of this kind which associate particular words with particular grammatical forms. This type of information has obvious input in helping to decide what forms of a word to highlight as typical.

In a fully developed grammatical system the verb phrase is the primary means of expressing time relationships, but adverbials play an important part too, and it is worth relating particular classes of adverbial to the meanings carried by the verb. We use the continuous tenses, for example, to express temporariness, among other things. Adverbials associated with temporariness in present time are: *at present, for the time being, for now, just now.* Temporariness in past time is expressed by: *at the time, at that time, for the time being, just then.*

Many language courses and pedagogic grammars associate adverbs of frequency with the simple tenses, particularly the present simple. Sometimes the use of adverbs of frequency with the present continuous is explicitly ruled out. However, as we pointed out in Section 5.2, these adverbs can be found with all tense forms, including the present continuous. Some adverbs of frequency, for example, are often found with a particular use of the perfective tenses. When we are talking about experience up to an established time we may say, *I've never been to New York.* We may also enumerate our experience saying, *I've been to San Francisco twice.* It is worth drawing this class of adverbs together and looking at their behaviour. One way of recycling the use of tense forms is by looking at the way they are used with different classes of time adverbial.

Many English courses spend a good deal of time contrasting two ways of expressing duration:

> *We have lived in Cumbria **for seven years**.*
> *We have lived in Cumbria **since 1996**.*

These forms are strongly associated with the present perfect tense, and there is often an implication that they are not found with the past simple, which is taken as standing in contrast to the present perfect. But this is mistaken. Phrases and clauses with *since* are closely associated with the present or past perfect and, in British English at any rate, are not found with the past simple. But phrases of duration with *for* can be found with any tense form:

> *We lived in Birmingham for ten years.*
> *I will be on holiday for two weeks.*

It is certainly useful to classify adverbs and adverb phrases, and to look at the way they are used with particular verb forms. In some cases we will be able to make statements associating particular adverbials with particular tense forms. Phrases and clauses with *since*, for example, are associated with the perfective forms. They are not found with other forms of the verb. The same applies, in British English, to the adverb *yet*. Conversely, adverbs which refer exclusively to past time – *yesterday, last week, ___ ago* etc. – are not found with the present perfect tense.

Adverbials, therefore, are useful ways of focusing on and illuminating tense forms. In a few cases it is possible to offer secure generalisations about the association between adverbs and particular tense forms, between *yet* and the perfect tenses, for example. More often however, adverbs provide an opportunity to recycle tense forms and encourage learners to think about their meaning and use.

8.3.2 Class and the organisation of information

In Section 6.3 I listed eight devices for organising text and gave examples for each category. Since these devices are used to organise text, it is important to highlight them as they occur in the texts learners experience. As learners become more experienced in handling English text, it is useful to bring together examples of these devices. Teaching Activity 6.1 in Section 6.3, which focuses on clefts and similar devices, provides an example. We listed sets of words used to mark contrast: *actually, in fact, in point of fact, as a matter of fact, in reality, in practice, really.* We could equally well have listed words and phrases to mark addition: *also, as well, besides, in addition, moreover, too, not only ... but also.*

We noted the importance of phrases like: *the thing is that ...; the problem is that ...; the best way is to ...; one proposal was to ...; this technique ....* This highlights the importance of general words used to refer back to elements of text. These words are particularly important when language is used to organise information in order to argue a case or offer an explanation. They assume a great importance in academic English, for example.

There are classes of verb which behave in particular ways to allow flexibility in the way text is organised. One of the eight devices we noted was the metaphorical use of words. As an example we cited the clause: *The cost prohibited covering the two reservoirs ...* Strictly speaking, only people can prohibit things but the language allows us to use words metaphorically, and in this case the word *cost* is used as the subject of the verb *prohibited*. One class of verbs which behaves in this way is **ergative verbs**. These verbs are like passive verbs in that 'the same verb can be used transitively, followed by the object, or intransitively, without the original performer being mentioned'. We can say, for example:

He closed the door behind him.
I rang the bell.

or

The door closed behind him.
The bell rang.

Sinclair's (1990) grammar lists these verbs and allocates many of them to specific topic areas:

Cookery: *bake, boil, cook, fry.*
Movement: *drop, move, turn.*
Change: *begin, open, dry, shut.*

The class of reciprocal verbs offers a number of possibilities. We can say, for example:

John hugged Mary.
Mary hugged John.
John and Mary hugged.
John and Mary hugged one another.

Each of these would have a slightly different emphasis and might be employed according to the way the text needs to be structured. Common reciprocal verbs are: *fight, meet* and *kiss.* Some reciprocal verbs, such as *agree, disagree, quarrel* and *mix*, must take the preposition *with* before the phrase *each other* or *one another.*

There is a very common class of verb known as **delexical verbs**. The commonest delexical verbs are *give, take, have, make* and *do.* They are used delexically when they depend for their meaning on the noun which accompanies them, as in:

*They were **having a drink**.*
*I **had** a quick **shower**.*

Typically, these verbs are followed by the indefinite article and a given noun. One of the important uses for delexical verbs is to enable us to add information by using an adjective in front of the noun. The forms:

> *He gave an interesting lecture.*
> *I had a quick shower.*

are much more likely than the forms:

> *He lectured interestingly.*
> *I showered quickly.*

So, if we want to comment on an action by describing it in some way, we can make use of a delexical verb.

There are things teachers and materials writers can do to help learners realise the potential of classes of verb like these. We can draw attention to them as they occur in text, we can summarise their behaviour and use and we can list the most frequently occurring items, those which students are most likely to meet outside the classroom.

8.4 Summary: Class and the lexical syllabus

There have been a number of proposals for a lexically based syllabus, notably Sinclair and Renouf (1988), Willis (1990) and Lewis (1993). O'Dell (1997) cites these three sources, and comments that: 'There is now an increasing tendency to give pride of place in the EFL syllabus to lexis, rather than grammar, notions or functions'. If we accept the following premises we can see why syllabuses should be built round lexis:

- Basic clause structure is very simple: N + V + ? The complications in clause structure arise from the patterns associated with particular verbs, and from the positioning of adverbials within the clause. Verbs can be allocated to classes according to the patterns they are associated with. Similarly, adverbials can be allocated to classes according to their position within the clause.
- The structure of the verb phrase and the noun phrase are fixed. But the realisation of the structure of the noun phrase, particularly post-modification, depends on the noun which is central to the phrase. Particular nouns are likely to be postmodified in particular ways. These nouns can be identified and allocated to classes.

- The first stage in learning is improvisation, which is lexically based. Learners tend to string together words and phrases and to build the grammatical system gradually as increasing demands are made on their communicative system.
- The acquisition of the grammar of orientation depends heavily on exploration. Teachers can provide useful guidelines to help learners with the selection of verb tense. Similarly teachers can provide guidelines for the use of the article system and for the use of devices which enable us to organise text in a receiver-friendly way. But if they are to develop workable systems of orientation, learners need plenty of opportunities to explore text and see for themselves how these systems operate.

Thus, language learning is mainly a matter of learning the meanings and uses of words and phrases. As learners become acquainted with words and phrases, they begin to work with them and allocate them to classes. At the same time, they are gradually building up the ability to deploy these words and phrases in a way which is receiver-friendly. This receiver-friendliness depends firstly on how explicitly the message is related to the outside world by the systems of verb tense and the use of determiners, and secondly on how linguistic items are used to allow the message to develop in a predictable way, generally from given to new. Teachers can help learners to develop appropriate systems by highlighting them in text (recognition) and by pointing to regularities in the way they are organised (system building), but the whole process must be kick-started by the acquisition of lexis. As lexis is acquired, so it is possible to expose learners to more and more texts, and provide more and more opportunities for exploration.

9 The grammar of spoken English

9.1 Spoken and written language: Some differences

Here is an extract from a discussion between two people talking about their fear of heights. It contains several features which are common in spoken English, but unusual or non-existent in written English.

1. CB: I don't particularly like heights. Erm. Heights, er, at the top of a mountain, or a hill, where it's possible to fall. Erm, the top of something like a lighthouse or something I don't mind, because there's a barrier around you. But heights where you think you may be able to fall.

2. BB: Yeah. I was okay until I had a rather nasty experience about er, height. Until then I was okay. I could go anywhere. But er, I was er, on a lighthouse actually. We were being taken round it. We went up all the stairs and to the light, er, room. And then the chap says 'Oh, come on. Right, we'll go out here.' I went through the door. And I was on this very very narrow little parapet ...

3. CB: Yeah.

4. BB: ... with a rail about – perhaps eighteen inches high ...

5. CB: Mm.

6. BB: ... and then a sheer drop of about a hundred feet or something. I was absolutely petrified. I've never been as scared like that before or since.

7. CB: That's very frightening.

8. BB: And, you know, I sort of edged round. I couldn't go back through the same door. I edged round and managed to find the other door. And that's it. Ever since then if I go up a ladder I'm scared stiff now. It really is, it's er, changed my whole life, you know. Absolutely frightening, that.

Task 9.1:

Look at the dialogue above and answer these questions:

1. Look at turns 1 and 2. There are several occurrences of *er* and *erm*. What function do you think these noises serve?
2. Why do the speakers say *something like a lighthouse **or** something; I **sort of** edged round*?
3. In turn 2 BB says, *I was okay until I had a rather nasty experience about er, height. Until then I was okay.* Why does he repeat himself?
4. Are there any words in turn 2 which you would not expect to find in written English?
5. What is unusual about the structure of the sentence, *The top of something like a lighthouse or something I don't mind*?
6. How many sentences are there in turn 1?
7. What is the verb in the last sentence in turn 8?
8. Is turn 6 grammatical?
9. At turns 3, 5 and 7, CB actually interrupts the narrative. Is she being rude?
10. It is often said that you should not start a sentence with *and* or *but*. How many sentences in this extract start with *and* or *but*? Why do you think this is?
11. What is unusual about the final sentence in turn 1?

1. Most spoken discourse is composed in real time. Speakers are working out what they want to say and producing language at the same time. This is no simple task. It is not surprising that even native speakers sometimes need time to gather their thoughts. So one of the functions of *er* and *erm* is to allow time for them to do this. Very often the *er/erm* occurs just after a possible completion point, a point at which the speaker may be seen to have finished a turn. This may well be the cause for the following:

> I don't particularly like heights. **Erm.** Heights, er, at the top of a mountain, or a hill, where it's possible to fall. **Erm**, the top of something like a lighthouse or something I don't mind ...

*Er*s and *erm*s are often referred to as 'fillers', as though they had no meaning or function, but they clearly serve a purpose. *Er/erm* often means 'Please let me continue. I haven't finished what I want to say, and I'd like a little time to gather my thoughts.'

Often you will hear *er/erm* at the beginning of a turn in response to a question. Here it means something like: 'Yes, I have heard your question and I intend to answer it. Please allow me a moment to work out my response.' It is misleading to think of *er*s and *erm*s as being without meaning or function. Hardly anything in language is there without a good reason.

2. The phrases *or something* and *sort of* are examples of what is often called **vague language**. Again, because spoken language is produced in real time, we sometimes don't have time to find the exact word or phrase that we want. We acknowledge this by using vague language. You will sometimes hear people, often teachers, complaining about this, saying that we should be more precise with the language we use. But vagueness is a common feature of spoken language. Everybody uses it – even the people who complain about it when they notice it being used by others. If you use a lot of vague language while delivering a prepared lecture, then you might rightly be criticised for not having prepared carefully enough. But if you are speaking spontaneously, you will certainly find yourself relying very often on vague language.

3. There is often repetition in spoken English. When we are reading we can go back over the script if we have not understood what has been said. Obviously we cannot reread spoken language, so the speaker often builds in redundancy by repeating parts of the message. In this case, the speaker even goes on to say, *I could go anywhere*, which is simply a further explanation of what he meant by *I was okay*.

4. The words *okay* and *chap* are much more likely to be found in informal speech than in writing. There are a number of words and phrases like this: *kids* for *children*; *guy, fellow, bloke* for *man*; *Mum and Dad* for *mother and father*; *loads of* or *heaps of* for *a lot of*. There will certainly be forms like this in the learners' first language too. We also have the word *yeah* which fulfils an interactive function, which is not found in written language.

5. The object of the verb (*the top of something like a lighthouse or something*) comes at the beginning of the sentence. Normally we would expect, *I don't mind the top of something like a lighthouse*. In spoken English we quite commonly put the topic of the sentence at the front and then go on to say something about it.

6. If by a sentence we mean something which starts with a capital letter and ends with a full stop, then the turn has been transcribed as five sentences. One of these is simply *Erm*. Presumably this is because there was a definite pause before and after it. Leaving aside *Erm* there are four sentences. But two of these: *Heights, er, at the top of a mountain, or a hill, where it's possible to fall*, and *But heights where you think you may be able to fall*, are not sentences according to the normal definition. Again this is not unusual in spoken English. There is no problem in under-standing these two non-sentences, and we certainly cannot describe them as ungrammatical. In fact when we are speaking we are not thinking of producing sentences at all, we are thinking of putting together units of meaning. Many of these units will be in the form of sentences. Some of them will not.

7. There is no verb. Again this utterance, *Absolutely frightening, that*, is not a sentence according to the criteria usually applied to written English. In spoken English we often leave out elements which can be easily understood. It is easy enough to expand this statement to its full form: *That was absolutely frightening*. This draws attention to the fact that the word *that*, which is the subject of the full form, is found not at the beginning, but at the end of the shortened form. This has the effect of highlighting the evaluation, *Absolutely frightening*, and of making it very prominent. The apparent ungrammaticality is in fact stylistically very effective.

8. Turn 6 contains the sentence, *I've never been as scared like that before or since*, which is certainly unusual and probably un-grammatical. The speaker was probably in two minds as to whether to say, *I've never been scared like that before*, or *I've never been as scared as that before*. Under the pressure of real time production he fell between two stools and produced a mixture of the two. Lapses of this kind are not unusual in spoken language. We have all heard people say things like *Not in the sleast*, a mixture between *Not in the least* and *Not in the slightest*.

9. CB is showing a polite interest in what BB has to say. Her interventions should not be seen as interruptions. As we listen to someone speaking we are expected to comment briefly to show that we are listening with interest. We may do this with a single word like *really?*, *mm*, or *right*, but we often make an

evaluative comment like, *That's very frightening,* or *That's amazing* or *That's awful.*

10. There are two sentences beginning with *But* and four with *And.* This is very common in spoken but not in written language. In written language we often have complex sentences with subordinating conjunctions like *because* and *although.* In spoken discourse, particularly in informal spoken discourse, we often string utterances together with words like *and, but* and *so,* adding one item of information to another.

11. The last sentence of turn 1: *But heights where you think you may be able to fall,* is in fact not a sentence at all. Again this is not unusual in spoken language. We add items of information one after another in units which are usually, but by no means always, like the sentences of written English.

Of course not all spoken language is produced in real time. I referred above to a prepared lecture. There are occasions on which a spoken message is carefully prepared beforehand and may therefore have many of the characteristics of written language. It will use much less vague language and very few *ers* and *erms.* There will be virtually no ungrammatical utterances, such as *I've never been as scared like that before.* But even when we have plenty of time for preparation we still need to take account of the fact that what we say in a lecture still has to be processed by listeners in real time. Good lecturers include interactive moves like *right* or *OK* or *now* to mark different stages in the development of their discourse. They give a careful introduction to what they have to say, and ensure that there is plenty of repetition so that their listeners have time to process what they are saying. So there will still be differences between a well prepared lecture and a chapter of a book on the same topic. The lecture comes somewhere between written English and spontaneous spoken English.

Most grammatical descriptions are based on the written language. This is not surprising. Written language is easily accessible. All you need to do is pick up a book and you have plenty of data to work with. Spoken data needs to be recorded and transcribed. This is a time-consuming business, but a full transcription is almost impossible. A full account of the grammar of spoken English would certainly include a description of intonation. Units of spoken language are marked by pauses and often by a falling intonation. It is a difficult and time-consuming process to include these in a transcript, and it requires specialist training to transcribe and read something intonationally. The data is elusive and difficult to gather and as a result grammar is usually in effect the grammar of written English. When we describe the spoken form we tend to take the written form as standard and describe spoken language, rather as I have done above, in terms of how it differs from the written. This is odd because it treats the spoken form as though it were somehow derivative and unnatural. If anything, it is the written form which is derivative and unnatural. There are many languages which do not have a written form, but all languages have a spoken form. Certainly, almost all of us experience much more speech than we do writing.

We will go on to look at a number of the important differences between spoken English and the standardised written form, and then to propose teaching strategies to take account of these.

9.1.1 Spoken language appears to be untidy

Sometimes when we look at a written transcript spoken language appears to be untidy. It doesn't say exactly what it means and we have to work out what is being said. Here is an extract where two people are talking about the high prices that are sometimes paid for works of art[2]. They have just been talking about Van Gogh's *Sunflowers* which sold for around twenty million pounds while it is well-known Van Gogh had lived and died in total poverty:

SJ: … it was a vast amount. Mm.
EL: Mm. But it seems sad, that it's – it's a famous saying that a painter has to die before he er … .
SJ: That's right. It's sad for Van Gogh.
EL: Yeah. Erm. But it's a pattern that just seems to repeat itself doesn't it, again and again? People while they're alive …
SJ: Mm. Mm. Mm. Mm.
EL: I don't suppose there's enough distance to judge whether it's a great work of art or not.

EL says, *It seems sad that it's a famous saying that a painter has to die before he er … .* Of course he doesn't really mean that the fact that there's a famous saying is sad. He means that the fact that a painter has to die before his work is highly valued is sad. It is interesting, however, that SJ has no problem at all in understanding what EL is saying.

It is difficult to see how EL might have completed the sentence, *People while they're alive …,* but his intended meaning is clear enough.

---

[2]This extract is taken from Willis & Willis, 1989.

If we were to write a report of this exchange we would have to do a good deal of tidying up:

> *It is often said that a painter has to die before his work is really appreciated. This was unfortunate for Van Gogh, and it is a pattern that is repeated again and again: people's work is not appreciated while they are alive.*

9.1.2 Spoken language omits words and phrases

One of the features of the discussion of Van Gogh, above, is that words and phrases are omitted. This is a common feature of spoken English. At the end of a good dinner the host or hostess might say '*Coffee anyone?*'. In the shared situation it is not difficult to interpret this as, *Would anyone like a cup of coffee?* But according to the description we have established that *Coffee anyone?* is not a clause. It does not have the structure N + V + ?. This is a common feature of spoken English. We often omit elements which can easily be understood from the context. This omission, which grammarians call **ellipsis**, is common in spoken English, particularly in conversation. Many questions in conversational English consist simply of one or two questions words: *What time? Where?* Parents with young children will be painfully familiar with the one word utterance *Why?* Someone who is accused of something may well respond: *Who, me?* Answers to questions are often similarly elliptical. When a teacher asks the class, *Is anyone absent?*, a student might well reply, *Yes, Jenny.* In the extract above, the sentence: *But heights where you think you may be able to fall,* is interpreted as: *But (I am frightened of) heights where you think you may be able to fall.* Spoken language often omits elements which can easily be retrieved from the context.

9.1.3 Spoken language is additive

In the discussion above about heights there are many occurrences of *and* linking one phrase or clause to the next. The effect is to build up the narrative, bit by bit in an additive fashion. This is particularly clear in: *And, you know, I sort of edged round. I couldn't go back through the same door. I edged round and managed to find the other door.* In the written form this would probably be something like: *Because I couldn't go back through the same door, I edged round and managed to find the other door.* In the spoken form we have a series of short statements and the listener builds up the picture of what happened.

In the sentence, *The top of something like a lighthouse or something I don't mind,* we have noted that there is a topic–comment structure.

The speaker begins by establishing the topic: *the top of something like a lighthouse* and then goes on to comment on this. This is a common feature of spoken English and, far from being accidental or 'wrong', is a useful way of organising information. The listener holds in mind the first item of information, in this case the topic, and then adds to it, interpreting whatever comes next in the light of what is held in mind.

This is very common not only in the structure of the clause, but also in the structure of the noun phrase. There is an excellent example in the CANCODE corpus: *His cousin in Beccles, her boyfriend, his parents bought him a Ford Escort for his birthday.* In written English, this might well be a complex noun group, something like: *He has **a cousin in Beccles whose boyfriend's parents** bought him … .* These complex noun groups pack information very densely. They are difficult to put together in real time, and also difficult to process for understanding. Therefore, spoken English often simply strings items together instead of nesting them inside one another in a complex noun group.

His cousin in Beccles, her boyfriend, his parents bought him a Ford Escort.

9.1.4 Spoken language is often repetitive

In the discussion on heights we noted the repetition in: *I was okay until I had a rather nasty experience about er, height. Until then I was okay. I could go anywhere.* This kind of repetition is necessary to give the listener time to process what is being said and sometimes to add emphasis. Because of this, repetition is a feature even of carefully prepared speech. If you listen to politicians speaking you will probably hear lots of repetition. British politicians, for example, often say things like: *It's good for business, it's good for the consumer, and it's good for Britain.*

9.1.5 Conversation is interactive

If there are two or more people involved in the production of a discourse they make use of mechanisms to organise turn-taking, and to ensure, as far as possible, that all participants are on the same track. Here is a short extract where two people are exchanging addresses[3]:

[3]This extract is taken from Willis & Willis, 1988.

1 DF: Okay. Can you give me your address? And your phone number? And I'll get it down here.
2 BG: Fifty-three ...
3 DF: Yeah.
4 BG: Cleveland Square.
5 DF: Cleveland Square.
6 BG: London west two.
7 DF: Is that the postcode, or –?
8 BG: Yeah.
9 DF: Just west two?
10 BG: Yeah.
11 DF: All right. Have you got a phone number?
12 BG: Yes, it's two six two
13 DF: Two six two—
14 BG: o six one nine.
15 DF: o six one nine. So it's er, Bridget Green, fifty-three Cleveland Square, London, west two, two s- and the phone number two six two, o six one nine.
16 BG: That's right.

The two participants are constantly checking to see that information has been successfully transferred. They say things like *Yeah* and *That's right*, and they repeat what the other person has said to check it out. In an information exchange this kind of feedback is typical. In a story-telling exchange like that in Section 1 above we have *Mms* and *Yeahs* from the listener to show attentiveness, and evaluative comments like *That's very frightening* or *That's amazing* or *Wow!* The important thing is that successful discourse is the responsibility of both participants. Even someone who is simply listening to a story is expected to play an active part. If you doubt this you might try a small experiment. Next time someone tells you an interesting story, try showing no reaction. Maintain the same facial expression and offer no comment on what they have to say. Before very long the story-teller will begin to look a bit worried and will probably stop and say something like: *Are you OK?*

9.1.6 Exchanges are formulaic

There are conventions governing interactions which are almost as important as the rules governing grammatical structure. In Italian, for example, thanking someone is always a two-part exchange, and the two parts are fixed:

A: *Grazie.*
B: *Prego.*

It is regarded as rude to omit a response after *grazie*. The usual response is *prego*. This may be replaced by *di niente* or just *niente*, but politeness always demands some acknowledgement. In English, however, there is no need to acknowledge a *thank you* if the service or favour is relatively trivial and straightforward. If I go into the newsagents and buy a newspaper, it is polite to say *thank you*, but I would not necessarily expect the newsagent to acknowledge this. If he did acknowledge he could use a range of utterances such as: *okay; right; cheers*. There is no formulaic response. If, however, the service or favour is more significant then some acknowledgement would be expected after *thank you*. There are a number of possible responses. English appears to be much more flexible than Italian in this respect. We would have an exchange like:

A: *Thanks.*
B: *Okay./That's okay./ That's fine./You're welcome./Not at all / Right.*

In learning a foreign language it is important to learn the formulae which govern basic exchanges and the forms of language which realise these exchanges. We have, for example:

Requests:

A: *Can / Could / Would you ... please?*
B: *Certainly / Of course / Sure / I'm sorry ... / I'm afraid not ...*
A: *Would you mind ___ing?*
B: *Not at all / Certainly / Of course / I'm sorry ... / I'm afraid not ... / I can't I'm afraid ...*
A: *Could I have ... please?*
B: *Certainly / I'm sorry ...*

Offers:

A: *Can / May / Could I ...*
B: *Thanks / Thank you very much.*
A: *Would you like ... / Would you like to ...*
B: *Thanks / Thank you very much.*

Some interactions are embedded in others. For example:

A: *So, can you come round on Friday?*
B: *On Friday?* ⎫
A: *Yes.* ⎬ *(request for clarification)*
B: *Sure.* ⎭
A: *Thanks.*
B: *Okay.*

Here we have a request for clarification embedded in another request and followed by a thanking exchange. It is, then, possible to build up fairly complex interactions on the basis of formulaic exchanges.

There are a large number of formulae which exist to service interaction. Question tags play an interactive function. There is a host of responses, such as *I (don't) think so; so/neither do I; I'm not sure; of course*, which comment on previous utterances. Many of these, like *I think so*, need to be identified for learners. They are lexical phrases which cannot be generated from general grammatical rules.

9.1.7 Some speech acts are governed by typical routines

When someone tells a story, they usually follow a basic routine. They will normally begin with an utterance which gives an indication of what is to come. In the story about fear of heights, BB begins by saying: *I was okay until I had a rather nasty experience about er, height. Until then I was okay. I could go anywhere.* There is then a description of the situation: *But er, I was er, on a lighthouse actually. We were being taken round it. We went up all the stairs and to the light, er, room. And then the chap says 'Oh, come on. Right, we'll go out here.'* Next comes a complicating factor, usually a problem: *I went through the door. And I was on this very very narrow little parapet ... with a rail about – perhaps eighteen inches high ... and then a sheer drop of about a hundred feet or something.* This is usually accompanied by some kind of evaluation: *I was absolutely petrified. I've never been as scared like that before or since.* Next comes a resolution: *And, you know, I sort of edged round. I couldn't go back through the same door. I edged round and managed to find the other door. And that's it.* Finally there is something which looks back on the experience and draws a conclusion: *Ever since then if I go up a ladder I'm scared stiff now. It really is, it's er, changed my whole life, you know. Absolutely frightening, that.*
   It is possible to link this routine to a number of formulaic utterances:

Opening: *I had a funny / dreadful / frightening experience once / the other day / a few years ago ...*
Introducing a complicating factor: *Suddenly / And then ...*
Evaluation: *It was awful / terrifying / really funny. Everybody laughed. / We were all terrified.*
Looking back: *So that's what happened. / So it was really frightening / funny.*

There is, therefore, a good deal of predictability in story-telling and a knowledge of how a narrative develops can be of great value to learners, both in producing and in understanding narratives.

If someone asks for directions to a particular place, the usual response is to look for some kind of orientation:

A: *Can you tell me how to get to the post office?*
B: *Well, you know the Town Hall on the High Street?*

As directions are given, they are accompanied by hints to help the listener check progress:

B: *You turn left at the Town Hall and you'll see a set of traffic lights at the end of that road.*

Directions are often followed by utterances checking that the information has been assimilated and these are acknowledged by the listener:

B: *You turn left at the Town Hall. Okay?*
A: *Right.*
B: *And you'll see a set of traffic lights at the end of the road. Right?*
A: *Traffic lights. Yeah.*

The final location of the post office is clearly marked and is clearly acknowledged by the listener:

B: *And the post office is right by the traffic lights on the left. You can't miss it.*
A: *Okay. Great. Thanks.*

Again, if these routine moves are familiar, this is a useful aid to both production and comprehension.

9.1.8 Spoken language is vague

Although we talk about vague language, this is actually misleading. In both spoken and written language we are as precise as we need to be and as we can manage to be. When speaking, there are a number of reasons why we are relatively imprecise. We sometimes do not have time to find the exact word we want. We find the following exchange in an interview situation:

BS: *And we raided the er, costumes department of the local little er – people that get together and do little plays and things like that.*
INT: *Drama society. Yes.*

Momentarily BS was unable to recall the term *drama society*, so had recourse to *people that get together and do little plays and things like that.*

English has a number of words and phrases which are used to refer to people and things when we can't recall the exact word: *stuff; people like that; things like that; sort of ...; kind of ...; or something; thingy; what's his name; you know ...* . I once transcribed a recording in which one participant, on being asked to describe something, said: *It was a – you know – a kind of a sort of a thing.* All languages have words and phrases like this, because all languages need vague language.

Sometimes it is not necessary to be precise. In the discussion about heights BB talks about: *a rail about – perhaps eighteen inches high ...,* and *a sheer drop of about a hundred feet or something.* Of course we sometimes use similar language in written English. In this chapter I have used vague words and phrases like: **several** *features which are common in spoken English* and **a number of** *the important differences between spoken English and the standardised written form.* But generally the purpose of written language is to transfer information, and in order to meet this purpose effectively we need to be precise. In spoken language the purpose is very often to make friends or to pass the time happily in the company of others. This is what is happening in the discussion about heights. In this kind of social exchange precision is less important than in an information exchange.

9.2 Teaching the spoken language

Some aspects of spoken language are very teachable. We can demonstrate typical exchanges, such as those used for offers or requests. In doing this we can focus on interactive markers like *right, okay, fine* and so on. We can point to the use of vague language and list ways of saying numbers: *about/around a hundred; at least a hundred; just over/under a hundred* and so on. All of these elements have an identifiable value which can, in principle, be made available to students.

As most spoken language is, of its very nature, spontaneous, some aspects are very difficult to teach. How can you explain to learners when they should put in *er* or *erm?* How do you teach them to say *mm* or *really?* at the appropriate time? What are the rules governing noun phrases like: *His cousin in Beccles, her boyfriend, his parents ...* . We cannot explain the grammar of spoken English, partly because it is so variable and partly because we do not yet have adequate descriptions to work from. We can, however, make students aware of the nature and characteristics of the spoken language. We can give them opportunities to analyse and to produce spontaneous language. Most important of all, we need to recognise the dynamic nature of spoken language. Language is the way it is because of the purposes it fulfils. The same applies to learner language.

One thing is sure: if we are to illustrate the grammar of spoken English we need samples of genuine spoken interaction. But this too creates problems. As we have seen, spoken language can be untidy with lots of false starts and instances of speakers talking over one another. This can make it difficult to process. Spontaneous spoken language is often delivered rapidly, unlike the carefully modulated language we hear in most language teaching courses. In the real world, the processing of spoken language often depends on shared knowledge and is consequently highly inexplicit. There are jokes about the married couple who engage in exchanges like:

A: *Have you er ...?*
B: *Yes. Erm, yesterday.*
A: *And did they ...?*
B: *They didn't say. I don't think they will, but they might ... you know.*
A: *Right.*

Such exchanges are readily comprehensible to the couple involved, but completely incomprehensible to anyone else.

It is difficult, but not impossible to make spontaneous recordings for classroom use. Much of the data used here is taken from published language teaching materials (Willis, J. and D. Willis 1988). Native speakers working in a recording studio were asked to carry out a series of tasks. The same tasks were later used with learners in the classroom. Learners, for example, first listened to the recording in 9.1.5. They were told that this was a recording of native speakers finding one another's addresses and telephone numbers. This meant that learners had a clear idea of what they were listening for. The recording featuring in 9.1 can be introduced in the same way as the written text about the eight-year-old robber used to illustrate a task-based methodology in Chapter 3. Learners can be given pointer questions or hints to provide an outline for the story. It is, therefore, possible to devise techniques to make spontaneous recordings accessible to learners, even at an elementary level. Learners can then carry out a similar task themselves. Finally, with teacher guidance, they can look at features of the language used in the spontaneous recording. It is very important to find ways of making such spontaneous recordings available and accessible to learners. It may be that teachers will feel the need to work with a standardised or tidied-up version before exposing learners to spontaneously produced data. But until we find ways of using spontaneous data in the classroom it will not be possible to prepare students fully for the sort of language they will meet in the real world.

9.2.1 *Applying appropriate standards*

One of the most important things we can do as teachers is recognise that spoken and written language are different from one another in important ways, and to apply appropriate standards to the different forms. In the past I have tried to teach students to speak written English. I remember teaching picture composition lessons in which students produced stories like:

> **A.** *There was a little boy and he was cycling down the street and a car came round the corner. The driver didn't see the boy and he tried to stop, but it was too late ...*

Given this kind of production I used to encourage students to produce a more measured text – something like:

> **B.** *One day, as a little boy was cycling down the street, a car suddenly came round the corner. Unfortunately the driver didn't see the boy coming towards him. Although the driver tried to stop it was too late ...*

Version A has all the characteristics of a spoken narrative; version B is much more like a written narrative. Because I was not aware of the structure of spoken narrative, I tried to impose on my students a form of language which was much more appropriate to the written language. It would be extremely difficult, however, even for a native speaker, to produce a version like B without careful preparation. It is entirely unreasonable to expect learners to produce written language under the real-time constraints which apply to spoken language.

It is not unusual for teachers to insist on written forms, even where a short form would be more appropriate. Many teachers have a tendency to insist that students speak in complete sentences, and to encourage them to produce complex sentences with subordinate clauses, even though native speakers rarely produce spoken language like this.

9.2.2 *Highlighting differences between spoken and written language*

It is useful to encourage students to recognise that spoken language can be untidy and includes elements like false starts and *er*s and *erm*s. This can be done by looking at transcripts of natural language, like those shown earlier in this chapter, and devising exercises which focus on the differences between the spoken and written forms.

Teaching Activity 9.1: From spoken to written language

BB: Yeah. I was okay until I had a rather nasty experience about er, height. Until then I was okay. I could go anywhere. But er, I was er, on a lighthouse actually. We were being taken round it. We went up all the stairs and to the light, er, room. And then the chap says 'Oh, come on. Right, we'll go out here.' I went through the door. And I was on this very very narrow little parapet ...

CB: Yeah.

BB: ... with a rail about – perhaps eighteen inches high ...

CB: Mm.

BB: ... and then a sheer drop of about a hundred feet or something. I was absolutely petrified. I've never been as scared like that before or since.

CB: That's very frightening.

BB: And, you know, I sort of edged round. I couldn't go back through the same door. I edged round and managed to find the other door. And that's it. Ever since then if I go up a ladder I'm scared stiff now. It really is, it's er, changed my whole life, you know. Absolutely frightening, that.

Rewrite BB's story as though it were part of a letter. Begin with the words:

I have been frightened of heights ever since I had a frightening experience a few years ago ...

Commentary on Teaching Activity 9.1:

This exercise would be done after learners have already processed the dialogue for meaning as part of a task cycle. In order to produce a written version of the story, learners will have to do a lot of work on the spoken version.

Obviously they will need to cut out *ers* and *erms*. They will change colloquial forms, like *I was okay* and *the chap*, to written forms, like *I was all right* or *I was not frightened* and *the man*. They will rewrite the ungrammatical form *I've never been as scared like that*. They will rewrite non-sentences, like *Absolutely frightening, that*. In making these adjustments they will be focusing on the differences between spoken and written language.

Teaching Activity 9.2: From written to spoken language

You are going to read a story which appeared in a popular magazine. The first sentence is:

I never used to worry about heights until I had a rather frightening experience a few years ago.

The last sentence is:

Now I get nervous even if I have to go up a ladder.

Here are some of the words and phrases from the story:

Lighthouse keeper – small room – light – small door – parapet – low rail – eighteen inches – one hundred feet – much too frightened – back to the wall – other door – frightened of heights.

What do you think happened?

I never used to worry about heights until I had a rather frightening experience a few years ago. We were on holiday by the coast, and we went to look round a lighthouse. The light-house keeper took us to the top of the tower and into the small room where the light was. Then he showed us through a small door. Suddenly I found myself on a tiny narrow parapet. In front of me there was a low rail, about eighteen inches high, and beyond that a sheer drop of about a hundred feet. I was petrified. I was much too frightened to turn round to go back through the original door. I kept my back to the wall and inched my way round the parapet till I came to the other door, and back into the room. I have never been so frightened in all my life. Since then I have been terrified of heights. Now I get nervous even if I have to go up a ladder.

Commentary on Teaching Activity 9.2:

This is a prediction task after which you would encourage class discussion before showing the written text. You could then play the original recording as given in Teaching Activity 9.1 and show students the tapescript. You could ask them to identify features of spoken English from the tapescript and go on to lead a class discussion focusing on the aspects of spontaneous spoken language we highlighted in Task 9.1 in Section 9.1.

Like Teaching Activity 9.1, this is an attempt to highlight differences between spoken and written forms. This exercise may be rather easier because it starts from the written form, which many students find easier to handle.

In highlighting differences between spoken and written forms it is important to make it clear that the forms are different because they fulfil different functions. It is not a matter of one form being superior to the other. In order to make this clear it may be useful to look at spoken forms in the learners' first language. The first language will certainly have noises which are equivalent to *er* and *erm*. It will certainly use vague language and units other than sentences. It is useful to look at transcripts of spoken language in the learners' first language to identify these features. If learners are not convinced that these are necessary features of spoken language, ask them to tell a short story or describe something in their own language without *er*s and *erm*s or hesitations, without vague language and in complete sentences. There is a game on BBC radio, called *Just a Minute*, in which celebrity guests are asked to speak for one minute on a topic without hesitation, repetition or deviation. Very few manage to do this.

In most transcripts you will find plenty of examples which illustrate the additive and repetitive nature of spoken language. The story above, for example, is basically a string of simple statements linked by the words *and* and *then*. It is important to point this out to students and to explain that this is typical of spoken language. In Section 9.1.3 we noted the additive structure of the noun phrase: *His cousin in Beccles, her boyfriend, his parents bought him a Ford Escort for his birthday.* When looking at the structure of complex noun phrases in the written language it is useful to point out the looser structure of the spoken form. When we look at standard written forms it is often useful to look at alternative spoken forms.

Teaching Activity 9.3: Quantifiers and possessives

A. In spoken English we often put a quantifier after its noun:

People in London, some of them spend hours travelling to work.
Young children, most of them love making a noise.

Can you rewrite these sentences so that the quantifier is after the noun?

Most of my family live abroad.

A lot of the old houses were destroyed.
Some of the spectators were attacked.

B. In spoken English possessives are often expressed like this:

Instead of saying: *Her neighbour's dog*, we can say: *Her neighbour his dog.*
Instead of saying: *His daughter's neighbour's dog*, we can say: *Her daughter her neighbour his dog.*
Instead of saying: *My friend Peter's daughter's neighbour's dog*, we can say: *My friend Peter his daughter her neighbour his dog.*

What could you say instead of the following?

my cousin's wife
my cousin's wife's mother
my cousin's wife's mother's boss
Mary's teacher
Mary's teacher's husband
Mary's teacher's husband's partner

Commentary on Teaching Activity 9.3:

There is no need to spend a lot of time on exercises like this. But it is important for learners to recognise alternative spoken forms.

9.2.3 Demonstrating the interactive nature of spoken language

Teaching Activity 9.4: Listening to interaction

Look at this transcript of a dialogue:

DF: Okay. Can you give me your address? And your phone number?
BG: Fifty-three, Cleveland Square. London west two.
DF: Have you got a phone number?
BG: Yes, it's two six two o six one nine.

Now listen to this longer version:

DF: Okay. Can you give me your address? And your phone number? And I'll get it down here.
BG: Fifty-three ...
DF: Yeah.
BG: Cleveland Square.
DF: Cleveland Square.

BG: London west two.
DF: Is that the postcode, or –?
BG: Yeah.
DF: Just west two?
BG: Yeah.
DF: All right. Have you got a phone number?
BG: Yes, it's two six two
DF: Two six two—
BG: o six one nine.
DF: o six one nine. So it's er, Bridget Green, fifty-three Cleveland Square, London, west two, two s- and the phone number two six two, o six one nine.
BG: That's right.

(Here the teacher should play the recording without showing a transcript.)

What differences are there between the two versions? Can you rewrite the first version so that it is more like real spoken language?

Commentary on Teaching Activity 9.4:

An exercise like this will certainly focus on interactive moves like repetition and the use of *Yeah* to show that the message has been received. It would be too much to expect learners to reproduce the full version exactly. You might build up to the writing exercise by playing the full version once then asking students to identify differences, then playing it again before asking them to produce their version. You can finish the exercise by showing them the full transcript.

Teaching Activity 9.5: Evaluations

Look at these exchanges:

A: Hey, I've just heard I've passed all my exams.
B: ...
C: I've just heard that Jack has failed all his exams.
D: ...

Choose comments suitable for B and comments suitable for D:

All of them? That's awful – Congratulations – That's terrible – That's great – Great – Oh dear, I'm sorry – That's marvellous – Wonderful – Well done.

Commentary on Teaching Activity 9.5:

This exercise focuses on evaluations which, as we have seen, play an important part in spoken interaction. You might usefully ask learners what evaluations they might employ in their own language. Once you have established the idea of evaluations, you can take note of them as they occur in the language learners are exposed to.

Teaching Activity 9.6: Some discourse markers

WELL:

1. You use *well* to show you have come to the end of a conversation:

    Well, I think it's time for lunch.
    Well, I'm afraid I have to go now.

2. You often use *well* to preface an answer to a question to show that you have heard the question and are considering your answer. You often do this if you are unable to answer a question directly:

    A: What time is it?
    B: Well, it must be nearly time for lunch.

    A: Who is that?
    B: Well, it's not the manager.
    Well, I don't know really.
    Well, I'm not sure.

3. You use *well* to change or correct something you have said:

    He's nearly seventy now. Well, he's certainly over sixty.
    I'm going home now. Well, in a few minutes.

4. You use *well* to add a comment to something or to introduce a story you want to tell:

    You know Mrs. Brown? Well, she's got a new job.
    I went to George's last night. Well, there was nobody there, so ...

What would you use for *well* in your own language?

Commentary on Teaching Activity 9.6:

Words like *well, right, okay* and *so* are very common in spoken English. It is difficult to say what they mean but it is possible to show how they are used. The best way of getting learners to think about their use is to relate them to the first language.

9.2.4 Building up formulaic exchanges

Teaching Activity 9.7: Functional dialogues

Can you arrange these sentences to make a short dialogue?

> *What time?*
> *I'm sorry, I can't. I have a computer class.*
> *What about Friday?*
> *Thursday?*
> *About seven.*
> *Sure. That's fine.*
> *Can you come round one evening?*
> *Sure. When?*

Commentary on Teaching Activity 9.7:

This is a short problem-solving activity, to be done in pairs. It focuses on the formulae to do with requests and asking for supplementary information. It is important to provide the problem-solving element in order to oblige students to pay careful attention to the wording of the dialogue.

There is more than one way of putting the dialogue together. After learners have completed the task they can read out their dialogues and compare solutions.

Finally, they can be asked to act out their dialogue from memory. An alternative would be to ask one student to produce the first utterance and then select another student at random to reply, then another student, and so on until the whole dialogue is built up.

The exercise can be varied by offering alternative realisations of the moves:

(I'm sorry, I can't / I'm afraid not / Sorry) I have a computer class.

(Can you / Could you / Do you think you could) come round one evening?

Alternatively learners can be asked to rewrite the dialogue using their own variations. Finally, learners can listen to a version of the same exchange, possibly one incorporating plausible additions to the original:

A: Can you come round one evening?
B: Sure. When?
A: Thursday?
B: *Thursday?* I'm sorry, I can't. I have a computer class.
A: *Oh.* What about Friday?
B: *Friday?*
A: *Yeah.*
B: *I don't know.* What time?
A: About seven.
B: *Seven? Sure.* That's fine.
A: *Okay, thanks.*
B: *Right.*

They may be given a written version without the additional, italicised utterances, and asked to identify the additions as they listen. The important thing at each stage is to provide a problem-solving element to provide a reason for carrying out the activity.

9.2.5 Establishing typical routines

Teaching Activity 9.8: Narrative structure

Listen to these stories again. Write down the following:

- the summarising sentence that comes at the beginning of the story;
- any evaluations;
- the summarising sentence that comes at the end of the story.

BG: I once had a dreadful journey home. My parents live in Sussex – and I remember catching a train once on a Friday night to go home, go down to Sussex, and it usually takes about an hour and I was very tired and I fell asleep half-way and ended up in Hastings which is about two and a half hours, two hours, erm, which was really annoying, 'cause it meant I had to wait for another train to come back again. It was awful.

> JV: A friend of mine had a similar experience on a Greenline bus after an office party. So you can imagine that he went to sleep and the Greenline bus went all the way to its terminus at one end, and then all the way back to the other one and was on its third trip ...
>
> BG: Oh no!
>
> JV: ... before they finally woke him up and said 'Are you sure – where are you supposed to be going to?' So that journey certainly went wrong.
>
> **Commentary on Teaching Activity 9.8:**
>
> These are both stories which the students have heard before. They may have just finished working on the stories, or they may have heard them some time ago. The purpose here is to highlight the way stories are built into a conversation and the way they are structured. You may then go on to ask how these stories might be introduced in the students' own language, and how they might be summarised at the end. Go on to list possible story introductions and conclusions in the L1 and in English.

You can carry out similar exercises with other routines, such as asking for directions, which was discussed in Section 9.1.7. Because the elements in these routines serve basic communicative functions they tend to be similar in most languages. It is, for example, difficult to imagine a language which did not structure the giving of directions with orientation and checking moves.

9.2.6 Focusing on vague language

> **Teaching Activity 9.9: Vague language**
>
> How many examples of vague language can you find in these exchanges:
>
> > A: *How far is it to Edinburgh?*
> > B: *I don't know. About a hundred miles I suppose.*
> > A: *A hundred miles. Mm. How long does it take to drive?*
> > B: *Well, a couple of hours or so. It depends on the traffic. Yeah, not more than a couple of hours.*
> >
> > *

> *A: What does it look like?*
> *B: Well it's sort of brownish. It's got a handle thing on the side.*
> *And it's about the same size as a smallish suitcase.*

Commentary on Teaching Activity 9.9:

Vague language is obviously very important for learners. They can use it to make up for vocabulary items they do not know or are not sure of. There are a few vague language items which can be used in a range of contexts. The phrases *sort of* and *kind of* can be used with virtually any adjectival expression. *About* and *or so* can be used with numbers and quantities, as can expressions like *just under, just over, not more / less than*. The suffix *-ish* can be added to colours and to common adjectives like *big, small, old* and *young*. If we are not sure of the right word for something we can choose a similar word and add the word *thing*. So a computer monitor can be described as *a television thing* or *a sort of television thing*. It is not difficult to equip learners with a good basis for vague language. Once you have done this it is useful to point out other examples of vague language as they occur.

9.3 Summary

It is clear that spontaneous spoken language differs in important ways from the standard written form. Many of these differences will be similar to differences between written and spoken forms of the learners' own language. It will certainly be useful to make constant comparisons between the characteristics of spoken English and the spoken form of the learners' first language. It would also be useful for learners to have a general understanding of the nature of spoken discourse and the differences between spoken and written forms. One of the problems we face in the classroom is finding something to talk about and something to read about. One of the obvious things to talk about is language itself. There is a strong case for introducing the study of language as part of the subject matter of the language classroom, and a principled comparison between L1 and L2 should be part of this discussion.

In Section 9.2 I acknowledged the difficulties of providing spontaneous spoken data in the language classroom. But I also argued that it is a priority for the ELT profession to find a way of making this kind of data available and accessible. We will still be largely dependent on grammars based on standard written forms. But once we have made spontaneous spoken language available in the classroom we can begin to work systematically at introducing learners to the characteristics of spoken language in the ways proposed here.

10 A final summary

10.1 Language learning and language development

In Chapter 1 I began by pointing out that what is 'taught' is very often not learnt. There is a gap between learners' ability to manipulate language as a system of rules, and their ability to use that language for spontaneous communication. If we think of learning as learning to use the language system, then we cannot predict or control what will be learnt. Some relatively simple items like the terminal third person-*s* in the present simple tense, or the formation of *do*-questions are oddly resistant to teaching. It is hardly surprising that, in the short term, complex systems like tense are not affected at all, even by careful teaching.

How, then, do learners progress? It seems that, to a large extent, learning is a natural developmental process. Yet, at the same time, there is evidence that instruction does help learners. Given the right kind of instruction, learners are likely to progress more rapidly, and to reach a higher standard of attainment. But what sort of instruction is most likely to help learners? Both research and our experience in the classroom suggest that learning is unpredictable. If teachers attempt to control what is learnt they will certainly fail. If they take the elimination of learner error as their overwhelming priority, they will certainly fail. It may even be the case that control and a focus on eliminating error often challenge rather than reinforce the developmental process.

Just because students do not always learn exactly what is taught, this does not mean, however, that they are not learning. I referred in Chapter 1 to a group of teachers who were dismayed at their failure to eradicate basic mistakes frequently made by their students. But I noted that, although these teachers failed in their attempts to teach specific language items, they were successful in helping their students develop a usable competence in the language. Learning appears to be resistant to teaching if we measure learning in terms of highly specific syntactic goals, like the use of *do*-questions. On the other hand, we have no difficulty in seeing that learning takes place if we look at language in more general terms as a meaning system, and consider the growth of learners' vocabulary and their ability to engage in more and more complex communication. What we need to do is look for ways to assist this general developmental process.

10.2 'Learning how to mean'

Language learning is constrained partly by the way our minds work, and our perception of language learning is very much affected by our concept of what a language is. Most approaches to language teaching give priority to the controlled production of acceptable sentences. Most testing procedures measure the ability to produce a range of acceptable sentences. This suggests a view of language as an amalgamation of acceptable sentences, and language learning as the ability to control an ever increasing variety of sentence forms.

Language use involves, however, much more than the ability to produce sentences. It is much more useful to think of language in Halliday's (1975) terms, as a system of meanings, and to think of learning a language as learning how to mean. When children learn their first language they begin by linking lexical items together. They rapidly acquire basic word order, but structural words and syntactic markers are built in gradually. It is quite some time before children consistently produce sentences which would be judged grammatical according to the standards of adult language use.

We should beware of overstating the similarities between the acquisition of the first language and the learning of a new language in the classroom. But it does seem that learners, like those acquiring their first language, begin by stringing words and phrases together and gradually build in more complex grammatical systems. It seems likely that learners begin by improvising. They gradually acquire a stock of words and phrases, which they string together as best they can in order to communicate basic messages. They are not concerned primarily with the production of sentences, but with the exchange of meanings. As they become more experienced language users, a number of things happen. Their exposure to a growing range of language forms provides them with the raw material for language development. Their vocabulary increases and they begin to experiment with an increasingly complex grammar.

We should not underestimate improvisation. It is a highly creative process, and one which comes naturally to all language users. We all strive to make meanings. It is a necessary starting point for language learning: if we want to develop and refine a meaning system, we can only do this by exchanging meanings. Improvisation lays the foundations for **consolidation.** Learners have a store of language which they are aware of, but which they cannot command in spontaneous speech. If they are given time to prepare what they want to say, language which is on the threshold of spontaneity may be incorporated into their performance. First they need to get meanings across (improvisation), then they can work to refine those meanings (consolidation). Consolidation is a stage on the road to spontaneous mastery, giving us the following progression:

Improvisation → Consolidation → Spontaneous use

There is a danger that a methodology that tries to insist on accurate production at all times denies learners the opportunity to improvise. This cuts them off from a dynamic natural process which is at the foundation of learning to use language.

10.3 Individual priorities

I suggested in Chapter 1 that learners display the following priorities:

Basic message → Concern for reader/listener → Presentation of self

In this view, their first concern is simply to get a message across: *Me Tarzan.* Next they will be concerned to make their communication clear and precise: *Hello. My name Tarzan.* Finally they will be concerned with the presentation of self. For a language learner this is likely to involve, among other things, a concern with grammatical accuracy, even though they may not achieve this.

It is important to recognise that there is often a conflict between these priorities. A concern for the listener involves a compromise. On the one hand, we want our message to be as clear as possible. On the other hand, concern for the listener demands that we produce language at an acceptable speed. When using a foreign language as a beginner or intermediate learner, we find that very often we cannot achieve both these goals at the same time. There may be a conflict between concern for the listener and presentation of self. What happens if we want to be formally polite but do not have control of the appropriate polite forms in the target language? Do we say: *Please, close the window*, or do we go for a longer, more polite form which may involve grammatical error: *Please, I excuse. You can close the window?* Once we recognise these conflicts we can see clearly that there is more to language than the production of acceptable sentence forms.

It is, of course, an oversimplification to suggest that all learners have the same priorities. Some learners are so extroverted and self-confident that getting their message across is almost their only priority. They show little concern for their listener and give low priority to the presentation of self. Such learners are not greatly worried about formal accuracy and may be quite impatient with the study of language form. They are content with a largely lexical mode of communication and, as a result, there is a danger that they will fossilise at a relatively low level of achievement.

At the other extreme, some learners are anxious to present themselves in a favourable light right from the beginning. This anxiety may manifest itself as an almost obsessive concern with formal accuracy, or as a reluctance to use the language at all for fear of embarrassing failure.

These are extreme cases. Most learners will have a more balanced set of priorities, and these priorities will shift according to the circumstances of language use. The important thing in a teaching context is to devise a methodology which has the following six features:

- an acceptance that the aim is to support general language development rather than to teach discrete language items;
- a recognition of the fact that learners are engaged in building a meaning system;
- the provision of opportunities for learners to improvise with the language they already have;
- incentives for learners to refine their language to meet different communicative demands;
- classroom procedures which will encourage learners to think carefully about how language is structured and how it is used;
- ample exposure to spoken and written texts to provide opportunities for learners to explore language for themselves.

This is what we attempt to do with a task-based learning (TBL) approach. We need to bear in mind, however, that priorities vary from learner to learner – some learners will need careful support and nurturing to encourage them to use language freely in the classroom, others will need to be reminded of the need to focus on accuracy.

10.4 The communicative framework

In Chapter 3 we looked at a basic task cycle involving three stages: **task → planning → report**. Before this task cycle there was an introductory stage in which the teacher explained the task and provided some of the lexis which would be needed to carry out the task.

A task involves improvisation. This is true even of native speakers who are working with new ways of meaning. Observe a group of trainee language teachers, who are struggling with new concepts and new terminology. They will be involved in stretching their language resources to cope with new meanings. Clearly this is even more true of learners at an intermediate level. They will have to stretch their limited resources even to put together a relatively simple narrative. Fortunately, as they work on a task, they are working in a sympathetic communicative environment. Other members of their group are also struggling to get their meaning across. Everyone is concerned with meaning, rather than looking too hard at the form of the message. Communication will be improvised, possibly with a heavy reliance on lexis and relatively little concern with grammatical markers.

At the **planning** stage in the cycle, learners are asked to prepare to talk to the class as a whole. They are preparing to move from a situation in which they were working in a small group to a situation in which their findings are to be presented to the class as a whole. There are a number of important differences in these communicative situations:

- In the small group, learners are concerned with solving a problem. They are thinking about the problem, and, at the same time, working with language. At the **planning** stage learners have already found their solution to the problem. They have decided what they want to mean. They now have time to think about how to express their meanings, to think about the language they need.
- They will need to make their meaning explicit. In a small cooperative group meaning emerges gradually as the members of the group make their contributions. When someone stands up to deliver a monologue to the class they will need to be precise and explicit. They will need to take account of the listener.
- They will be anxious to present themselves in a favourable light. In a small group everyone is involved in a cooperative venture. There is a joint concern with solving a problem rather than with making judge-ments. In talking to the class as a whole speakers will be exposing themselves to the judgement of the class – and the teacher.

After the planning stage comes the report. One member of the group will present the findings of the group to the class. The need to be precise and explicit and the need to present the group in a favourable light will create a need for grammatical accuracy.

Let us try to relate these classroom activities to language use. As we have seen, the **task** phase involves **improvisation**. The **planning** stage moves towards **consolidation**. In order to achieve the required clarity and presentation learners will draw on language which is on the threshold of spontaneity. At the **report** stage the speaker has to work out priorities. How much can they rely on consolidation? How far do they sacrifice accuracy in order to achieve a reasonably rapid delivery? Let us summarise this section by linking the elements we have been looking at:

Introduction	Enables **improvisation** by providing required lexis.
Task	The communicative situation allows **improvisation** with little need to attend to the listener and little concern for presentation.
Planning	The communicative situation demands a focus on form to take account of the listener and the presentation of self. This will demand **consolidation**, requiring learners to call on language systems which are on the edge of spontaneity.
Report	The speaker needs to compromise between **consolidation** and **spontaneous use**. This involves decisions as to how much they can move from improvised language to incorporate the insights from the planning stage.

This communicative task-based framework needs to be supplemented by opportunities for language study. This means that in addition to producing language for themselves they need exposure to relevant language. In the task cycle in Chapter 3 there was a written text which provided language input. This could be supplemented by a recording of experienced users of English, possibly native speakers, telling their versions of the story. In a lesson based entirely on spoken language learners might listen to recordings of experienced speakers carrying out tasks parallel to the tasks they have engaged in themselves (see Willis, J., 1996).

10.5 Language description and learning processes

We have set out a model which organises grammar under three headings: structure, orientation and pattern. The grammar is linked to lexis through the notion of class, which groups words and phrases into classes according to their behaviour.

Some aspects of language are relatively easy to learn. As an example of this I gave my lexical store of menu items in Spanish. Some grammatical items, however, are relatively easy to describe or explain, but seem to present real learning difficulties. The terminal -*s* in the present simple, *he runs*, is an obvious example. The formation of *do*-questions is another. But some aspects of language defy description. What guidance can we give learners to help them choose between the past perfect and the past simple? When is it appropriate to use the passive form of a verb? We can give broad hints which might help learners with these questions, but we cannot provide a comprehensive answer.

We can think of this in terms of learning processes. Some vocabulary items simply involve a process of **recognition**. I can identify the Spanish word, *cerveza*, with the English, *beer*. Ideally I need to have experienced a range of Spanish and English beers to understand the true relationship between *cerveza* and *beer*, but recognising an equivalence between the two words will take me quite a long way.

Some language learning involves **system building**. I can, for example, provide a learner with a pretty good description of the structure of the noun phrase in English. I can explain why *The big black cat sitting in the garden* is an acceptable noun phrase, whereas *The sitting in the garden black big cat* is not. It may be some time before the learner reaches the stage of being able to produce these complex noun phrases with an acceptable level of fluency, but this is not because the underlying concepts and rules are impossible to describe.

The same applies to *do*-questions. I can demonstrate these to learners without too much difficulty. Many learners will quickly be able to manipulate these forms while they are thinking carefully about them, but it will be quite some time before they can incorporate them into spontaneous use. The problem is one of moving from improvised question forms which come readily and naturally to the learner, to the incorporation of the more complex *do*-questions in spontaneous use.

Finally some language learning involves **exploration**. Some language systems cannot be fully explained because they are simply too complex. I have given two examples above: the choice between the past perfect and the past simple, and the decision as to when to use a passive verb. Pattern grammar involves exploration for quite another reason. In theory, patterns are accessible to classification and exemplification, as Francis *et al.* (1996; 1998) have demonstrated; but there are so many patterns, and they are so open-ended that they cannot be listed exhaustively for learners. We can provide hints, but learners have to discover for themselves the range of patterns and their exponents.

So some basic lexical items can be learnt and put to use almost immediately. Some systems, like the structure of the noun phrase, or *do*-questions, can be learnt fairly readily, but require time before they will be used with any consistency. There are yet other systems that defy explanation either because they are too complex (the distinction between past perfect and past simple; the use of the passive) or too wide-ranging (pattern grammar).

The grammar of class enables us to group words according to the way they pattern with other words. As learners are exposed to more and more language they realise that different words behave in different ways. In learning to use complex words like *agreement* learners need to relate the word to a number of classes. They need to recognise that *agreement* may be countable or uncountable; that it is often post-modified by a *to*-infinitive as in *an agreement to return to work*; that *agreement* is one of those words commonly found with verbs of motion – we *reach* or *come to* an agreement, a conclusion, a decision or a verdict. Learners are constantly exploring the grammar of class. What ways are there of classifying words, and what words belong in which classes? Broadly speaking we can relate different language systems to different learning processes:

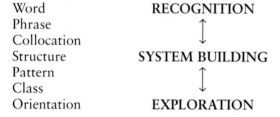

10.6 Implications for teaching

I have suggested that language develops through improvisation via consolidation to spontaneous use, and I have outlined a basic task cycle which encourages this development. The question to ask now is: how can we supplement this with language instruction to assist that progression?

Recognition can take place on a number of levels. All learners are likely to recognise words and to attempt to relate them to meanings. Many learners, however, are not consciously aware of collocation, or of the importance of fixed phrases. They need to be made aware of this at an early stage. This can be done both by finding examples in English and by asking them to look at the phenomena in their own languages. The same applies to pattern and class. It is useful to build up recognition of these gradually. This can be done by identifying the words which are found with a particular pattern, and asking learners to allocate them to semantic groups, while pointing out that meaning and pattern are related. In Section 2.3 in Chapter 2, for example, we looked at the adjectives that are found in the pattern:

It + BE + Adj. + *to* + Verb

We listed these under the headings: GOOD/BAD; EASY/DIFFICULT; USUAL/UNUSUAL; WISE/FOOLISH. Again it may be useful to look at the same phenomenon and at parallel examples in the first language.

In some cases, as we have seen, recognition can lead more or less directly to learning. It is worth asking learners to commit words and phrases to memory. This might usefully be done in preparation for a task. The day before completing a task focusing on travel, for example, learners might be asked to review or learn relevant words and phrases.

Where system building is involved, teachers can help learners by explaining and illustrating systems – how questions are formed, what verbs are followed by a *to*-infinitive and so on. The explanation and exemplification may be teacher-led or learner-centred. Teachers may take the lead in formulating rules, or they may offer data, on the basis of which learners can formulate generalisations for themselves. Testing procedures may help to clarify or reinforce this kind of learning.

As we have seen, **exploration** is a necessary part of learning for some systems, particularly pattern, class and orientation. After texts have been processed for meaning as part of a task, we need to use a range of activities to encourage learners to look carefully at the texts. We might, for example, simply ask learners to list the verbs in a given text which are followed by the *to*-infinitive, and then go on to list other verbs in the same class. We might work with a progressive deletion exercise focusing on particular language forms, or we may set a rewriting task or a grammaticisation exercise. The purpose of these activities is to encourage learners to look carefully at language forms and to think about those forms. When we select examples for learners, it is important to use language which is familiar to them as much as we can. This involves looking at texts they have already processed. Language is much more likely to be recalled and remembered if it has real meaning.

10.6.1 The communicative framework and language study: The interface

We need to recognise that recognition, system building and exploration do not normally lead directly to spontaneous use. They need to be supplemented by opportunities for language use. Imagine a group of learners who have looked at question formation in English, including *do*-questions. These question forms have been highlighted and recognised. The underlying system has been demonstrated and explained. The learners are aware of what is to be learnt, they have yet to put it into practice. Let us assume that they are then set a task which involves asking questions:

List five questions which a tourist visiting your town might ask.
How would you answer these questions?

During the task stage, most learners would use improvised forms for questions: *Your town have good restaurants? We can do good walks near your town?* and so on. At the preparation stage, at least one or two people in a group would try to correct these forms. Discussion might contest the relative merits of *Does your town has good restaurants?* and *Does your town have good restaurants?* They may even ask the teacher to arbitrate. Finally, at the report stage, one of the group will list the questions for the rest of the class, and the teacher will provide corrections where necessary. They will then listen to questions from other groups. At the report stage there can be no guarantee that learners will use correct question forms. Even if they do, this is no guarantee that all members of the group will continue to produce appropriate question forms. But, almost certainly, the exposure, the discussion and the attempts to encode questions will have some effect. They will take learners a little closer to spontaneous use.

In the example cited above there is a clear focus on question forms involved in the task. But any task is likely to involve a whole range of language forms. Any task will involve selecting appropriate verb forms and determiners. Any task will involve organising information. Different learners will be at different stages of development with regard to these systems. Some will be on the verge of incorporating *could* and *might* as modals expressing possibility into their spontaneous usage. Others may be happy to rely entirely on the adverbials *perhaps* and *maybe* to encode these meanings. The first group may achieve the breakthrough they need during a particular task cycle. As a result the second group will have exposure to alternative forms within a closely defined communicative context. This exposure is likely to take them closer to their own breakthrough.

The important thing to recognise is that we never know what aspects of the grammar are about to become a part of the learner's spontaneous use. Language study activities bring forms to the learner's attention. It is essential that we incorporate these within the communicative cycle. The communicative activities involved in the task cycle are designed to enable learners to bring these forms gradually into their spontaneous repertoire.

10.7 An integrated model

Very often, teaching and learning are seen as focusing on a particular language item, which is introduced to learners, who are then expected to move more or less immediately to spontaneous use. We have seen that these expectations are quite unrealistic. For the learner, different aspects of language are at different stages of development. In a given teaching unit we may be asking learners to **recognise** one language feature. We might, for example, ask them to underline all the question forms in a given text. Another feature may be the focus on **system building**. We may, for example, look in detail at complex noun phrases and ask learners to produce noun phrases of similar complexity. We may also encourage **exploration** of yet another feature by focusing, for example, on alternative ways of talking about the future.

All of this will be taking place within a task-based framework. As part of this learners will be improvising, using the language they have to create new meanings, and, as a result of this, preparing the way for new learning. Some language features will be consolidated. Learners will identify their value in a communicative context and produce them as part of the planning stage. Finally, some aspects of language will become accessible for spontaneous use.

The learner's language system is dynamic. It grows and develops in unpredictable ways. This means that any attempt to characterise learning, to characterise changes in the system, will be a vast over-simplification. This also applies to the brief summary of the model I have given above, but this model does at least acknowledge that a number of different learning processes and communicative processes are involved, often simultaneously, and that learning does not proceed in a simple linear fashion, with one item of language following another in a controlled way. Any realistic model of learning must recognise at least this level of complexity.

10.8 Implications for syllabus design

Traditionally people think of a language syllabus as an inventory of grammatical, lexical and functional items which represent learning aims. The problem with this notion of syllabus design is that it sees language as a series of discrete items. It takes little account of complex systems of orientation, and it has little to say about the way language is used to structure information. It also leads us easily to the assumption that language is learnt one item at a time. It takes no account of the kind of dynamic and interrelated learning processes we have been talking about here.

In my commentary on Teaching Activity 7.3a in Chapter 7, and also in the Summary of Chapter 7, I introduced the notion of the pedagogic corpus. The pedagogic corpus is made up of those texts which learners have read or listened to in the course of their studies. The best way to exemplify language for learners is to draw their attention to these texts, texts which are familiar to them. The best way to encourage learners to explore text for themselves is to demonstrate to them the value of the texts they have experienced.

Another way of thinking of the language syllabus is to base it on the pedagogic corpus. Instead of identifying an inventory of language items we see syllabus construction as the assembly of a corpus of texts which learners will process for meaning in the way the eight-year-old robber text was processed in Chapter 3. Once a text has been processed for meaning it is available for language study. If we take this view of syllabus design there will be six parts to the process of materials writing:

1. List the lexical items which you believe learners at a given level should become familiar with. If you are working with learners of general English, you can go about this by looking at frequency lists. By the end of the intermediate level learners should be familiar with at least the most frequent 2,500 words in the language. If you are working with a special-needs group, English for academic or occupational purposes, you will need to assemble a sample of the kind of texts they are likely to be exposed to as readers or listeners.

2. Identify a set of topics likely to be of value and interest to your target learners and at an appropriate level of difficulty. Design a pedagogic corpus by assembling a set of tasks and associated spoken and written texts which cover these topics as far as possible. Spoken texts may be recordings of tasks learners will be asked to carry out in the classroom.

3. Order your texts and tasks according to the level of difficulty. There is no objective way of doing this. The most effective procedure is to enlist the help of a group of teachers who are experienced in teaching at your target level. Ask them to order the tasks for you.

4. Analyse your texts for coverage of lexical items identified at stage 1. The frequent words of the language which are not covered in the texts should be covered in supplementary exercises. Teaching Activity 3.5, for example, was designed to supplement the verbs in the text which occurred in patterns with the *to*-infinitive.

5. Identify elements of the grammar (structure, orientation and pattern) illustrated in the texts you have assembled. Decide in which order

they are to be treated as part of language study. This ordering does not imply control and simplification. Learners will, for example, be exposed to a range of question forms before any formal attempt is made to recognise and systematise all of these forms. They will also have opportunities to ask questions before they have made a formal study of questions. When they move on to formal language study, it will build on their experience of question forms, both the accurate forms they have encountered in the input, and their own improvised question forms.

6. Design a set of language-focused activities which will focus on the target items in context. Items which are treated at an early stage for recognition will be recycled later as part of system building, and some items, particularly those concerned with orientation, will be recycled yet again with exploratory activities.

The texts selected for the pedagogic corpus should be natural texts rather than texts specifically designed for language teaching. Natural texts may include texts which are simplified for specific purposes, to make them accessible to children or to a non-expert audience, for example. But as a general principle we should avoid texts which have been created simply to illustrate a particular grammatical point. There are at least four reasons for this:

1. There is a serious danger that specifically designed texts will show the language not as it really is, but as the course writers imagine it to be or would like it to be. Adverbs of frequency, for example, will be found only with simple tenses, never with continuous tenses.
2. Language is shaped by its communicative purpose. Language users take decisions on the grammar of orientation according to how they want to organise information and highlight it for their reader/listener. Concocted texts have no communicative purpose. Given this, there are no real criteria for the organising and highlighting of information. Text organisation will be arbitrary.
3. If we accept that a lot of learning takes place through exploration, we should welcome a variety of language and acknowledge the need for exposure to a variety of language forms. A look at concocted texts in any coursebook which relies on concocted language will show that it is very limited in the picture of the language that it presents.
4. Real language provides a refreshing link between the classroom and the world outside, so learners are more readily motivated by real language than by concocted texts.

Artificially contrived language may be useful for recognition and system building. It is, I think, reasonable to concoct examples to illustrate the structure of the noun group, or the way questions are formed. But language exploration should always, as far as possible, focus on naturally occurring text. Exploration focuses on language which is too subtle or too wide-ranging for explanation and exemplification. It seems to follow from this that we cannot hope to teach this language by contriving texts. It is possible to make a case for using artificial examples at the recognition and system-building stages, even for the grammar of orientation. But for exploration learners need to be exposed to natural text.

If we see the pedagogic corpus as central to syllabus and materials design, we can go beyond the view of language learning as the accumulation of a series of language forms. We can see learning as the learner's growing familiarity with a valuable body of language. This in turn encourages the learner to take a positive view of learning. Learning is contextualised by the communicative framework, it is communicative activity in the classroom which enables learners to develop their spontaneous communicative repertoire, but the catalyst for this development is the exploration of text. The learning processes of recognition and system building are important in that they facilitate exploration and communication, but, important though they are, they are simply facilitating processes, paving the way for real language use.

10.9 In the meantime ...

This book incorporates a number of recommendations for syllabus and materials design. I hope that those of you who are engaged in these activities will have found something of value here. I hope that it will also be of value to teachers working to supplement the materials they are currently working with. It may be, for example, that your materials fail to recognise the importance of pattern grammar. If this is the case, you might usefully refer to a description of pattern grammar such as that provided by Francis, Hunston and Manning (1996; 1998). This will help you to analyse the texts which your students are exposed to in their course and to design supplementary activities to introduce them to the grammar of class. It may be that your course provides generally good coverage of lexis and grammar, but does not provide opportunities for exploration. If this is the case, you can provide supplementary exercises designed to encourage your learners to look carefully at language for themselves. Perhaps you feel your learners have too few opportunities for language use, for improvisation and consolidation. In this case you could refer to J. Willis (1996) and see how you might design tasks to supplement the topics and texts covered in your coursebook.

I began Chapter 1 by saying that, whenever we do anything in the classroom, we are acting on our beliefs about language and language learning, and by acknowledging that our beliefs about language learning and teaching are shaped by our training and our classroom experience. Teaching is an endlessly challenging occupation. Like language learners, the best teachers move from improvisation to consolidation and finally to spontaneous use. We begin by doing what seems to make sense. This experience is then revised by training and by reading. We consolidate good practice. That practice is constantly refined by exploration. It is unlikely that you will agree with everything you have read here. Nevertheless, I hope that what you have read will prompt you to explore your classroom experience and, perhaps, to experiment in the classroom with new techniques.

References

Biber, D., S. Conrad and G. Leech. 2002. *Student Grammar of Spoken and Written English*. Harlow: Longman.

Brazil, D. 1995. *A Grammar of Spoken English*. Oxford: OUP.

Francis, G., S. Hunston and E. Manning. 1996. *Grammar Patterns 1: Verbs*. London: Harper Collins.

1997. *Verbs: Patterns and Practice*. London: Harper Collins.

1998. *Grammar Patterns 2: Nouns and Adjectives*. London: Harper Collins.

Halliday, M. A. K. 1975. *Learning how to mean: Explorations in the development of language*. London: Edward Arnold.

1978. *Language as Social Semiotic: The Social Interpretation of Language and Meaning*. London: Edward Arnold.

1994. *An Introduction to Functional Grammar*. London: Edward Arnold.

Hughes, R. and M. McCarthy. 1998. From Sentence to Discourse: Discourse Grammar and English Language Teaching. *TESOL Quarterly* 32/2.

Lewis, M. 1993. *The Lexical Approach*. Brighton: Language Teaching Publications.

Long, M. 1983. Does second language instruction make a difference? A review of the research. *TESOL Quarterly*, 17, 359–82.

1988. Instructed interlanguage development: In: L. Beebe (ed.) *Issues in Second Language Acquisition: Multiple Perspectives*. Newbury House.

Nattinger, J. and J. DeCarrico. 1991. *Lexical Phrases in Language Teaching*. Oxford: OUP.

O'Dell, F. 1997. The Pedagogical Context. In: N. Schmitt and M. McCarthy. *Vocabulary: Description, Acquisition and Pedagogy*. Cambridge: CUP.

Sinclair, J. and A. Renouf, 1988. A Lexical Syllabus for Language Learning. In: R. Carter and M. McCarthy (eds.) *Vocabulary and Language Teaching*. Harlow: Longman.

Shortall, T. What Learners Know and What they Need to Learn. In: Willis, J. and D. Willis (eds.) 1996.

Sinclair, J. M. 1988. Collocation. In: Steele, R. and T. Threadgold. *Language Topics*. Amsterday: John Benjamins Publishing Company. (Republished in: Sinclair, J. M. 1991. *Corpus, Concordance, Collocation*. Oxford: Oxford University Press.)

(ed.) 1990. *Collins Cobuild English Grammar*. Glasgow: Collins Cobuild.

Skehan, P. 1992. Strategies in second language acquisition. In: *Thames Valley University Working Papers in English Language Teaching*, No. 3.

Widdowson, H. G. 1989. Knowledge of language and ability for use. *Applied Linguistics,* Vol. 10: 128–37.

Willis, D. 1990. *The Lexical Syllabus.* Glasgow: Collins Cobuild.

Willis, D. and J. Willis. 1996. Consciousness-raising activities. In: Willis, J. and D. Willis. 1996.

2000. Task-based Language Learning. In: Carter, R and D. Nunan (eds.) *The Cambridge Guide to Teaching English to Speakers of Other Languages.* Cambridge: CUP.

Willis, J. 1996. *A Framework for Task-based Learning.* Harlow: Longman.

Willis J, and D. Willis. 1998. *The Collins Cobuild English Course, Level 1.* Glasgow: Collins Cobuild.

1990. *The Collins Cobuild English Course, Level 2.* Glasgow: Collins Cobuild.

1996. *Challenge and Change in Language Teaching.* Oxford: Heinemann.

Subject index

Name index

Lightning Source UK Ltd.
Milton Keynes UK
UKOW031057010312

188151UK00002B/56/P